The
Quiet Man

The
Quiet Man

═══════

*The Indispensable
Presidency of
George H. W. Bush*

John H. Sununu

BROADSIDE BOOKS
An Imprint of HarperCollins*Publishers*

HarperCollins books may be purchased for educational, business, or sales
promotional use. For information, please e-mail the Special Markets Department
at SPsales@harpercollins.com.

Unless otherwise noted, all photographs are courtesy of the George Bush
Presidential Library and Museum.

FIRST EDITION

Library of Congress Cataloging-in-Publication Data has been applied for.

ISBN: 978-0-06-238428-7

15 16 17 18 19   OV/RRD   10 9 8 7 6 5 4 3 2 1

This book is dedicated to my family—
who have always played the largest role in my own journey.
Their support has made it all worthwhile.

CONTENTS

INTRODUCTION

"I'M A QUIET MAN, BUT I HEAR THE QUIET PEOPLE OTHERS DON'T."
—George Herbert Walker Bush, 1988 Republican
Convention Acceptance Speech

I n early 1993, after the inauguration of President Bill Clinton, I was invited to speak to a business group about my life in government and years of service to the man Clinton had defeated the previous year—former president George Herbert Walker Bush. As governor of New Hampshire for three terms, I had worked with Bush long before he was elected to the Oval Office and helped him through a contentious GOP primary against a host of other Republican candidates. Later, as his chief of staff, I served the president faithfully for almost his entire term of office. During the speech, I summarized for the group what I felt were Bush's accomplishments in both foreign and

domestic policy. In the question-and-answer period that immediately followed, I was asked why I felt the president had lost his
reelection bid.

After touching on what I believed were the inadequacies of his
campaign, I noted the historical precedents of losing an election
immediately after leading a nation through a great shift in the
foreign policy landscape.

"The most notable example is Winston Churchill, whom everyone credits with having been the heart and soul of England's
victory over Hitler in World War II," I told the group. "Then,
immediately upon the end of that war, there was an election in
England, and Prime Minister Winston Churchill's party was
voted out of office."

Looking at some of George Bush's partners from the end of
the Cold War, we see very similar results. Mikhail Gorbachev
lost his presidential election in 1991 and Prime Minister Margaret Thatcher lost the leadership of her own party. President
François Mitterrand of France lost an election, as did Brian Mulroney in Canada. Chancellor Helmut Kohl of Germany lost, too,
in 1998. Even the Australian prime minister lost his election, as
did the prime minister of Italy. The Japanese prime minister had
to step down, and his ruling party lost a reelection bid for the
first time since World War II.

I referred to all of this as the "Churchill Effect," and it seems
to afflict leaders after a great foreign policy burden is lifted from
an electorate's shoulders. There is an almost immediate shift in a
nation's agenda. People refocus their attention on domestic needs
and desires, and the new priorities send them in search of new
leaders. It is quite possible that in 1992 George Bush was just a
victim of the Churchill Effect.

George Bush had not just one, but several Churchill moments.
Not only did he orchestrate one of the largest and most successful

military campaigns in history when he drove Saddam Hussein out of Kuwait, but he also adeptly led the world through the most dramatic and remarkable political transformations of the modern era—the fall of the Berlin Wall and the reunification of Germany, the restoration of democracy in Eastern Europe, and the collapse of the Soviet Union. George Bush gently guided America as it stepped onto the stage as the world's lone superpower.

Regrettably, those international achievements have overshadowed President Bush's successes on the domestic side. During the 1992 presidential election campaign, Bill Clinton often accused our forty-first president of not having a domestic agenda, but nothing could be further from the truth. Unlike his successor, who passed only a couple of major bills during his two terms, George Bush was an enormously effective president. Except for Franklin Delano Roosevelt's legislative blitz during the Great Depression and Lyndon Johnson's masterful and opportunistic policy-making run in the aftermath of the assassination of President Kennedy, the domestic legislation of George H. W. Bush is the most prolific, consequential, and precedent-setting of all the modern presidents'.

Ronald Reagan had a great capacity for communicating conservative principles and a conservative agenda. George Bush may not have had the rhetorical skills of the "Great Communicator," but his style of quiet, effective leadership produced policies and legislation that, when considered as a whole, were even more conservative than those of his iconic predecessor. Committed to family values and conservative social principles, George Bush went into office intent on cutting spending, reducing taxes, minimizing regulatory burdens, and using America's strength to maintain peace and stability throughout the world. He was a free-market conservative through and through, and his record in both foreign and domestic policy reflected it.

I believe George Bush was the right man for his time. He was the last American president of the so-called Greatest Generation, which came of age during World War II. Internationally, the time called for a man who inherently understood the historical imperatives of postwar Europe, who was unafraid to project power in the face of tyranny, and who respected the power of his position enough to use it judiciously. The time also called for a man who knew why he loved America and was willing to make it better.

George Herbert Walker Bush is much too modest a man to brag about what he accomplished as the forty-first president of the United States. The conventional wisdom regarding his administration ignores many of his great achievements. Here I put into context not only how he reshaped the face of the world, but also his extraordinary domestic achievements, which have not received the recognition they deserve.

George Bush came into office with a clear vision of what he wanted to accomplish for his country and how he wanted to do it. He guided and sweated out the details with his domestic policy team just as diligently as he attended to foreign affairs with his national security team. In a way, his domestic achievements are even more exceptional because he had to deal with a very partisan and Democratic-controlled Congress throughout his term.

President Bush signed into law more than a dozen major pieces of domestic legislation during his four years in office, including the 1990 budget bill, his energy deregulation legislation, the Clean Air Bill, the Farm Reform Act, his crime bill, the Civil Rights Act of 1991, and the Americans with Disabilities Act. His Education Summit with America's governors produced the first set of "national performance goals" to spur the improvement of education in our K–12 schools. He also passed precedent-setting child care legislation, led the effort to resuscitate the savings and loan industry after the system's collapse, reinvigorated Latin American economies by restructuring bonds under the Brady Plan, and negotiated the North American Free Trade Agreement.

Many of the issues George Bush faced when he took office in 1989 had been lingering for decades—the struggle against communism, instability in Latin America, social inequality, threats to the environment, struggling schools. Solving those issues was a fitting last mission for the former fighter pilot who once told the American people, "I see my life in terms of missions—missions defined, and missions completed." George H. W. Bush's last public mission in the national arena set the stage for a new century and, to use a phrase often heard in those years, a new world order. It was also, not coincidentally, the last time an administration really got it right—working for the country's common interest, above partisan sniping and electoral self-interest.

As an added dividend, the George H. W. Bush administration brought into the national spotlight some figures who would become household names then and in the years that followed. The Bush administration brought Dick Cheney, a member of Congress and former chief of staff for President Gerald R. Ford, to national prominence as secretary of defense. It elevated Colin Powell to chairman of the Joint Chiefs of Staff and international celebrity. With Clarence Thomas, it placed on the Supreme Court the most ardent and principled originalist in American history. And in Roger Ailes, Bush found a political consultant who would go on to transform the American media landscape.

Writing this book required me to break a promise I made to myself when I left the White House in 1992. Back then I made a firm decision not to write any book about my experiences as chief of staff. I did not want to do one of those "kiss and tell" books so often churned out by retiring political figures. At the time, when

I mentioned this decision to the president, he seemed quite satisfied. George Bush was not a great fan of those tell-all books.

Recently, however, I began to have second thoughts about not writing, and I conveyed those thoughts to President Bush during one of our regular lunches at his family home in Kennebunkport, Maine, in the fall of 2013. The Bush compound sits on one of those rugged, rocky stubs of land jutting into the ocean along the Atlantic coast. For well over a century, it has been the place for seven generations of Bushes to gather, bond, relax, recharge their batteries, celebrate victories, mourn defeats, and strategize about the family's future endeavors. The president and Barbara call it the family nest. It is locally known as Walker's Point after the president's mother's side of the family, who originally purchased the property in the late nineteenth century.

That brisk autumn day, my wife, Nancy, and I drove past the Secret Service agents who still guard the compound's gates, then embraced with hugs and handshakes as fine a First Family as has ever lived in the White House. The Bushes were gracious and welcoming as always. We met the president in his little office about a hundred yards from the residence. We lingered there for some time, and our cordial conversation quickly escalated to a fairly raucous, humorous exchange. I teased him about the obnoxiously colorful socks he had started wearing to all his public appearances. We even brought him a couple of pairs to add to his collection.

Eventually, it was time for lunch and, with a young aide pushing his wheelchair down the path, we made our way to the main house, where Barbara, wearing a bold pink sunshield of a hat, joined us. We sat down on the back deck overlooking the Atlantic Ocean for a leisurely lunch of lobster salad and other trimmings. The first hour of conversation focused on what was happening around the country and the world. As lunch wound down, our discussion turned to whether or not the president would consider another parachute jump on his ninetieth birthday in June (he had celebrated his seventy-fifth, eightieth, and eighty-fifth birthdays by skydiving). He was all for it, but I could tell from the stern look on Barbara's face that perhaps she was not sold on it yet. She would later relent, however, and the president would spend part of that birthday drifting earthward under a red-white-and-blue parachute with veteran members of the US Army's Golden Knights group.

Changing the subject that day, I told both Bushes that I felt it was time for the full story of his administration to be told—to document what he had achieved in both the domestic and the international arenas during his presidency. I lamented that so many of his accomplishments were still unappreciated and perhaps even unknown to members of the younger generation.

"I have been thinking about writing the book I said I would never write," I told him.

They both responded quickly and supportively. "Great idea. Go to it," the president said.

That is how this book was born.

No one spends more time with the president than his chief of staff. There were very few meetings at which I was not in the room, and I had the opportunity to hear the president's candid opinions and see how he shaped his decisions. This book, the first from a White House chief of staff in more than twenty-five years, tells the story from the perspective of a hands-on participant who was there to witness everything as it happened in the Oval Office. I believe it will change what people think they know about George H. W. Bush, the forty-first president of the United States.

I examine the president's decision-making process during the Gulf War, during the fall of the Soviet Union, and during his meetings with world leaders such as Mikhail Gorbachev, Margaret Thatcher, François Mitterrand, Boris Yeltsin, and Helmut Kohl. We see his determination as he directed steps to fix the savings and loan crisis, put together the 1990 budget, and pressed for and signed other major pieces of legislation. All were important events for people here in the United States and around the world. I know how President Bush dealt with each one of these issues, and how the decisions he struggled with were ultimately made.

The chapters that follow provide behind-the-scenes details of the Bush presidency, beginning with my efforts to help George H. W. Bush win the 1988 Republican nomination for president when I was governor of New Hampshire and ran his primary campaign, and ending with my last days in the White House in 1992. It is not, nor is it intended to be, a definitive history of President Bush's administration; rather, it is one man's recollections of and perspectives on some of the most important events of the last generation.

The
Quiet Man

1

Journey to the White House

━━━━━━━

One of the first visitors to the Oval Office after President George Herbert Walker Bush was inaugurated in January 1989 was his mother, Dorothy Walker Bush. A small-framed woman with wavy blond hair and a complexion perpetually freckled by long summer days in Maine, Dorothy Bush was the embodiment of good manners and breeding. Her influence over her son, it was said, was of an order of magnitude greater than that of anyone else in his life, so it was fitting that on the day after he took the oath of office, President Bush guided the eighty-eight-year-old great-grandmother gently by the elbow to one of the off-white chairs dominating the most powerful sitting area in the world.

He sat by her protectively while a gaggle of reporters and photographers were allowed to gather in the doorway for a photo op. It was, she told the assembled group, "the most exciting day of my life so far." Bush beamed and pointed to her. "This is the one that told me not to brag about myself, and bend my knees when I volley."

The directives from his mother may have originally been meant for the world of sports, but I believe the president kept them both front and center throughout his career in politics as well. His mother came from and existed in a world of privilege, but took great pains to see that her children were not spoiled by it. Her edict not to brag about yourself not only influenced her son's reluctance to tout his accomplishments but also implied an obligation to perform well enough so there would be successes about which you could modestly refrain from bragging and leave to others to acknowledge.

And the admonition to "bend your knees when you volley," a tennis reference, reminded the president that competition was good, and that when you competed—be it athletically, politically, or diplomatically—there was a proper, correct way to be most effective. The president's daughter, Dorothy "Doro" Bush, spelled it out well. "My father has lived his life by certain standards, by a certain set of rules, and with a certain way of doing things that go a long way towards explaining the man he is today."

When George Bush spoke about the "certain standards," he often put them in the context of attributes his parents had, but they clearly were attributes he inherited as well and practiced in every facet of his life. He said of his mother, "She never hurt anyone's feelings. She always tried to see the other guy's point of view." And his description of his father, Senator Prescott Bush of Connecticut, certainly applied to the president: "Big. Strong. Principled. Respected by all who knew him. A leader. Wonderful sense of humor."

When I heard George H. W. Bush speak those stirring words "I do solemnly swear . . ." on January 20, 1989, I think I was almost as excited as his mother. I was looking forward to serving as his chief of staff at a time when it looked as if the world was poised to make historic changes. I saw few other people in political life better suited to maneuvering in those choppy waters than Bush. In addition to his impeccable upbringing by Dorothy Walker Bush, he had a top-notch education and had served his country heroically in the military in World War II. He successfully ran a business, served two terms in Congress, and then was America's envoy to China and our ambassador to the United Nations. He ran the CIA before serving two terms as the country's vice president. One doesn't come across résumés like that much anymore.

Born in 1924, still a child during the Great Depression but largely shielded from its effects, Bush entered Phillips Andover Academy, a prestigious boarding school in Massachusetts, in the fall of 1938 and graduated four years later. Many of Bush's character traits gelled at Andover, among them a knack for leadership as captain of the baseball team and the soccer team and a respect for tradition. Phillips, he said, "was a huge influence in my life, more so than college."

After graduation, just months after the Japanese attack on Pearl Harbor pulled the United States into World War II, he enlisted in the United States Navy on his eighteenth birthday, and after eleven months of aviation training he earned his wings and a promotion. He was eventually assigned to the aircraft carrier USS *San Jacinto*.

The youngest aviator in the US Navy at the time, he flew fifty-eight combat missions in the Pacific. In June 1944, after completing a torpedo run on an enemy radio site, his plane was shot down by Japanese antiaircraft fire. His two crewmates were killed, but George Bush parachuted into the ocean and, after floating in a life raft for a short while, he was rescued by the submarine USS *Finback*. Amazingly, the recovery was captured on film. The jerky black-and-white footage shows a jumpsuited Bush being dragged onto the deck and then walking purposefully toward the hatch. At one point, the young Bush looks straight at the camera with uncharacteristic alarm in his eyes. I think it's the only time I have ever seen him look really shaken up.

Underneath his kinder and gentler exterior are a bona fide toughness and a commitment to complete his missions. After he was shot down—he was awarded the Distinguished Flying Cross for his heroism—he arrived in Hawaii for reassignment. He was offered a choice of returning to the United States or rejoining his old squadron, which was still battling in the Pacific. Bush elected to return to his squadron.

Bush stayed with the squadron until just before Christmas 1944, when he returned to the United States. The following month he married Barbara Pierce, whom he had met three years earlier at a dance in Greenwich, Connecticut. He returned immediately afterward to finish out his war service in a new squadron, but the war ended before the unit was deployed back into action. That fall, as part of the wave of GIs returning to civilian life, he enrolled at Yale University, and quickly distinguished himself there, too. He earned entry into the honor society Phi Beta Kappa and the prestigious secret undergraduate society Skull and Bones, and was selected captain of the almost–national championship Yale baseball team. There is a great photo of George Bush with Babe Ruth, taken just a few months before Ruth lost his battle with cancer. Bush is in his baseball uniform, accepting the original manuscript of Ruth's autobiography for the university library.

Bush himself described the event. "I was the captain of the ball club, so I got to receive him there. He was dying. He was hoarse and could hardly talk. . . . His whole great shape was gaunt and hollowed out." I was so struck by the photo linking one of my baseball heroes with the president I worked for that I later chased down a copy and asked Bush to sign it for me.

Rather than rely on family patronage after graduation, Bush insisted on making his own way and in 1948 moved himself and his young family to West Texas, where the young veteran launched a career in the oil business. He began in the oil equipment business, but within a couple of years he had started his own company on the production side of the industry. He soon merged his firm with that of two brothers, Hugh and Bill Liedtke, and they named the new enterprise Zapata Petroleum Corporation. Bush and his colleagues at Zapata turned out to be pioneers in the then-developing field of offshore drilling.

In 1964, after succeeding in the private sector, George Bush, mindful of his family's tradition that those of means give back to a society that has been good to them, turned to public service. He won the Republican primary for a U.S. Senate seat from Texas, but lost in the general election to Democrat Ralph Yarborough, an incumbent buoyed by fellow Democrat and Texan Lyndon Johnson's overwhelming presidential win. Two years later, Bush gave national office another go, and this time he was elected congressman from the state's Seventh Congressional District. At the time, he was one of only two Republicans in the twenty-three-person Texas congressional delegation.

In his first term as a congressman (1967–69), Bush demonstrated his commitment to principle even in the face of strong political headwinds. Congress was debating the third major civil rights bill to be passed during the Johnson administration, the Civil Rights Act of 1968 (also known as the Fair Housing Act). The bill was very controversial, particularly in the South and in Texas, where pockets of opposition to equal rights remained. In spite of some serious constituent pressure and even threats, George Bush voted in favor of the bill.

Bush was reelected in 1968 with little serious opposition. He took advantage of the light load required in his own campaign by stumping aggressively on behalf of Richard Nixon's presidential effort. Former vice president Nixon had come into Texas to support Bush in 1966 and later asked him to be one of a small group of surrogate speakers in his 1968 campaign.

Throughout his life and political career, George Bush demonstrated a commitment to personal loyalty that inspired me and everyone around him. Despite any philosophical differences he may have had with Lyndon Johnson, Bush remembered the kind words the president had for his father, Prescott Bush, when the two men served in the U.S. Senate together in the 1950s, and he stood beside Johnson to the end—literally. On Nixon's inauguration day, Bush skipped the swearing in of his fellow Republican and trekked out to Andrews Air Force Base to join in the farewells for President Johnson and Lady Bird Johnson. Surprised to see the young GOP congressman there among the well-wishers, Lady Bird Johnson, never one to mince words, later described Bush as "not only a strong Republican but . . . a warm and caring man who wrote the book on friendship."

In 1970, Bush tried once more to win a U.S. Senate seat representing Texas, but was again defeated in the general election, this time by Lloyd Bentsen. After the loss, in December 1971, President Nixon called on Bush to serve as ambassador to the United Nations. In 1973, Nixon named him chairman of the Republican National Committee.

Bush headed the RNC during the last tumultuous months that Nixon was in office. Somehow, he was able to maintain a deep and lasting friendship with Richard Nixon even though, at Nixon's last cabinet meeting, George Bush was one of the few with the courage to tell the president to his face that it was time to resign. Again, in a handwritten note delivered to Nixon the next day, Bush told the embattled president that it was his "considered judgment" that he should step down. "It would now ill-serve a president whose massive accomplishments I will always respect and whose family I will always love, if I did not now give you my judgment," he wrote.

Gerald Ford, Nixon's vice president, and Bush, as head of the RNC, together rode out those difficult days leading to Nixon's resignation, and Ford, when he took over as president in August 1974, rewarded Bush by naming him envoy to the People's Republic of China. Nixon had surprised the world two years earlier by opening diplomatic relations with the most populous country in the world, and potentially one of the most powerful. George Bush understood the importance of that new relationship and was willing to take a chance on the distant and untested position because he was certain China would some day be a global power.

The China service proved to be a dream assignment for Bush. Although he often felt frustrated by his lack of access to leaders at the very top of the Communist Party's power structure at the time, the friends he made then would later be in the top ranks when he was president, and those friendships would prove important as he dealt with the Tiananmen Square crackdown in 1989.

Bush would remain in China for only about a year. In 1976, President Ford asked him to return home and take over as director of the Central Intelligence Agency. It was not a position Bush had actively sought, and in some circles it was considered detrimental to one's political ambitions, but he told Ford that he had been raised by his father to "serve his country and his president."

His year at the CIA (January 1976 to January 1977) gave Bush an even stronger appreciation for the quality of our men and women in the intelligence service and the value of their service to the strength of the nation. Following the crises of the Vietnam War, Watergate, and the Church Committee's findings, he worked hard to restore America's faith in the intelligence community and rebuild the working relationship between the intelligence agencies and Congress. The bond Bush developed with the men and women of the CIA was both intellectual and emotional, and instead of hurting him politically, the tenure, though brief, ended up helping him through the rest of his career.

George Bush and Jerry Ford were old and good friends. Bush, in his typically self-deprecating manner, had a laugh at his own expense when he released a letter he wrote to Congressman Gerald Ford in 1966 when Ford was the Republican House minority leader. Bush started the letter with the salutation, "Dear Gerry." The correct spelling of Ford's nickname, as everyone else in political life knew at the time, was with a J—"Jerry." Bush sheepishly admitted that he had not figured that out yet.

Four decades later, when Bush gave the eulogy at Ford's funeral in January 2007, he knew how to spell his old pal's name correctly. In his remarks, Bush made a point of saying that Jerry Ford was "a good man" and that his "word was always good." These were traits he valued highly in others, and traits he also carried himself, as Ford noted when he swore Bush in as head of the CIA. Bush, he said, was "a good man," with strength of character.

When Bush was president, he called Ford every now and then to let him know what was happening in the rapidly changing world. And Ford would sometimes call me, as chief of staff, with a message for the president when he did not want to bother Bush directly or, on a couple of occasions, to ask for my assistance with the messy and complicated logistics of being a former president. I grew quite fond of Ford, and always found him to be a very supportive and empathetic individual.

After I announced my own resignation, Ford was one of the first people with whom I met. I called on him at his home in Rancho Mirage, California, and he went out of his way to let me know that he thought I had served George Bush the way Ford would have wanted his own chief of staff to serve. He also confided to me that Bush knew I had been "catching the arrows and spears for him." As usual with Ford, the meeting was warm and cordial, and lasted more than a couple of hours.

One of the many things I admired about George Bush was that he was smart enough to use those relationships with former presidents to good advantage, and humble enough to seek their advice as often as he saw fit. Bush knew Nixon, Ford, and Ronald Reagan, with whom he served two terms, very well. He did not know Jimmy Carter as well, but went out of his way when he was in office to keep the Georgia Democrat informed on issues in which the former president had a special interest, such as the Middle East. I believe George Bush felt that of all the former presidents, Nixon had the best grasp on the tough policy issues Bush was facing when he was later in office himself. On occasion, he would call Richard Nixon just to keep him up to date. Nixon often reciprocated with calls offering a suggestion or two.

In 1980, Bush ran for president of the United States against Ronald Reagan, but withdrew from the race a couple of months after losing the New Hampshire primary. Bush had shocked the Reagan campaign and the experts by winning the 1980 Iowa caucuses and riding into the New Hampshire primary with what he felt was big momentum, or "Big Mo," as he put it in his Iowa victory speech. But "Big Mo" did not carry the day in New Hampshire, and Reagan won a decisive primary victory. The Bush campaign hung on through a few more states, but by the last week in May he and his campaign manager, Jim Baker, decided there was no way they could remain competitive.

On May 26, 1980, the Bush team took off on a campaign plane for a scheduled stop in Houston. Just after they were airborne, the plane audio started playing the hit song Kenny Rogers had released a couple of years earlier, "The Gambler." When Kenny got to the line "You've got to know when to hold 'em, know when to fold 'em," the staff got the message. When the plane landed in Houston, Bush told the press his campaign was over.

At the Republican National Convention, Ronald Reagan selected him as his running mate, and the Reagan-Bush ticket defeated incumbent President Jimmy Carter by a landslide in the November election. On January 20, 1981, George Bush was sworn in as vice president, and he served dutifully and actively through both of Reagan's historic terms.

When the time came for Bush to make another run for the presidency in 1988, he turned to Lee Atwater, who had been deputy manager of the Reagan campaign in 1980, to run the show. Atwater was only thirty-five years old when Bush tapped him, but he had already built a reputation for running hard-hitting, winning campaigns for Governor Carroll Campbell and U.S. senator Strom Thurmond in his home state, South Carolina. Lee Atwater was an especially talented competitor with a good nose for issues that could be used effectively to peel off segments of voters who might otherwise be indifferent or even opposed to his candidate. Reagan had him to thank for identifying the most compelling issues to attract the so-called Reagan Democrats who helped swing the election in favor of the Republicans. For Bush, he ran a well-funded, tough, aggressive campaign that attacked the record of his opponent, Massachusetts governor Michael Dukakis, on issues such as crime, the environment, national security, and taxes.

I found Atwater to be a hardworking, focused, and very smart political operative. He understood the American electorate better, perhaps, than anyone else in the political game at the time. Early on, he discovered that the American voter generally has a very limited personal list of priorities and if candidates could address those priorities, or even just one of them, with a hard-hitting message, those voters could be won over. He also appreciated the nuanced differences in priorities across the demographic groups in America.

Later, Atwater and I had long discussions about different groups who could be courted as swing votes during the general elections. We both felt that the Catholic vote in America was quickly evolving into one of the most important swing votes because many Roman Catholics, when polled on issues, clearly looked as if they belonged on the conservative side of the spectrum, although they tended to vote on the more liberal side. Their beliefs looked Republican, but they often voted Democratic.

Those voters were the Czechs and Poles in the manufacturing Midwest, the autoworkers and the steelworkers of the Rust Belt, the Irish vote in New York and Boston, the Hispanics in California and Cubans in Florida, and the French-Canadians I knew in New Hampshire. Atwater and I both believed that with the right message, these constituencies could be attracted to the Republican side. The message did not involve religion, however: each regional packet was moved by different nonsectarian, political issues specific to its circumstances.

In 1980, Atwater helped Reagan develop a message to capture the interest of these voters in the Midwest. Catholics with Eastern European roots, often union members, had been voting Democratic for a generation or more out of sheer habit. Atwater helped Reagan focus on an anticommunist message with rhetoric condemning the Soviet occupations in the Eastern European countries, peeling those voters away from the Democratic side and broadening the Republican base. They were the blue-collar Democrats—the Reagan Democrats—who were, at least temporarily, part of the evolving conservative majority of the 1980s.

One evening, after Lee Atwater had been named chairman of the Republican National Committee, I stopped in at his office at the RNC on my way home from the White House. A television mounted on the wall was tuned to a channel carrying wrestling.

"What are you doing watching wrestling?"

"I am not watching wrestling!" he insisted.

"What's with the half-naked guys grappling each other with armlocks and choke holds then?"

"I'm not watching them," he said. "I'm watching the audience. That audience is a big part of the swing vote in America."

My thoughts returned to the simple wisdom of that statement a couple of years later, in 1991, when Atwater died after a year-long struggle with brain cancer. It was a tragic loss to all who knew him. I'm fairly certain that if he had survived to manage the president's reelection bid in 1992, Bush would have sailed into a second term.

My own dealings with George Bush date to 1979, when he came to New Hampshire during his first presidential campaign. The principal contenders for the Republican nomination that year were Bush and Ronald Reagan. Because my wife, Nancy, was chair of the State Republican Committee and had to remain neutral, I made no public declaration of support for either of the candidates, though I ended up voting for Ronald Reagan in the primary election. Since the candidates in New Hampshire presidential primaries are very accessible to all voters—not just to family members of senior party officials—I had a number of opportunities to meet and get to know George Bush.

After the presidential primary that year, I myself entered the race for the U.S. Senate seat held at the time by Democrat John Durkin. That primary was held in September 1980, and I came in second to New Hampshire's attorney general, Warren Rudman, in a field filled with a number of significant Republicans, including former governor Wesley Powell and several state legislative leaders. Rudman was the only notable Republican moderate in the race, and it was important to encourage our more conservative voters to support him against the Democratic incumbent, so, after the primary, I agreed to chair Rudman's general election campaign to help unify the party. Rudman went on to narrowly win the race, riding Reagan's coattails in the "Reagan Revolution."

President Reagan and Vice President Bush developed a very strong and warm personal relationship. From the beginning of their days in the White House they shared a weekly lunch, and over that lunch they discussed Reagan's agenda, the issues of the day, and the ups and downs of politics. In his conversations with President Reagan, Bush was candid and direct with his opinions, but always made sure they were kept confidential.

When Reagan was shot by John Hinckley on March 3, 1981, Bush handled the crisis in a firm but low-key manner, and got great credit for his sensitive demeanor. He demonstrated the capacity to do what was necessary without appearing to be overly eager to fill the role.

As vice president, George Bush focused primarily on deregulation and Reagan's war on drugs. He also represented the president at so many state funerals around the world that he often, but discreetly, used the self-deprecating motto "You die—I fly." Reagan and Bush ran again as a team in 1984 and were easily reelected.

As vice president, Bush helped Ronald Reagan dramatically change the political landscape in eight short years. The Reagan defense buildup clearly altered the balance of geopolitical power in America's favor. By the end of the Reagan terms, a plausible path to a more stable and peaceful relationship with the Soviet Union was beginning to emerge. The U.S. economy had been stabilized. The runaway inflation of the 1970s had been tamed and jobs were once again plentiful. There remained a growing gulf between what the U.S. government spent and the revenue it raised in the form of taxes, but at least the private sector was back on its feet. Most significant, perhaps, was that Ronald Reagan's faith in and optimism about America had restored pride and hope across the country.

Following Reagan's election in 1980, during the next election cycle, in 1982, the party asked me to run for governor against the incumbent Democrat, Hugh Gallen. I agreed, even though the governor looked as if he would win easily in a midterm election year that would heavily favor the Democrats. In September 1982, I won a fairly tight Republican primary and had only eight weeks to prepare for the general election.

Our compressed election cycle made it difficult for any primary winner challenging an incumbent to raise the money necessary to run a successful campaign. I needed to quickly pull together a major event to do just that. The day after the primary, I called Vice President George Bush and asked if he would come up to speak at such an event. Without hesitation, he said, "Count me in." Less than two weeks later, he spoke at a political dinner in Manchester that raised virtually all of the money we needed. It was the first time I called on Bush for a political favor and, in typical George Bush style, he immediately said yes and delivered on his commitment.

Election day in 1982 was, for me, the typical long-wait day that all candidates experience at the end of a campaign. By then there was nothing else to say. Every endorsement had been made. Every hand had been shaken. Mailers were sent. Ads were run. There was nothing more that could possibly be done. Our last poll, taken on the Sunday just two days before the election, had me trailing the incumbent governor by five points, so I was somewhat resigned to the likelihood that the election would not finish with a win in the Sununu column.

Even though I had that in mind, Tuesday was still a day of nervous waiting. I dropped by several voting precincts to thank volunteers who continued to support my campaign down to the last moments by getting voters to the polls and holding up signs with my name on them outside the polling places. I made the decision to spend most of the day on the West Side of Manchester. That part of the city was home to many of the wonderful, working-class New Hampshire citizens whose families had emigrated to the state from Quebec in the early 1900s to find jobs in the once thriving mills. Though primarily Democrats, they were classic blue-collar, hardworking conservatives by nature, so I had made a concerted effort to court them and even cut a couple of ads in French for the two French-speaking radio stations in the area. As I walked that day around the West Side schools and community centers where people were voting, I was struck by the kind and friendly reaction I got from people walking in and out to cast their ballots. Many of them went out of their way to stop and chat and to compliment my family and me. Still, recalling the results of my own Sunday poll, I harbored no illusions about actually winning the contest.

As was typical for any candidate, regardless of the polls, we had scheduled our "victory party" at the Highway Hotel in Concord. Expecting a loss, Nancy and I went out to dinner with two of our very closest friends. On the way back to the party after dinner, at about 7:55 p.m., we turned on the car radio. The polls closed at 8:00, and at about 8:05, the news stations began reporting that, on the basis of exit polling, I was going to be the upset winner of the election. When we finally had a chance to look at hard numbers later, we discovered that I had nearly won the heavily Democratic city of Manchester, with a surprisingly strong showing on the West Side and from the other blue-collar, ethnic neighborhoods in the city.

Voter registration in Manchester in 1982 was about two to one in favor of the Democrats. In my three terms as governor (1983–89) I worked hard to court blue-collar Democrats. I made a concerted effort to connect with them on family values issues and to manage the state budgets in much the same way they ran their household budgets—frugally and efficiently. The strategy was a successful one. By the time I left office seven years later, Republican registration in Manchester had grown significantly, to the point that there were almost as many Republicans as there were Democrats on the rolls. That shift in party support was happening not just in New Hampshire: it was happening across the country, and would be a critical part of the political landscape for years to come.

From the time I first took office as governor of New Hampshire in January 1983, Vice President Bush was very supportive of what I was trying to accomplish. He continued to be just as supportive when I was elected chairman of the Republican Governors Association in 1985, and chairman of the National Governors Association in 1987. At that time, like many other governors across the country, I was working in a bipartisan way to get Congress to understand the value of giving the states some flexibility in the manner in which they implemented federal programs. Bush understood that, and we communicated often during those years.

During my own reelection campaign in 1986 I began seeing quite a bit more of Vice President Bush as he and Lee Atwater, soon to be his campaign manager, became regular visitors to New Hampshire. Atwater lobbied hard to convince me to make a public commitment to support Bush for president as early as possible. I had come to know George and Barbara Bush fairly well by then, and had already decided in my own mind that he was the presidential candidate I would support in the 1988 primary. Not long after I was sworn in for my third term in 1987, I publicly endorsed the vice president and agreed to serve as cochair for his campaign in the state. I let him know I would do it by calling him and saying, "As a good friend once said to me, 'Count me in.'" He laughed heartily, and a relationship both professional and personal was cemented.

I began organizing the Bush campaign in early 1987 along with former governor Hugh Gregg and his son, then congressman Judd Gregg. Joining us was Andrew "Andy" Card, who had worked in the Reagan White House and, with his Massachusetts roots, was an astute observer of New Hampshire primaries. Andy would later serve as my deputy chief of staff in the Bush White House.

Our first task that year was to sign up a Bush chairman and a vice chairman in every town and voting precinct. The U.S. senator Warren Rudman and former attorney general Tom Rath were doing the same on behalf of the man who would be Bush's main opponent in the campaign, U.S. senator Robert Dole of Kansas. The Dole camp had the same objectives, but the leverage and perquisites I had as governor trumped the influence of a senator working in Washington, even when that senator was Warren Rudman.

The campaign kickoff took place at the Gregg family homestead. Thousands of volunteers and voters showed up. It was the perfect place to begin our yearlong quest to get Bush to shake fifty thousand hands and be photographed with five thousand supporters. After all, if people have a picture of themselves and the vice president on the living room mantel, they will work very hard to make it a picture of themselves and the president.

Bush described the day in his diary:

We fly to Greenfield, NH to the Judd Gregg home and there is a crowd in excess of 2,000 people. One of the biggest crowds, if not the biggest, that I've ever seen in NH. It was fantastic. Judd

Gregg, John Sununu and I spoke. They were very brief, and I was informal. Sununu told me that I had fire in my belly and it was the best he had ever heard me give. . . . I shook every one of those hands, and it took two hours, walking up and down the rope line, endless pictures, autographs and literally, by the time I got finished, just before I spoke, my tendon and arm hurt.

One of the interesting discoveries I made when I became governor was how strongly coveted low-digit automobile license plates were. For some reason, everyone with a car in New Hampshire wanted to have just two or three or even four numerals under the "Live Free or Die" state motto on their license plate. It was a brag of sorts. By tradition, when a low-digit license plate was turned back in to the state because the registrant moved out of state or died, the governor, via the director of Motor Vehicles, got to choose who received that number when it was reissued. When I became governor, I wasn't sure on what basis I could or would decide how to reissue those numbers, so I temporarily ordered that none of them be reissued until I resolved the process in my own mind. During my first four years in office, a few hundred of these plate numbers piled up. Most were four-digit plates that were quite coveted, but also in the mix were a few three-digit ones and, most prized of all, a handful of two-digit numbers. They turned out to be a gold mine.

Once we got the Bush campaign rolling, I quickly decided how I wanted to put those plates to use. As we rode around the state encouraging the more influential political figures to join us on the Bush team, we quickly discovered that whenever one of the more desirable opinion leaders was having trouble deciding whether to support Bush or Dole, the promise of a low-digit license plate was a very effective tiebreaker. In 1987 and 1988, we built the deepest, broadest, and most effective political campaign machine ever assembled in the state. I attribute much of that success to making good use of that hoard of license plate numbers tucked away in the bowels of the DMV.

The 1988 Republican primary stands out as a classic example of what makes the New Hampshire primary phenomenon unique and so important. The reason the Granite State has had such a significant impact on American presidential elections isn't just that it is early and so many candidates are still in the race. Rather, it's that the citizens of New Hampshire take their role in the process seriously. They commit a great deal of personal time and effort to meeting and getting to know the candidates.

With that in mind, our team had George and Barbara Bush campaign across the state throughout 1987. Coffees in people's living rooms. Luncheons at local VFW posts. Rallies in small town squares. County fairs. Factories. Schools. We hit them all. These traditional opportunities allowed Bush the candidate to explain his positions and let New Hampshire voters see and hear him in person, shake his hand, and get a photo. We wanted to create a firm, positive perception of who George Bush really was before the closing days of the campaign, when we knew the rhetoric would get hot and tough. On the surface, it was a very smooth, good old "see-me-touch-me-feel-me" New Hampshire campaign. Behind the scenes, though, it was a frantic but focused year of preparation for what we all knew would be a very intense eight days between the Iowa caucus and the New Hampshire primary.

New Year's Eve in Concord was fairly typical. We took over a furniture store downtown during that city's First Night celebration, rearranged the sofas and chairs to give the place a homey feel, and invited anyone and everyone to come by to shake hands with the Bushes and get a Polaroid picture taken. It was a bitterly cold evening, but the line still stretched around the block. Judd

Gregg and I hustled around delivering cups of hot chocolate to the throngs standing on line, shuffling their feet and blowing into their cupped hands. By the end of the evening, I believe, something over a couple of thousand people passed through. And each one of them got a personal "Thank you for joining us tonight" along with a heartfelt handshake or embrace. The warmth of the Bushes on that cold New Hampshire evening impressed a lot of voters.

Another special day that proved the value of "see-me-touch-me" politics was also in December 1987. I asked the vice president to interrupt his Christmas holiday quiet time in Maine to come down to Manchester and do a half-hour interview with the political reporter for the local ABC affiliate, WMUR-TV. He asked me, rather sternly I must say, "Why do we have to do this?" I really didn't have a good answer other than to assure him that one day it might prove helpful. He was clearly not happy about it, but he trusted me, so he and Barbara agreed to make the hour-and-a-half drive down.

When the Bushes arrived to tape the interview, the station manager and staff were all there waiting with their families. George and Barbara graciously and patiently chatted with everyone and smiled for all the snapshots. Later, on the final weekend before the primary, when we decided at the last minute to change our advertising spot to one that was critical of Senator Dole's position on taxes, the manager of WMUR was more than happy to come back in to juggle things at the station despite the inconveniently late hour. He was, he said, happy to accommodate his "dear friend the vice president." Later that same evening, when I saw the vice president, I told him how the manager had gone out of his way for us.

"Remember when you asked me why you had to come down to WMUR over Christmas?" I teased him. "That's why."

Bush seemed pleased with our campaign efforts on his behalf in New Hampshire, and as we approached the end of 1987 and our primary election day, he urged me to get more involved in the national effort. Although any significant work outside the state was somewhat limited by the reality of my responsibilities as governor, there were some very interesting and exciting opportunities that I simply could not pass up.

For one, Vice President Bush invited me to meet Mikhail Gorbachev, the leader of the Soviet Union, a couple of months before the vote in New Hampshire. General Secretary Gorbachev was in Washington for a series of meetings with officials in the Reagan administration and invited Bush to have breakfast with him at the Soviet Embassy on December 10, 1987. The vice president asked me and his then chief of staff Craig Fuller, as well as former congressman T. Cooper Evans (R-Iowa), to join him at the breakfast.

It was my first chance to see Gorbachev up close and personal. I was impressed at how animated he was in conversation and how frequently he smiled, especially considering how tough things were for him at home. It was obvious to me that Gorbachev wanted to ensure that if Bush won the election in November he would continue to work with Gorbachev to expand the initiatives that had already begun under Reagan. I also think that in putting me in the room with the Soviet leader, Bush—besides sharing a little bit of history with me—wanted to see how a governor from a small state like New Hampshire might fit within the political and diplomatic cauldron of Washington. Considering that he kept urging me to get more and more involved after that breakfast, I suspect I passed that review, and I agreed to work to get endorsements for him from my Republican gubernatorial colleagues.

In Washington, James Baker, Lee Atwater, and Roger Ailes, a veteran television producer and consultant with political roots going back to the Nixon era, were leading Bush's national strategy, and we all worked closely together on the critical first primary in New Hampshire. They didn't have my hoard of license plates, but they understood New Hampshire better than most DC political consultants. Equally important, both Atwater and Ailes understood the power of hard-hitting messages and television commercials to define the differences between candidates. Unlike the tepid team that would run Bush's 1992 reelection campaign, they were more interested in making sure their candidate won than just looking good to their friends in the press.

Ailes was a close friend of George Bush and joined the campaign to direct the media activities. One of his most successful efforts on the candidate's behalf was in managing an interview Bush did with *CBS Evening News* anchor Dan Rather. CBS had been pressing for an interview with candidate Bush for a long time, and the campaign finally agreed to do it in January 1988. At Ailes's insistence, however, Bush would not do the interview on tape. He knew that the notoriously liberal Dan Rather and CBS could edit a taped interview to make Bush look bad regardless of how the interview actually took place. Instead, Ailes said Bush would do the interview only if CBS aired it live and uninterrupted. Rather and CBS agreed.

Ailes helped Bush prepare for a variety of contingencies. He also warned the vice president that CBS, rather than just asking about the campaign in general, might choose to home in on a particular unflattering issue such as the Iran-Contra affair. As expected, CBS aired a prerecorded segment on the Iran-Contra situation before beginning the live interview of Bush by Rather.

Ailes and Bush had been tipped off by one of their few friends at CBS that Rather and his team were bragging about how their interview would "take Bush out" from the campaign. Ailes made sure Bush understood how adversarial the interview was likely to be, and emphasized to the vice president how important it was for him to do his homework. "They are prepared, you are not," he warned Bush.

Beyond the factual preparation, Ailes made sure that the vice president realized that he had to stay on the offensive. In case the interview really began to get out of hand, Ailes suggested that Bush bring up an embarrassing tidbit from Rather's own career—a time the previous year when the anchor had a temper tantrum and stormed off the set because his *Evening News* broadcast was preempted by a tennis match. A hundred or so CBS affiliates across the country aired seven minutes of silence and Rather was forced to apologize for his gaffe the next day.

During the interview, Ailes positioned himself just off-camera but in a spot where Bush could still see him. When Rather started getting overly aggressive in his questioning, Ailes signaled Bush to raise the dead air incident. "How would you like it if I judged your career by those seven minutes when you walked off the set in New York?" Bush asked. Rather sat there for a moment in stunned silence, his lips pursed angrily. The famously combative anchor never really recovered, and Bush came out of the interview the clear winner. Ailes's advice to and support of Bush made a huge difference in the image the vice president was able to project on network television.

We knew that the Iowa caucus—next door to Dole's home state, Kansas—was the first significant hurdle. In 1980, George Bush had shocked the Reagan campaign with an unexpected victory in Iowa, and Reagan had to scramble in New Hampshire to get his campaign back on track. We expected Bush to come out of Iowa again with a strong victory, but we made sure the New Hampshire operation had enough depth and strength to handle whatever happened in the Hawkeye State.

Finally, the Iowa caucus arrived. This time the result was far different from the outcome in 1980, and much worse than what we expected. Bush lost badly, coming in third, behind Senator Dole and the Reverend Pat Robertson, a favorite of Christian conservatives. It was a devastating political blow. The reaction in the press and through much of the political chattering classes was that Senator Dole had the momentum after Iowa and George Bush was fading fast. That meant the New Hampshire organization was going to be tested. We were prepared.

George Bush had been defining his positions and personality with New Hampshire voters for more than a year. He had met with them, listened to them, and shared time with them. Whether or not they agreed with him on every issue, most voters knew he was a good man.

When George and Barbara Bush arrived in New Hampshire for the last week of handshakes and stump speeches, they were both a bit down after their unexpected loss in Iowa. I tried to let them know we were absolutely ready and prepared, and told them to relax. My message was clear: "Iowa picks corn. New Hampshire picks presidents." The campaign was ready to cash in on the fund of goodwill and support it had accumulated over the past year. I was confident that he could and would sail to victory, and I told them so: "New Hampshire will be about a ten-point victory," I told the Bushes—and I meant it.

Everything we did that last week was designed to remind voters why they supported George Bush. The personal contact continued. Three fast-food breakfasts a day, in the driver's seat of an eighteen-wheeler at a regional truck stop, rallies, an ice-fishing stop with baseball great Ted Williams during a snowy trek to Wolfeboro to show he cared about the North Country, and visits to malls, town halls, and schools—all with hordes of national media in close pursuit.

Not only was George Bush a quiet man; he was a nice, kind

man. He became somewhat uncomfortable when discussing his opponent during a campaign, especially if the discussion took on negative undertones.

The late 1980s were a period of evolution in campaign advertising. Candidates began running harder-hitting messages and harder-hitting ads against their opponents. In the 1988 Democratic primaries, in New Hampshire, it was Tennessee senator Al Gore who first introduced the issue of Willie Horton, a convicted murderer serving a life sentence in Massachusetts for having raped a woman during a weekend furlough from prison, in an attack ad against rival Massachusetts governor Michael Dukakis. Although many in the media later blamed Bush, and Roger Ailes, for recycling Gore's Willie Horton issue, it was actually an independent group that used it against Dukakis in the subsequent general election. Most of the attack ads between Bush and Dole in the primary concerned issues like taxes and national security. Those commercials, for both sides, were a bit tougher and more direct than had been the norm up to that time, and were initially a bit difficult for the "old school" George Bush to accept, but once his opponent started pounding him, he was smart enough to understand that this was a new era in campaigning.

I had been willing to take the lead in responding to Dole's early attacks on the vice president, and supported a tough response in our debate over whether to run an ad in the primary attacking Dole for flip-flopping on taxes. As a result, when the campaign became more intense, I found him relying on me more and more to provide the counterpoint against the opposition. Eventually he became more comfortable and responded to some of the charges himself, but all the way through to the end, I found myself in the role of delivering the really tough messages.

There wasn't much difference between Dole and Bush on national security issues. They both had been lifelong supporters of a strong defense and were very comfortable with Ronald Reagan's theme of "peace through strength." So, seeking an advantage, the Dole camp stole a page from Reagan's 1980 campaign playbook and tried to out-conservative the vice president. In the earlier race, Reagan had effectively labeled George Bush as a moderate Republican, but that was actually a mislabeling dating all the way back to 1968, when Bush had voted in favor of the Civil Rights Act of 1968, also known as the Fair Housing Act.

Senator Dole's campaign stepped up his attacks on the vice president, charging that Bush was not a worthy conservative successor to Ronald Reagan. The Dole camp began pounding away on the theme that Bush wanted to increase taxes. The charge was false, but it was effective. Ailes prepared a tough response going after Dole for voting for taxes. It was an ad that I thought would resonate in our staunchly antitax state of New Hampshire. Roger, Lee Atwater, and I urged the Bush campaign to put the ad on the air, and when we finally got the vice president's reluctant approval, Roger and I scrambled to get it added into the mix on the Boston and New Hampshire TV stations. It was this ad, the so-called straddle ad, that our friends at WMUR went out of their way to get on the air in Manchester, and it was this ad, I believe, that put Bush squarely on the path to winning.

Bush beat Dole by more than 9 percent, almost the 10 percent victory we promised when the Bushes landed. Once again, a New Hampshire primary victory would stimulate a successful presidential run. Once more, New Hampshire voters had, in effect, picked a president. On victory night, Vice President Bush said it all in four simple words: "Thank you, New Hampshire." From there, it proved to be a relatively downhill glide to locking up the nomination. One perfect volley after another, bent knees and all.

2

Framing the Mission

―――――

George Bush had effectively been running for president since 1978—since about the middle of the Carter administration—when America's needs were defined by worrisome confrontations between the superpowers, a stagnating economy, a military demoralized by the loss in Vietnam, and a population dispirited by the resignation of a president. This was the world Ronald Reagan and George Bush inherited when they first entered the White House in 1980.

The world George Bush confronted in 1988 was a world very different from that of 1980. He was proud of what Reagan had accomplished, but recognized that the legacy left its own unique set of opportunities and challenges.

Bush knew the ballooning federal budget deficits were unsustainable. He understood the need to address the environmental issues neglected over the previous decade. Overregulation by Democratic Congresses had hobbled American productivity during the previous forty years and had to be brought under control. Internationally, Vice President George Bush had a very clear vision of what was going on in the world and how Reagan's policies had positioned the United States as one of the world's two superpowers. He saw an opening for great change in the world, especially if the improving relations with the Soviet Union could be nurtured into a real partnership. He was sure that he could go even further with the Soviets than just agreements on arms control.

Those who run for president usually have a general sense of how they believe they can best serve the country. But it isn't until a year or two before the actual election that they are able to frame their broad objectives as a specific agenda. The important issues change from year to year, sometimes even from month to month. Serious contenders may have an underlying political philosophy to guide them, but the specific issues emerging from that philosophy must be, by necessity, formed in the debate of ideas that takes place during the political campaign.

The conventional wisdom that George Bush came into office without a clear understanding of what needed to be done and how to do it—in his words, or more accurately in words added to the Bush narrative by *Time* magazine in early 1987, "the vision thing"—could not be further from the truth. He had to lay the groundwork for this vision without appearing overly ambitious, however, and he did this during his last two years as Reagan's vice president. When he finally began to present this platform to the world in the early months of 1988, it was clear that Bush did indeed have the vision that many partisan critics claimed he lacked. It was plain for all to see and hear as he ran for office, and later as he selected the team to help execute that vision. Those who failed to see it either were blind or chose not to look. George Bush did not take the oath of office intending to coast through four years responding to events as they happened; he knew what needed to be done, how to do it, and how to do it right.

The foundation of his agenda was solidly conservative, and Bush knew that he wanted to address his list of priorities in a manner that reflected his unwavering belief in the free market and capitalism. Domestically, he knew the federal government had become too intrusive, and he wanted to unleash the growth potential it had constrained. He wanted to help people solve problems themselves instead of doing the solving for them, and he recognized that different people had different needs. Though he really believed in a kinder, gentler nation and tried to adopt a kinder, gentler style, internationally, he realized that if America were to regain its rightful place on the world stage it would have to shake off its post-Vietnam hesitancy and begin to project power in a responsible manner. He wanted to help people at home and abroad as well, but in the teach-a-man-to-fish manner of the old Chinese proverb.

By the time Bush announced his candidacy, I already had been getting frequent visits from Lee Atwater, whom Bush had officially hired as manager of his presidential campaign. Although it was apparent that Atwater's principal objective in these visits was to get me to agree to chair the Bush primary election campaign in New Hampshire, we had a number of long discussions about campaign themes and issues. It was evident to both of us that George Bush, by virtue of his service in China, the UN, and the CIA, and as vice president, had a clear sense of the international situation and had built a solid network of relationships with knowledgeable and effective foreign policy advisors. We could see that he was crafting a specific and purposeful international vision and had a clear idea of what he could accomplish in that area. Since the vice president's strengths tended toward international affairs, Atwater asked me to put together some suggestions on how Bush could frame and present a set of domestic policy objectives that reflected his conservative philosophy and the goals he had accomplished as vice president.

After nearly two terms as governor of New Hampshire, I had developed a great respect for the political acuity and productivity of my fellow governors. I found that governors, because they live among their constituents, have a better sense of, and appreciation for, the needs of their own individual states and, in most cases, those of the entire country. I had found them capable of seriously discussing how to deal with tough issues such as education, welfare, jobs, the environment, energy, and the nation's infrastructure without the partisan bickering that so often encumbered talks on these issues in Washington. Through the National Governors Association and the various regional governors' groups, they had been very effective at finding ways to work together and develop practical solutions to some of these critical problems.

My strongest recommendation to Atwater was that Vice President Bush begin to cultivate closer personal and political relationships with Republican governors, not only for the boost it would give his campaign but also because they would be a valuable source of advice as he developed a meaningful domestic policy agenda. Atwater agreed, and we began to build this governor-centric approach into the vice president's political trips during the 1986 midterm elections and into 1987.

As part of that strategy we brought groups of governors to meet with the vice president in Washington or to visit with him and Mrs. Bush when they were in Maine. The Bush family home outside Kennebunkport proved to be a boon to Bush both as a candidate and, later, as president, when it became a surrogate White House. The spectacular but comfortable setting—as well as the genuine warmth and hospitality George and Barbara Bush extended to their guests—put many visiting dignitaries, both American and foreign, quickly at ease. The governors were no exception.

Southern Maine is notorious for its infrequent but violent summer storms, two of which have virtually destroyed the main house at Walker's Point over the last century, but on the occasions when we brought governors in for meetings, we were blessed with lovely weather. Most of the gatherings occurred during the summer or early fall, and would begin around noon with a light lunch on the deck of the main house. Anywhere from three to six governors would come at a time, and Bush would spend the better part of the day discussing the problems they faced and the solutions they proposed. They wanted to talk about the environment, about law and order, and about individual rights. They wanted to tell Bush about the problems they faced with federal education and welfare policies. Always attentive and curious, listening more than talking, Bush would get an earful for hours, and then everyone would break for happy hour before returning to the nearby Nonantum Inn for the night.

At these Maine meetings and others held in Washington, Bush heard from Lamar Alexander of Tennessee about education challenges in K–12. California's George Deukmejian told him how federal immigration policies were weighing on the states, and not in a good way. Jim Thompson of Illinois spoke about the need for better management of the Great Lakes, and Terry Branstad of Iowa talked about the plight of small farmers. Carroll Campbell of South Carolina and Jim Martin of North Carolina discussed the need for federal policies to keep American businesses competitive with the rest of the world. Tommy Thompson of Wisconsin wanted to talk about reform of federal social programs, and John Ashcroft of Missouri about modernizing the equipment used by state and local police. Norm Bangerter of Utah wanted control of some federal open lands out West to revert to the states, and Arch Moore of West Virginia told Bush of the problems faced by the coal mining areas of America. I spoke to Bush about acid rain and the uneven availability of affordable energy across the country. And we all told him how important it would be to reform the welfare system.

During these conversations, the governors shared anecdotal and factual evidence that convinced Bush that the general approach from Washington of providing one-size-fits-all programs was a serious mistake. The vice president began to appreciate the value of flexible programs that allowed governors of smaller states to implement them differently from those of larger states.

The governors told the vice president that the existing welfare structure was not working. They asked for more flexibility and the ability to spend money on job training to help welfare recipients develop the skills they needed to find work and get off the welfare rolls. They explained how the nation's principal welfare program, Aid to Families with Dependent Children (AFDC), was creating a generation of families reliant on handouts without ever reaching those who need it most. AFDC, they said, was one of the prime examples of how well-intentioned Washington programs often hurt more than they helped. Through the governors, Bush also learned that money from many federal programs was denied to groups that could multiply the impact of such support simply because these groups used facilities and volunteers from church-based organizations.

From these discussions the vice president also came to see that the biggest problem in education in the country was the poor performance of students in kindergarten through high school, or K–12. Governors emphasized the importance of local control of education. The perspective from Washington, by contrast, was that federal mandates could solve any problem. The governors stressed that education was best managed when policies and programs were controlled and made accountable by the states and their own school districts.

Environmental issues presented a special challenge. Pollution often affects people and places very far from the source. Acid rain is a perfect example, and one that I discussed with the vice president. Smokestacks in the industrial Midwest were generating pollution that was damaging the forests of New England, and any regulatory solution to the problem had to be carefully crafted and implemented in a way that was fair to both regions. All of this reaffirmed Bush's belief that for programs to be effective in both rural and urban areas, local officials needed the flexibility and capacity to match the details of the delivery systems with the best resources available within their own communities.

The vice president also heard of dissatisfaction among the governors with the federal approach to law and order. Their main complaint was that Washington failed to appreciate the benefit of flexibility in its financial support, particularly concerning the larger cities in America. Crime statistics were on the rise in these cities, and local law enforcement officials needed the ability to spend money in ways that would most effectively meet the needs of their individual cities instead of following the cookie-cutter approaches mandated by federal officials.

Most important, George Bush learned that voters around the country looked at issues and talked about them differently from the politicians in Washington. This came as something of a surprise to Bush, but he was a quick learner. As the governors explained their priorities, Bush began to appreciate how language can influence people's perception of government. In Washington, when talking about welfare reform, they spoke vaguely of "institutional restructuring." In the real world, people talked about "getting money to the families that need it." Governors, who live among their constituents, understood this better than many members of the House of Representatives and Senate and other Washington officials. Bush took note, and it became a valuable strength in the campaign. As a result, the domestic agenda he developed offered realistic solutions in language the voters could relate to.

Vice President Bush went to speak to meetings of the Republican Governors Association to hear collectively from the governors about their concerns. He also spoke at regional governors' gatherings and used all of these experiences to expand and hone his agenda. George Bush listened. In one-on-one meetings, group discussions, large forums, and informal conversations, he learned about the most pressing issues and about realistic solutions. He ran with those issues in the campaign and addressed them, not only in his speeches, but at events specifically designed to highlight his understanding of and commitment to them.

The approach worked well, and George Bush the candidate began to define a domestic program that included recommendations to address the nation's budget deficits, resolve environmental issues that had been sidelined for a decade, rebuild and strengthen the quality of education, put the nation on a sounder energy footing, stimulate the economy, help rebuild the nation's infrastructure, deal with a growing immigration problem, assist urban areas in their struggle against crime, and, in general, reinvigorate the role of the states in our federalist compact.

George Bush's commitment to this federalist approach—giving more flexibility and authority to the states—was quite similar to the approach later taken by his successor, former governor Bill Clinton. When Bush talked about welfare reform, he talked about changes that eventually would be adopted almost wholesale by the Clinton administration. He expressed his concern about dependency on welfare. He supported giving states more autonomy. He said he wanted our welfare programs to eliminate dependency, not create it. He wanted to add job training and a work requirement to the welfare process. He felt these changes would enhance the self-pride and the dignity of the welfare recipients. The big difference, of course, was that when Bush spoke of these things he was dealing with a Congress dominated by Democrats, many of whom had written the legislation for the most ineffective components of some of these programs.

A concise description of George Bush's domestic agenda would be that it was framed around goals defined by his supporters in the Republican Governors Association. On the campaign trail and in his debates with Democratic candidate Michael Dukakis in the fall of 1988, the vice president hammered home those goals and their policy components. Many of those goals came at a cost, however, and Bush realized that in order to fix the problems he was hearing about, he would have to get the federal deficits under control. He identified the budget as a top priority: reducing the deficits and implementing a "flexible freeze" on federal spending were critical. He also strongly supported a cut in the capital gains tax to stimulate the growth needed in the economy, and an amendment to the Constitution requiring a balanced federal budget.

George Bush the man knew where he wanted to be on all the issues. Now the candidate just needed to get his party in line behind him. And when the nomination process is as decisive as Bush's was in 1988, the nominee can control the party's platform process at the convention. The vice president asked me to chair the Platform Committee at the 1988 Republican National Convention in New Orleans.

He and I spent a great deal of time reviewing the way the last two Republican platforms had been constructed, and I received very clear directions from him, on an issue-by-issue basis, as to how he wanted the platform built for his election. The result was a platform that was pure Bush. It was a Republican agenda, a conservative agenda, a free-market agenda, a federalist agenda. And it became one of his principal assets in erasing the nearly seventeen-point lead that Michael Dukakis held in June 1988.

Because we spent significant time ahead of the convention meeting with many of the delegates on the Platform Committee, getting Bush's agenda into the platform turned out to be virtually painless. Every provision he wanted was easily adopted. The only item that got sticky had to do with missile systems, and it was easily resolved by a minor change in language. All the other issues—education, the environment, national security policy, civil rights, rights of the disabled—were defined in the platform as specific party and candidate commitments. They were commitments that George Bush had reached through an exhaustive process of listening, discerning, debating, and campaigning. They were things he genuinely wanted to accomplish as president. It was probably the most conservative Republican platform ever, even more conservative than the platforms of 1980 and 1984.

The convention also confirmed Dan Quayle as the vice-presidential nominee on the Bush ticket. I was not involved in the process of selecting Quayle, not only because Bush had been kind enough to put me on the list of "possibles," but also because he kept that process close and within a very small core group—a style that, as I would come to discover, he would use in the White House.

The tight secrecy of the process may have backfired. The media, particularly the liberal national press, had no clue that

Quayle was still in consideration, so when he was announced, reporters ripped into his background with a vengeance. The campaign team assigned to help him move into the role of nominee was not prepared for the intensity of the coverage, and it took a while for the team to recover. Unfortunately, that stumble set the tone for coverage of Quayle for the next four years.

I had known Quayle for a couple of years. After meeting him at a few social events in Washington, I found him to be a smart conservative with a good feeling for the election process, and he knew that you cannot change policy if you don't win elections. I thought he was a good choice as vice president. He was a favorite of conservatives. He had been a key Senate player on disarmament issues, so he had some credibility in international affairs, and had been an architect of job training reform, so he was well-versed in the domestic arena as well. He also was seen as a solid campaigner, having unseated an incumbent Democratic darling, Senator Birch Bayh, to win his election in the state of Indiana.

During the course of the campaign, I did not run into him much, but after the election, during the transition, we spent a great deal of time talking and trying to help Bush get the agenda and team together. While I served in the White House with Dan, I found him to be on target on all the tough issues, our best contact with Congress, and a very good source of sound political advice. Not only was he completely loyal to George Bush, but he was a great asset inside the White House. When we had a problem in the House or Senate, Quayle was the go-to guy. When we had a tough policy discussion, the guy who got into it and said the hard things was Quayle. He was a great vice president for Bush.

Bush's agenda for domestic legislative action, which carefully toed the delicate line between constructive action and debilitating overregulation, was more conservative and more aggressive

than what Ronald Reagan had been able to get out of the Democratic Congress. We had no illusions about how tough the battles
were going to be, but we were ready to take them on because
we felt there were better ways to get good results than had been
proposed and fought over in the past.

By the spring of 1988, well before the convention, it became
apparent that the Democratic nominee was going to be Massachusetts governor Michael Dukakis. Because Dukakis believed
his strength came from his experience in Massachusetts, the
Bush team sensed that his principal campaign issues would
revolve around America's domestic needs.

Dukakis thought he could blindside Bush on issues like the
environment, state highways and other infrastructure needs,
education, job creation, welfare, and the homeless. He assumed
that Bush had been isolated in the Washington bubble and would
not, in short order, be capable of debating these issues fluently
with him, a two-term governor. Bush, of course, was prepared to
meet that challenge.

What Dukakis failed to appreciate was his own gaping defi-
ciency in the arenas of international affairs and national security.
The governor thought he could catch up with Bush by sitting
through a few briefings by foreign policy experts. Those shortcomings were fatal to Dukakis because, at the end of the day,
George Bush was able to figure out how to go toe to toe with
Dukakis on domestic issues, but Dukakis never figured out how
to maneuver his way around the international stage anywhere
near as adeptly as the vice president.

Armed with an agenda and a platform blessed by the Republican rank and file, we hit the campaign trail confidently despite
polls that put us far behind our Democratic opponent. To
demonstrate the vice president's approach to dealing with the
environment, we went straight to Michael Dukakis's backyard—

Boston Harbor. Bush reminded people that his opponent had not started cleaning up the harbor until the state of Massachusetts was ordered to do so by a federal court. Bush laid out his own position on what should be done to address the needs of the environment, but, in campaign mode, he also made sure the voters heard that despite his rhetoric, Governor Dukakis had not taken action on a critical environmental issue in his own state.

Bush was taking issues Dukakis thought he had an advantage on and getting the upper hand with them, an approach that would serve him well. He avoided sounding like a Washington insider and used instead the language of governors and their constituents. In his campaign for president, George Bush was addressing the country's pressing domestic issues from the priority list of the governors. He spoke about the environment and energy. He addressed the problems of crime and drugs. He argued for holding down spending and taxes. He campaigned on expanding job opportunities and child care. The Washington press corps and the national press did not always give broad coverage to these issues, but the local press did, and the voters began to tune in to the substance of George Bush's speeches.

He talked about health care in the same context in which he had heard governors present their concerns. He emphasized how much more efficient health care delivery under Medicaid could be if states were allowed to implement programs in ways that matched the needs of their particular citizens, their particular state's structures, and the size and character of their hospitals and clinics.

Bush talked about the differences between him and Michael Dukakis on issues like law and order, where the vice president supported the death penalty and Dukakis opposed it. Bush also affirmed his strong commitment to strengthening the manufacturing sector. He felt that overregulation was chasing jobs out of

America, and he made a commitment to give America's competitiveness a very high priority in his administration. He called as
well for reform of the nation's agricultural subsidy system, which
was creating a generation of farmers dependent on handouts
from the federal government.

As the campaign against Michael Dukakis progressed, the
more mannerly side of Bush often hesitated to go on the offensive, so I found myself drawn into the role of the most outspoken
surrogate against Dukakis. I gathered a whole set of statistics
showing that although Massachusetts may have ranked among
the top ten states in the country on some favorable economic
indicators, it actually ranked sixth out of the six New England
states on virtually every important measure. Dukakis wanted
to talk about the "Massachusetts Miracle," but I labeled it the
"Massachusetts Mirage." I made sure my criticisms of the Dukakis record were fact-based and not ad hominem. I tried to be
direct and to the point, and because I was representing someone
else—the Bush candidacy—I made every effort to be sure that
everything I put in the public domain was accurate and correct.

With the party unified by a strong convention (August 15–18
in New Orleans) and a solid conservative platform, Bush closed
the gap. He kept up the pressure on his own record and the
issues. He talked about their differences on crime, on taxes, on
the environment, on defense, and on the role of government—
many of the same issues he had discussed with the governors in
those seaside chats at Walker's Point. In the end, he was able to
retain most of the "Reagan Democrats," won over the majority
of Lee Atwater's wrestling audience, and won the 1988 election
quite handily.

George Bush won the popular vote 53 percent to 45 percent,
took the majority of the vote in forty states, and won 426 elec-

toral college votes to Dukakis's 111. Remarkably, however, the Democrats actually gained one seat in the Senate and two seats in the House of Representatives. They retained solid control of the Congress. The new president would have to work with them to get any results at all.

DOMESTIC STRATEGY

After the election, Bush outlined his agenda for working with Congress for the next four years. He laid out for himself a very comprehensive and specific agenda for his first term in a memo he drafted by hand on December 26, 1988. He had it typed up into a talking-points paper for the first cabinet meeting, to be held on January 23, 1989. In fourteen triple-spaced pages, he outlined objectives for both his foreign policy and his domestic policy. The first page under the heading of domestic policy is titled "Education" and the second page is titled "Environment." His concern about needing to straighten out the budget crisis as soon as possible is referenced under almost every heading throughout his list.

The agenda's principal components, with the details shaped by months of input from listening to the governors, included:

The Budget

Bush made it clear that his number one domestic priority was to get the ever-growing budget deficit under control. He knew this wouldn't be an easy task, and indicated that he wanted to meet with his economic team immediately after the inauguration to begin to develop a strategy on how to prepare his first budget and get it passed through Congress.

Environment

During the campaign, the president highlighted his commitment to have the nation act on its responsibility to clean up the air and water. Amendments to the Clean Air Act (1970) had been stalled in Congress for more than twelve years. He would need to map out a detailed and acceptable proposal to send to Congress and break the logjam.

Energy

George Bush's experience in the energy business made him keenly aware that by overregulating and limiting domestic energy production, America had restricted both its own economic development and the range of foreign policy options in its diplomatic arsenal. The United States was overly dependent on foreign sources of energy because overregulation at home had inhibited development of the infrastructure needed to expand the production of domestic natural gas and oil reserves. Similar regulatory hurdles had stifled competition in the electric utility business.

Education

Bush was concerned about the continued deterioration of K–12 student performance, and he made improvement of primary education a major domestic priority. He agreed with the governors that K–12 education should mainly be the responsibility of state and local governments and not of the federal government. He knew he would have to come up with something innovative to meet their appeals for flexibility, local control, and effective solutions to a wide range of needs. Continued conversation and cooperation with the governors would be one of the tactics for developing a list of potential suggestions.

Civil Rights and an Americans with Disabilities Act

When Bush was vice president, C. Boyden Gray, Evan J. Kemp Jr., and Justin Dart Jr. had kept him informed on legislation pending in Congress that would address the needs of America's disabled. As president, Bush wanted to sign an Americans with Disabilities Act, but knew just how complicated it would be to craft laws fair to both the disabled and the business communities. Similar challenges were inherent in the civil rights legislation also before Congress at the time, but Bush was determined to find a way to get a good bill passed.

Immigration

With his Texas roots, the president was well versed in the immigration issue from all its varied perspectives. He had lived in a region where immigrant laborers and immigrant entrepreneurs were important components of the economy. Business leaders in the technology sector told him how beneficial it was to encourage citizenship for the talented and well-educated scientists and engineers in their firms, and he heard governors tell him how the structure of immigration laws often kept families apart. He wanted to prioritize the problems in this area and propose some specific solutions that he could ask Congress to consider in a future bill to reform immigration.

Crime

Although cities and states were trying to deal with crime, criminal networks had become larger and more complex, spreading far and wide. In 1988, violent crimes in America increased by more than 5 percent over the year before. Mayors and governors were unanimous in asserting the need for more support from the federal government, along with changes in laws and regulations to allow for better coordination among the federal agencies, states, and communities. In response, the president wanted to come up with a package of proposals that addressed those specific concerns.

Drugs

The Reagan administration and Congress had discussed an expansion of both the funding and the authority for federal action to deal with America's fast-growing drug problem. Congress had passed a law creating a cabinet-level position of drug czar, and the president was ready to go even further by actively increasing private sector involvement in the effort. Leaders in the private sector would, he believed, recognize the wide-reaching social benefits of dealing with this growing scourge. The president would need to prepare his recommendations to meet with those leaders to develop an effective partnership program.

Welfare

Virtually all the governors voiced the need for significant welfare reform. Bush knew it would be difficult to get the liberals in Congress to reform the very provisions that they had put in place over the previous decades, but he wanted to establish the criteria for a good welfare reform bill and try to pass as much of his proposal as he possibly could. With input from the governors, the president believed he could craft a package that he could send to Congress.

International Leadership

On the foreign policy side, Bush saw clearly the opportunities before him now that Mikhail Gorbachev had initiated serious reforms in the Soviet Union. Ronald Reagan's "peace through strength" policy had put America in a preeminent position militarily, and when it became apparent that Gorbachev, with his perestroika and glasnost (reform and openness, respectively), was moving to restructure the Soviet economy and its politics, Reagan reciprocated by opening the door to peace talks and arms control. George Bush, Secretary of State James Baker, and National Security Advisor Brent Scowcroft saw a real possibility of ending four decades of confrontation between the nuclear superpowers. It was Bush's top foreign policy priority.

Europe

Soviet initiatives to reduce the number of troops on the ground in Eastern Europe created a new opportunity for stabilizing the political and security environment of the entire continent. The president and his foreign policy team knew they needed a balanced, yet bold, series of responses to the changes that had already taken place. This was a once-in-a-lifetime opportunity, and the president wanted to work in concert with our NATO allies to restore freedom and democracy to all of Europe.

Arms Control

Although arms control was an agenda item that fell under the broader rubric of how to deal with the Soviet Union, the president and his team needed to broaden the discussion because the topic of medium-range missiles in Europe was becoming a sticky one. A key NATO partner in Europe, West Germany, was facing serious internal political strife because of the presence of nuclear weapons on its soil, a matter that had to be considered as part of the overall foreign policy agenda.

Central America

The United States' relations with its partner nations in the Western Hemisphere were not good at the time, largely because of our interventions in Central America in the 1980s, and President Bush wanted to fix that. The key, in his view, was economic partnerships. Those partnerships not only could shore up the economies of other countries, but could benefit our own economy as well by creating and expanding markets for American goods and services. This issue spanned both foreign and domestic policy. The president wanted to develop some specific new programs to tackle this critical need.

China

Since his days as the United States envoy to China (1974–75), George Bush knew how important it was to build on the initiatives begun by Richard Nixon more than a decade and a half earlier. He felt so strongly about this priority that before he even took office he began preparations for an early trip to the Pacific, with particular attention to China.

BUILDING THE TEAM

Near the end of the election cycle, the polls suggested that Bush would win the presidency. Although he didn't want to be presumptuous, Bush knew enough to start thinking about the tremendous amount of work that lay ahead should he emerge victorious. He knew there would be a transition period of only about ten weeks, and he wanted to make good use of every minute of it.

During that ten-week window, he would have to make final decisions on his principal appointments, frame a timetable to get things started, and prioritize his agenda for action. It was the time for the team members to get to know one another better and to figure out how to work together.

There are two kinds of transitions: one is a transition between the two political parties, and the other occurs when the same party as the sitting president has won. Surprisingly, it is harder when the transition is within the same political party, which was the situation we had to deal with late in the fall of 1988. It was especially difficult because many of the Reagan appointees wanted to stay on, but Bush wanted to encourage some of them to leave so he could clear the slate and appoint a team of his own.

After the election, of course, there was much press chatter about whom Bush would name as chief of staff. None of it was accurate. About a week before election day, the vice president asked me if I would come to Washington with him if he was elected. I had previously announced that I was not going to seek a fourth term as governor and was returning to the private sector. I told the vice president that, in fairness to my family, I really thought I needed to return to "a real job." He asked if there was any job *at all* in Washington that I would be willing to consider, and I told him the only one would be helping him directly as his chief of staff. In response, he told me I ought to have a chat with my wife and family to see how they might feel about my coming to Washington to do just that. A couple of days later I let him know that if he wanted me to serve as chief of staff, my family would support a decision to join the administration.

A few days after the election, Bush heard that I was headed to Florida to visit my parents. He suggested I visit with him there at the home of his good friend Will Farish in Palm Beach. I agreed, and drove over to the Farish residence and knocked on the door. Farish and Bush answered the door together. Bush immediately turned to his friend and said, "Let me introduce you to my new chief of staff." That's how I found out I had the job.

My tenure as governor of New Hampshire ended at noon on January 5, 1989. I immediately headed down to Washington,

DC, to prepare for a seamless transition and a fast start. By then I had completed conversations with the living previous chiefs of staff and had read Sherman Adams's book on his years serving Dwight D. Eisenhower. James Baker, one of Reagan's chiefs of staff, warned me that some department heads would be closer to the boss than others, and that managing the egos of those that weren't close was not easy. Ken Duberstein, who also served Reagan, stressed how important it was to keep the president from being overwhelmed. Every issue was the most important one to someone, but not all of the issues needed to end up on the president's desk. Almost all of the former chiefs of staff emphasized that I had a "constituency of one": the president himself. Everyone else's agendas, opinions, and needs were secondary to the president's. I would have to use the transition between election and inauguration to find out what Bush wanted me to do.

Overall, George Bush staffed his presidency with a very strong team. It was a talented bench that mirrored the president's inherent vision of what he wanted to accomplish. Most were people who had been successful in both private and public life and were part of the deep well of Republican experience available at the time. Many also were battle-savvy survivors who had fought political wars either as candidates or on the campaign side. For the most part, you could sense that they knew what had to be done, and how to do it—successfully.

On the international affairs side, for the post of national security advisor Bush turned to Brent Scowcroft, a former Air Force general who had served as deputy security advisor under Henry Kissinger in the Nixon administration and later as national security advisor for President Ford. Scowcroft and Bush had been friends since the pair met in Beijing when Bush was liaison there. Scowcroft served as a foreign policy advisor to the vice president during the 1988 presidential campaign.

James Baker was the president's choice to be secretary of state. Baker was from Texas and had run Bush's first campaign for president in 1980. When Bush was chosen to be Reagan's vice presidential candidate, Baker helped the ticket get elected and served as part of a troika running the White House during the first Reagan term. During Reagan's second term, Baker served as secretary of the treasury. Both Baker and Scowcroft worked with Bush throughout 1988 on policy and strategy, and when the election was over, they were ready to take on the world.

His choice of a core domestic policy team also revealed the president's knack for picking the right people for the right task.

Roger Porter, from Harvard, was considering a position in the Trade Office, but I was able to convince him to join the White House team as head of the Domestic and Economic Policy Office. Porter had been a White House Fellow, had served in both the Ford and the Reagan administrations, and understood how the gears of government meshed, better than perhaps anyone else around at the time. Porter not only was smart but seemed to work twenty-four hours a day, and that would prove critical when it came time to herd the various factions of Congress and the federal bureaucracy in the direction Bush knew they needed to go.

In Richard Darman, Bush found a budget manager who understood the financial implications and imperatives of what Bush wanted to accomplish and the complex ins and outs of how to weave those together in a way that worked. He had served in key positions at Treasury, at Commerce, and in the White House, and also on the faculty at Harvard. As director of Bush's Office of Management and Budget, he would be responsible for bringing federal spending under control in a manner that suited the president's underlying conservative philosophy.

In selecting me as chief of staff, I believe, Bush was turning to someone with deeply conservative principles and ties to the

Republican governors who could help him articulate his domestic agenda. My personal approach as a hands-on governor gave me experience with and comprehensive understanding of the issues because I had to deal with them on a daily basis during my three terms as governor of New Hampshire. I believe Bush also chose me to be his chief of staff because he appreciated the way the campaign had been managed. My private sector experience trained me to make fast, effective decisions and execute them quickly, a far cry from the long-drawn-out dance that is the decision-making norm in Washington. The president saw in me an engineer who understood policy and could keep the wheels moving.

Rounding out the domestic team was C. Boyden Gray, an old friend of the president's who had been serving as his legal counsel throughout his term as vice president. Gray had an exceptional understanding of language and the nuanced impact that a single word or phrase can have on legislation, and he was absolutely determined that the president's principles should be reflected in laws dealing with such disparate topics as clean air, civil rights, and disabilities.

Normally in Washington, a team of such enormous talents and egos would mix like oil and water. Staff tensions, which can be debilitating to a president, would inevitably arise. But ours ended up being one of the tightest-knit groups to ever occupy the West Wing. We had our disagreements, of course, but in the end we all got along incredibly well and adhered to what I call the Jell-O Dessert Theory of consensus building and action. Before a decision is made it's like a Jell-O dessert before it gels, with positions, postures, and perspectives moving around fluidly like pieces of fruit in a bowl of warm Jell-O. But once the president made a decision, once the Jell-O had cooled, those pieces of fruit, or positions, were set in place. To put it another way, the route was mapped and we all marched in that direction.

Besides this core team, the Bush White House included some faces familiar from the Reagan presidency. Lauro Cavazos stayed on as secretary of education, and Richard Thornburgh as attorney general. I knew each of these appointees personally because Thornburgh had served as governor of Pennsylvania during most of my own tenure as governor of New Hampshire, and Cavazos, coincidentally, was the dean of the dental school at Tufts University while I was the associate dean of the College of Engineering there (1968–73). For secretary of the treasury, Bush decided to keep Nicholas Brady, who had succeeded Baker at that post for President Reagan when Baker resigned to run the 1988 campaign. Brady had been a successful investment banker on Wall Street and a U.S. senator from New Jersey, and was a longtime advisor and confidant to George Bush.

Other than in the press office, the president allowed me to build out most of the key White House staff myself. After learning I was to be chief of staff, I persuaded Andy Card, who had been a member of Reagan's staff, to join me as my deputy. He had taken a few months' leave from his position in the White House to work in New Hampshire on the primary campaign. During the campaign, I discovered he was very effective and loyal to Bush, and I wanted him to be part of my own effort to support the president.

With Andy's help we sorted through an excellent list of political appointees and came up with a slate of recommendations, virtually all of whom the president then approved. The entire roster of cabinet choices was sent to the Senate at virtually the same time, the first week after the inauguration. All of them were quickly approved, with the exception of secretary of defense nominee John Tower.

President Bush had real strength and real diversity in his cabinet. He chose Elizabeth Dole to be his secretary of labor; he chose Dr. Louis Sullivan, president of Morehouse College, to be his secretary of health and human services; he chose Manuel Lujan, a former congressman from New Mexico, to be his secretary of the interior. He accepted the recommendation from Vice President Quayle and me that he appoint a couple of strong conservatives—Jack Kemp as secretary of housing and urban development and William Bennett as director of the Office of National Drug Control Policy, the so-called drug czar.

One of my own most critical appointments was selecting my principal personal assistant. It was a job that required a person who was smart, politically sensitive, and trustworthy. I knew there would be no better choice than my principal assistant from the New Hampshire governor's office—the name may surprise you—Jacqueline Kennedy. Jackie was the wife of New Hampshire's commissioner of administration, and our family had known Jackie and her family for years. She had been with me at the State House for all six years, and in that time she had to deal with every governor, dozens of senators and congressmen, and every presidential wannabe for two presidential election cycles.

Jackie could maintain a proper pace when the schedule was chaotic, and she kept my paperwork flowing and in order. Most important, I could absolutely trust her to be loyal to the president and me. As had been true in New Hampshire, I always got a kick out of the reaction of newcomers when they realized that the gatekeeper to the office of the Republican chief of staff turned out to be Jackie Kennedy.

SETTING THE ROUTINE AND THE TONE

During those days of contemplation between the time the president asked me to be his chief of staff and the time I accepted, about a thousand things were running through my head. Chief among them was the realization that one of my key responsibilities would be to catch the "arrows and spears" that would certainly be coming the president's way. As much as the president was inclined to be bipartisan in his leadership, I knew that Washington politics was a hardball game and partisanship almost always prevailed.

Besides being a target, there are many other aspects to the role of chief of staff. As James Baker warned me, one of them is insulating the chief executive from a lot of the petty problems that inevitably crop up in the high-pressure and ego-driven environment of Washington. If a cabinet member, let's say the secretary of commerce, wants to have coffee with the president, but the president would rather not, he may tell the chief of staff to pass along the message. There's a subtext to this directive. If the president doesn't mind the cabinet member's knowing of this preference, he would tell that person himself. By asking me, as chief of staff, to convey the message, he is asking me to take responsibility for saying no. That way, no one's feelings are hurt.

Interactions like this obviously contribute greatly to the perception that a chief of staff is the gatekeeper, not only facilitating meetings with the president but barring others from seeing him as well. In my practice as chief of staff, I used my daily morning meeting with the president to run all meeting requests past him to see which he wanted to take and how he wanted them handled. I worked hard never to freelance those important decisions. It was my job to make sure that his schedule, as well as the inevitable interdepartmental battles, would be managed in a way that allowed him to get involved in the issues he wanted to deal with, and graciously avoid those he did not. Our personal morning meeting became the best occasion for sorting all that out. It was the most important meeting of the day.

Every major decision by a president earns him at least one enemy and one friend. It was my job to absorb the enemies and leave the friends for the president. That doesn't just happen by accident or circumstance in Washington. The process must be carefully managed and maintained. That is the chief of staff's job: good things that happened and made people happy were credited to the president; bad things that happened and disappointed people were my fault.

Occasionally, personal issues surfaced during my morning meetings with the president. Once in a while he would ask me to call Bush family members to remind them of how closely the media microscope was trained on each and every one of them. Although I was pleased that the president was comfortable enough with me to confide his personal concerns and confident that I could deal with such issues tactfully, it was sometimes difficult and awkward.

One of the most challenging instances, in that it called for delicate handling, was actually one of the first, sometime in the middle of 1989. The president's brother, Prescott Bush, had gone to China on a business trip not long after the president himself had been there. Prescott was trying to put together a deal to build a country club golf course in Shanghai and was beginning to receive some criticism in the press about the endeavor. The president wanted me to let Prescott know that he ought to be working harder to keep a "low profile."

I called the president's brother and we had a nice, friendly conversation. I was able to make the point clear to him by reminding him of an old admonition. "You don't always get in trouble just for doing something wrong," I told him. "You can get in trouble for doing something right in such a way that your enemies can make it look as if you did something wrong." I'm proud of the fact that every time I ran into Prescott afterward, he thanked me for making that call.

When I took the job as chief of staff, I assumed it would be for a very short term. It didn't take more than a quick analysis to recognize that in Washington the usual tenure of the president's chief of staff was about eight or nine months. I assumed that I would probably be away from New Hampshire for no more than a year. But I believed that even during such a short time, I could help the president get started on his agenda and perhaps establish a framework that would help him get through his first four years. I believed I could make a difference for him.

Even before taking office, Bush had made it clear that he wanted to hit the ground running. "On our first full day in office, I want to have a cabinet meeting that afternoon," he told me.

On Monday, January 9, I had a long meeting with the president-elect and started peppering him with questions on how he wanted to structure the daily operation of his White House. From the experience of his eight years in the White House as vice president to Ronald Reagan, Bush was aware that the key operations of his staff would start a couple of hours before he arrived at the Oval Office. He was also sensitive to the fact that the European time zones were five or six hours ahead of Washington (Eastern Standard Time), and Moscow was eight hours ahead. Of course, in typical George Bush style, he wanted to get in as many solid working hours as possible, so he wanted his White House to start quite early in the morning.

We quickly settled on a general pattern, with a regular schedule that set aside certain times for certain responsibilities. The president began his formal day in the Oval Office with an 8:00 a.m. intelligence briefing that would include the president, the vice president, National Security Advisor Brent Scowcroft, and me. That meeting, the President's Daily Briefing (PDB), was presented by the CIA and would take ten to fifteen minutes. Following that, always on the calendar for 8:15, was a separate half hour for Scowcroft to bring the president and us up to date on all foreign policy issues arising from events that occurred overnight or were expected during the course of the upcoming day.

That briefing segued into a similar one at 8:45 that I would lead, addressing all other issues beyond foreign policy. Scowcroft usually stayed for that as well. My meeting was scheduled to end at 9:15. I recommended to the president that we generally block off 9:15 to 10:00 for some slack so we could go into further detail on any items that might have come up as a result of the earlier briefings. We also scheduled a half hour in the afternoon, usually at 4:00 or 5:00 p.m., for an after-the-fact look at the day's events. In between, George Bush would squeeze in all those other events and meetings that crowd a president's day.

Every minute of every day for the president was logged. April 4, 1989, was fairly typical. Among the more than seventy different interactions noted that day were a five-minute call with James Baker at 7:31 a.m.; another at 7:39 with Al Gore, whose six-year-old son had been seriously injured in a car accident; and yet another with Marvin Bush, the president's son, at 9:21 after the president's daily series of intelligence and national security briefings. At 9:37, he met with the president of Costa Rica, Óscar Arias Sánchez, for nearly an hour. At 11:00 he participated in a six-minute ceremony in the Rose Garden commemorating the fortieth anniversary of the North Atlantic Treaty Organization, this after a series of two-minute meetings with Brent Scowcroft, Vice President Quayle, and the First Lady. At 11:17, he spoke with Transportation Secretary Samuel K. Skinner for two minutes; he then met with Lee Atwater and several others for forty-nine minutes before having lunch with his secretary of education, Lauro Cavazos. During lunch, at 12:27, California Republican senator Pete Wilson called.

At 1:07 the president and Mrs. Bush met with the wife of the president of Costa Rica. At 2:06 the president attended a briefing for the members of the American Business Conference. At 2:51 the president chaired a National Security Council meeting in the Cabinet Room.

At 5:29, he participated in the first annual President's Sweet Sixteen Invitational Horseshoe Tournament; then, two hours later, he hosted a state dinner with President Hosni Mubarak of Egypt. Maureen McGovern sang for forty minutes beginning at 9:55 after the two presidents exchanged toasts at 9:40. At 11:15, the president "retired," as the log notes.

I organized my own schedule to work around this daily dose of constant movement, arriving at the White House at 6:15 a.m. and immediately diving into the pile of clips, memos, and reports that had come in overnight. I also did a cursory review of what was in the morning papers. From 6:45, I had an open-door policy that allowed for any member of the staff with something to discuss to come and sit with me.

At 7:15, an hour into my typical day, I had a daily formal meeting with Deputy Chief of Staff Andy Card and Ed Rogers, executive assistant to the White House chief of staff. From there, Card and I would go into a staff meeting at 7:30 with about twenty or so senior staff members to quickly review the key issues of that day for each of them. In that meeting, if necessary, I allocated staff and presidential time to address the most critical ones. That meeting, while short, allowed all of the senior staff to hear what the others were up to and allowed me to provide some guidance on how to deal with those critical issues.

That general schedule became the framework for the very regular and disciplined routine we set for the president and the White House team. The crucial meeting of the day for the president was that hour-and-a-half-plus meeting with the four of us starting at 8:00 a.m. It was there that all the tough issues were reviewed. It was there that Scowcroft and I received specific instructions from the president on how he wanted issues handled, how he wanted personnel matters resolved, and how he wanted to deal with Congress. It was there that we received our marching orders from President Bush.

Despite the president's commitment to this disciplined routine, there was also a sense of camaraderie and fun in the George Bush White House. Laughter was a great stress reliever, and there was plenty of it. The president himself was often at the forefront, believing that the team that laughs together works well together. He always had a couple of jokes and made an effort to keep things light.

Mrs. Bush sometimes walked her dog Millie through the Rose Garden in the morning and heard what she described as "raucous laughter" from behind the Oval Office's glass doors. She said she often wondered to herself how we managed to get anything done in there. Every once in a while she would even rap on the window. Occasionally it would get so loud that Patty Presock, the president's assistant, or even the Secret Service, would knock on the door and tell us to keep it down because we could be heard all the way to the press room.

Once, when Bush was being parodied regularly in Garry Trudeau's cartoon strip "Doonesbury" as an invisible president dubbed "President Skippy," Brent Scowcroft, Bob Gates, and I were briefing him in the Oval Office. Suddenly, in the middle of the briefing, he jumped up, excused himself, and went to the washroom.

While he was gone, I asked the ever-present White House photographer to take a picture of the three of us animatedly addressing the empty chair behind the desk. We had a large copy of the photo framed and all signed it "To President Skippy, from the Gang that sees through you."

The president accepted the picture with a great laugh, and then went rushing into the press room with it, causing a mad scramble among the reporters, who assumed—from the president's urgency—that there was a crisis of some sort. He promptly showed the photo to all of them, and jokingly accused the three of us of conspiring with Trudeau and planning a coup.

George Bush set and kept that tone and it had a ripple effect. It created a climate of camaraderie that helped our team become closer by making all of us feel more comfortable working with one another. He also made sure all those on the staff knew how much he appreciated their dedication and long hours. Often, his appreciation was expressed in surprising and unexpected ways.

A classic example involved the president's love of baseball. About a year and a half into his term, just after the 1991 baseball season had begun, our afternoon review in the Oval Office drifted to the topic of baseball. I mentioned that 1991 would mark the fiftieth anniversary of two of the greatest achievements in baseball history: Ted Williams's batting .406 and being the last player to finish a season over .400, and Joe DiMaggio's fifty-six-consecutive-game hitting streak. Perhaps we ought to do something at the White House to commemorate that historic baseball year, I suggested—perhaps a presidential medal.

His eyes lit up. "Why don't you see when we can get them here?" he said.

"Maybe we could do it on the day of the All-Star Game and then fly them in *Air Force One* up to Toronto," I said. The Major League Baseball All-Star Game would be July 9.

Bush loved the idea.

The next morning I called baseball commissioner Fay Vincent, a good friend, and told him about the plan. He loved the idea, too, and we agreed to call Williams and DiMaggio.

Since I knew Ted Williams well, I called him and Fay said he would call DiMaggio. The White House operator got Ted on the line for me and after a little friendly banter, I told him the plan.

There was silence at the other end of the phone.

"Ted, what do you think?" I asked.

More silence.

"John, I just can't accept," Williams said, finally.

I was shocked. "Ted, why not?"

"I just can't," was all he said.

Try as I might, I could not change his mind, so I called Fay immediately to get his take. He told me DiMaggio was all set. I then told him of my conversation with Williams.

Fay said he would call Ted himself, and get back to me.

About an hour later, he called back.

"It's all fine," he said. "Ted is honored and will accept the medal."

I asked him why Williams turned it down earlier.

"Ted said 'no' because he thought he would have to wear a tuxedo."

That afternoon I relayed the good news to the president: we were all set to do it on All-Star day. Then, in an aside that betrayed an ulterior motive for going to so much trouble, he said to prepare the baseball greats to be inundated by autograph requests from the White House staff. All along, one of his primary considerations was to make sure the legion of adoring fans who worked for him got to take advantage of one of the few perks of their position and to be sure Williams and DiMaggio were on board with that.

When I called Fay back to relay the president's request, he said, "Ted said the more the merrier; Joe grumbled but agreed to do it for the president."

Our scheme worked perfectly on All-Star day. Ted and Joe came to the White House, sat in my office, and chatted with a few key members of our White House team. As expected, the staff all brought something for their heroes to sign, and both Ted and Joe signed everything put in front of them, including a couple of boxes of baseballs I brought to distribute later to the staff members who couldn't join us in the office that day.

The president presented them both with their citations—we had learned that DiMaggio had already received a Medal of Freedom (1977) so we opted for Presidential Citations instead—in the Rose Garden. He lauded their statistics and then added, referring to their service in World War II, "Both men put off their baseball careers to serve their country. Their service deprived them of even greater statistics, but also enhanced their greatness in the eyes of their countrymen."

Then we stuffed them into *Air Force One*, where the president, Fay Vincent, and I, along with about a dozen staff members, friends, and relatives enjoyed a baseball junkie's ride of a lifetime to the 1991 Major League Baseball All-Star Game.

About a month later, the president decided to give the Presidential Medal of Freedom to Ted Williams, and through Fay Vincent I let Ted know that no tuxedo was required but that he might at least want to wear a tie for the formal presentation in the East Room. Fay said it would be the first and only time Ted would wear a tie since he left baseball, but that he would do it for George Bush.

At the ceremony in the Rose Garden before the All-Star Game, the White House photographer snapped an amazing image of the three men. I had both Bush and Williams sign a copy for me, but lacked DiMaggio's signature. I was never able to get DiMaggio to sign the picture. He always said he got "all signed out" at the White House.

Six years later, in 1997, when the George H. W. Bush Presidential Library was inaugurated at Texas A&M, the president and

Mrs. Bush hosted a breakfast in their apartment at the library for some special guests, including former British prime minister John Major, Lech Walesa of Poland, former Canadian prime minister Brian Mulroney, Lady Bird Johnson, and Nancy Reagan.

After breakfast, I was walking down a long hall talking with Nancy Reagan. My father had passed away a few months earlier after a long struggle with Alzheimer's disease, and I was speaking with Mrs. Reagan about President Reagan's own battle with it. During a break in the conversation—which was getting emotional for both of us—I noticed a copy of the same picture of Bush, DiMaggio, and Williams in the Rose Garden. This one had all three signatures on it, however. I told Mrs. Reagan I had the same photo, but lamented the fact that my own copy had only two signatures.

A couple of weeks after that conversation, I received a package at my home in New Hampshire. It was that same framed copy of Bush, Williams, and DiMaggio signed by all three that had been hanging on the wall of George Bush's apartment. Somehow the president had heard my story and sent me his own copy. A note in the package thanked me for having organized that event so many years earlier. That was George Bush being George Bush.

It takes just such a combination of grace, manners, gratitude, and humor to keep one's sanity in the combination of goldfish bowl and cauldron that is the White House. Bush was used to it; I had seen it to some extent as governor, but I was a bit surprised at how self-centered the battles were in DC. Every decision on every issue is subject to criticism from both sides, or, if it is a complex issue, from a dozen sides at least. Nothing gets done that doesn't eventually seep into the public domain, and you are, of course, fair game for all the reporters with a desire to immortalize themselves by breaking some scandal or skewering some significant public figure.

Ironically, those same reporters are comfortably ensconced in the White House with their own press room, humble as they may feel it is, and a chunk of White House staff, the press office, dedicated to making sure they get what they need for their stories and to helping them follow the president everywhere he goes. The pack forages not far from the Oval Office, and there has been more than one scoop because a reporter was close enough to the action to overhear something that wasn't meant for his or her ears.

In those pre-Internet days, everything that happened in Washington reached the public only after being filtered by the press. The Washington press corps is a very large, complex, well-funded, and self-endorsing network of egos determined to be not just reporters, but active participants in the governing process. They are unlike any other reporters in the country. They have their own cliques, their own rules, and their own self-indulgent sense of their role as guardians of all they alone think worth protecting in America.

Barbara Bush was especially annoyed by the negativity of the Washington press corps. At the first lunch she hosted for all the cabinet spouses, including my wife, Nancy, shortly after we arrived in Washington, she spoke to them of what was to come. Nancy admitted that she was somewhat accustomed to it already from her six years as first lady in New Hampshire when I was governor. At that time, she stopped reading the newspapers entirely and found that it made everything a lot easier. She suggested that Barbara try doing that.

A few months later the four of us had a chance to be together, and just as we were gathering, Barbara turned to Nancy and said, "I took your advice. I've stopped reading the papers and I'm a heck of a lot happier."

George Bush was no fan of the press either, and I, too, had

little respect for the quality of its product. I have always admitted this personal bias, and it explains why I restricted my contact with and access to the press while I served President Bush. It ended up being one of my biggest mistakes while I was in Washington.

Both Bush and I hated press leaks. For as long as I had known him, he thought that staff members who gave tidbits to the press were self-serving, disloyal, and disruptive to the team effort. As chairman of the Republican National Committee during Watergate, he had seen firsthand the self-serving leaks that became the basis of the daily attack stories by *The Washington Post* and *The New York Times*. As vice president, he watched staffers at both high and low levels jockey for turf and power by strategically leaking information about what was or was not happening in the West Wing.

The president made it clear to me he did not want that kind of White House.

On the other hand, Jim Baker told me that a disciplined, true-to-the-presidential-agenda background session with the press could be an important tool for a chief of staff. It could spell the difference between a good working relationship with the press and a bad one. Baker spent a lot of time during his White House years using his press contacts to their full potential. Baker's point was that a good relationship with the press would serve the president well in the long run.

I mentioned Baker's recommendation to George Bush while we were laying out how he wanted the White House run. He just frowned. "Let's leave that stuff to the White House press office." In retrospect, perhaps I should have tried harder to get him to let me take Baker's advice, but I did what the president directed and avoided any off-the-record briefings. I also focused on tightening up operations in general to eliminate other leaks. I made it clear to the staff how important this was to the president, and said there would be no exceptions to the rule.

Like many good intentions in Washington, it was an elusive goal. The temptation was too much, even for our extremely loyal staff. We still had the inevitable leaks of gossip about personality conflicts, policy battles, emotions, or appointments, all with barely a crumb of reality.

I let the press know that my interactions with it would always be on the record, but I didn't fully appreciate the media's addiction to the art of unidentified sources. The blinders were lifted from my eyes a couple of weeks after the inauguration when the two *Washington Post* reporters assigned to the White House, Ann Devroy and David Hoffman, asked to see me in my West Wing office. They both had covered the White House during the better part of the Reagan administration and were staying on to cover Bush.

They came in, and I answered their questions on the nominations and appointments we were making, our schedule for sending legislation to Congress for the first few weeks, and my first impressions of the job. Surprisingly, to that point, it was a very low-key interview.

Of the two, Ann Devroy was the more aggressive and competitive. Over the years, she clearly had put together a large network of people with whom she talked to get her stories. But she always seemed less interested in getting the story right than in getting something into print first, usually with a more sensational spin than most of the other reporters. Once, when I asked how she could print a story that she knew was untrue, she told me: "I don't worry whether something is true. It's my job to get into print what I hear, or what I can piece together from what I hear." David Hoffman was almost as aggressive, although he spent a little more time trying to get his stories to correspond to reality.

But David, too, when all was said and done, never let a need to report all the facts get in the way of a good leak.

At the end of the interview, just before our scheduled time was up, the pair suggested that we schedule a weekly time for an off-the-record background session. They argued that it would be a convenient way for me to brief them on what we wanted to accomplish, who in the White House was doing well and who was not, and what the president was thinking or saying. All this would be printed and attributed to an anonymous "White House official," they told me.

I declined their offer. They persisted, saying such interviews were "standard practice" and had been "done by all the chiefs of staff." They tried to convince me this was the best way for me to make sure their stories reflected my point of view. As they put it, it was the most effective way for me to let the world know that "the chief of staff is in control."

Again, I declined. Politely. Still, they hammered away at me. This time, they said that if I cooperated I could expect to get treated well in the stories. If I didn't, they said, then I probably wouldn't be happy with what they wrote. Once more I refused. This time I stood up from my desk, signaling that the meeting was over and the issue closed, and showed them to the door. I was thinking—or perhaps hoping—that it would be the end of the issue.

The next day, at my meeting with the president and Brent Scowcroft, I mentioned what had happened. When I told them that Devroy and Hoffman said "all chiefs of staff did it," they both made wry comments to the effect that some of my predecessors had developed the art form better than others. It was clear the president did not want me to indulge Devroy and Hoffman with any off-the-record access.

At first it appeared that nothing else was going to come of

that meeting with Devroy and Hoffman. But a few days later, I received a call from Katharine Graham, the principal owner and publisher of *The Washington Post*. Graham was something of an institution in Washington, and she asked to see me privately at the White House. Although surprised, I agreed.

When our meeting started in my corner office of the West Wing, Mrs. Graham graciously commented that the president, because of his experiences as vice president, would handle his new responsibilities well. She then turned the topic of the conversation to me and my new job as chief of staff. She said she hoped I would find my tenure as chief of staff to be a great experience.

"Washington is a great city," she continued. She loved "the tempo and character" of the district, she said, and told me to make an effort "to understand and enjoy it."

Then she surprised me. Referring to Devroy and Hoffman's earlier visit, she suggested that I reconsider my refusal to hold a regular session with them on background.

"You'll be pleasantly surprised at how mutually beneficial private briefings can be," she said.

"The president prefers that I not do them," I told her.

"That's not really in the best interest of the president or you," she countered. "In Washington, we do things differently than you were used to in New Hampshire. Washington has a lot of background interviews so that reporters can get all the details from you. Since they are getting some of the information from others, it is important to get the president's version into the story. Without these background interviews, you definitely will not like how the stories come out."

"That sounds like a threat," I said.

She said nothing in response and the topic was never broached again. We spoke a bit more about the expectations for the president, and she said the *Post* would like me to come down and meet some of the editors and other senior reporters. I agreed to do that, and the meeting ended cordially.

Beyond my attempts to be cordial, however, I was stunned. I asked Andy Card and Ed Rogers to come into my office immediately afterward, and I told them of the conversation with Mrs. Graham. Andy seemed as surprised as I was, but Ed just said, "She's right. That's the way things are done in this city. If you don't play the game, you'll get bit."

Mrs. Graham's admonition still sounded like blackmail to me.

Later that afternoon, in my wrap-up meeting with the president, I told him of my meeting with Mrs. Graham. "That seems like overkill," he muttered, and that was all he said on the subject.

Since he said nothing about appeasing the *Post*, I took that as a marching order to stay on the record. As time went on, I thought the newspaper's efforts to coerce me into giving its journalists special treatment by publishing negative stories about me would go away. I couldn't have been more wrong. It continued to print articles clearly intended to remind me that I should have cooperated with Devroy and Hoffman, not to mention Mrs. Graham. The articles ranged from the merely trivial—the fact that I wasn't, in their opinion, rich enough to be in government service—to the laughably absurd, such as whether my official car might have been in the high-occupancy vehicle lane on a Memorial Day holiday.

Not long after my meeting with Mrs. Graham, I mentioned that episode to Don Regan, who had come to Washington first as Reagan's secretary of the treasury, and later as his chief of staff. I had called Don with a new-chief-of-staff-to-an-old-chief-of-staff question, and when I mentioned the Devroy/Hoffman/Graham episode, he wanted to hear all the details. When I finished, he laughed and asked if I had read his book *For the Record*. I sheepishly admitted that I had not.

He told me to read it, since it recounted a similar incident with Don's deputy chief of staff. We lamented that it must be standard operating procedure at *The Washington Post*. Nothing, we agreed, can cover up a lack of real reporting talent so well as a few good leaks.

That was my introduction to the reality of the Washington press corps.

3

Clearing the Way

George Bush never enjoyed dancing. Getting elected president demanded that unpleasant duty, however, even for a man who didn't like it. On the day he took the oath of office, January 20, 1989, Bush had to attend no fewer than nine inaugural balls. And, true to character, he and Mrs. Bush waltzed around the floor at every single one of them. No matter how much it pained him, it was what was expected of the new chief executive, and George Bush always tried to exceed expectations.

The transition period had ended all too quickly. Psychologically we had been thinking we had right up to January 20 to complete our preparations. But by the close of business on January 17 we were being swept up in the glitz and glamour of the inaugural celebrations. There was not much to do in the next three days except enjoy the small perks of victory.

My memories of that inaugural weekend are of trying to enjoy the moment but being harried by a hectic schedule and a sense of obligation to be available to tens of thousands of "close and personal" supporters who had descended on Washington to be part of the celebration. We all felt it was the time to mix, mingle, and remain accessible as we celebrated together and expressed our appreciation for all their hard work and support.

All three days were filled with breakfasts, coffees, lunches, and receptions. Even with a very skilled military driver whisking us through the congested streets of the capital, half of them blocked off by one celebration or another, it was hard to maintain any kind of schedule. On the evening of January 18 alone, we attended three separate inaugural dinners.

The climax of the celebration, of course, was the evening of January 20, the day the president was sworn in, with those nine inaugural balls. The president and Mrs. Bush were great at being everywhere, taking it all in, smiling all the while. And dancing. We must have done a good job of sharing our time that evening, because to this day, I still run into loyal Republicans who fondly recall sharing the celebration with us that weekend.

Besides the Bushes, the other star of the inaugural weekend was Lee Atwater. Atwater had stealthily and efficiently taken control of an event titled "Celebration for Young Americans" on the official program. He turned it into his own personal rhythm-and-blues concert by gathering some of the greatest singers and musicians alive—Joe Cocker, Bo Diddley, Percy Sledge, Stevie Ray Vaughan, Ron Wood—for a nearly four-hour show. Even with all that star power in the house, it was Atwater, the thirty-seven-year-old from upstate South Carolina, who stole the show. He strapped on an electric guitar; snatched a pair of sunglasses from one of George Bush's sons, Marvin; and tore through an amazing rendition of Tommy Tucker's "Hi-Heel Sneakers." He got a standing ovation from the crowd and from the gaggle of pros who had gathered to watch and play with him.

The president arrived at Atwater's event just before Lee took the stage. He was presented with a white guitar inscribed "The Prez" and was put to work onstage playing backup to Atwater's song and dance. He looked to be having a genuinely good time.

After Bush had taken the oath that brisk Friday in January, he and Ronald Reagan descended from the inaugural platform together and went to the east front of the Capitol. There they exchanged salutes before Reagan and Nancy Reagan took off for Andrews Air Force base in a helicopter, and George and Barbara Bush went to the Congressional Leadership Luncheon in Statuary Hall in the Capitol. They then joined the Inaugural Parade to the White House.

The scheduled events had all gone off without a hitch. There was but one variation from tradition. Normally the president and president-elect, along with their spouses, rode from the White House to the Capitol in one car, and the vice president and vice president–elect and their spouses in another. Only four sitting vice presidents had ever been elected president of the United States—John Adams, Thomas Jefferson, Martin Van Buren, and George H. W. Bush. Because of his status, Bush could not ride with Dan and Marilyn Quayle to the ceremony. Instead, the Quayles gave Representative Tom Foley of Washington and Senator Ted Stevens of Alaska, both of them from the Congressional Inaugural Committee, a ride to the ceremony.

Unlike some presidents, Bush made few significant decorative changes to the Oval Office. He removed the Remington statue and other western-themed paraphernalia of his predecessor, and on the table behind his desk, between the U.S. and presidential flags, Bush replaced Reagan's photographs with about two dozen or so pictures of his own extended family. He also chose to replace the famous Resolute desk, which Reagan and many other presidents used, with another traditional desk that had never been used in the Oval Office (though it had been used in the Oval Office Study), the C&O desk, which Bush moved over from his office in the Capitol. When Bush first set foot in the Oval Office as president, there was a note waiting for him in one of the drawers of the Resolute. "Don't let the turkeys get you down," it said, in Reagan's handwriting.

At about the same time that day, I wandered into my own office just down the hall. My predecessor, Ken Duberstein, had stoked the fireplace. Ken had also left me a note. "Keep the fires burning," it said.

Presidencies, even historic ones, often lose their steam and allure in the second term, and Reagan's was no exception. Bush entered the Oval Office with a very clear vision of what he wanted to accomplish in both the foreign and the domestic arenas. He knew he had a wonderful opportunity to dramatically change the world. As loyal a vice president as he had been, Bush was keenly aware of a number of problems that had stalled the presidency in the previous years, and he was determined not to leave them all to fester and risk additional impediments to moving his own agenda forward. He had to quickly repair and resolve those problems.

First and foremost, he needed to deal with the bad blood that existed between the Reagan administration and Congress over military aid being given to the Contra insurgency in Nicaragua. Congress felt it had been lied to—some members even felt Reagan had broken the law—and the Democratic leadership had been flogging the issue to generate public support for a Democratic presidential bid. The "chorus of discordant voices," as Bush described it in his inaugural address, had become nearly deafening. He needed to develop a new strategy in Latin America that would bring real reform and democracy to those nations, and to have any hope of success he needed to fashion an expanded level of cooperation with Congress.

Additionally, Reagan's defense buildup had overstressed the budget, and the economy was paying the price. There were signs of a real slowdown. The stagnation was compounded by a rapidly growing crisis in the financial markets caused by imprudent lending at many of the savings and loan banks across the United States. Although warning signs had flashed previously, there had been no sense of crisis up to that point, but in the few weeks before the inauguration, things got worse. The more we learned about the S&L problem during the transition, the more concerned we became. Our well-laid-out agenda for serious legislative proposals to boost the wider economy and on a host of other domestic concerns was endangered by a potentially huge drain on the federal treasury.

Secretary of the Treasury Nick Brady and budget director Dick Darman scrambled to get a sense of the size of the S&L problem during the first few days of the Bush presidency. They quickly realized how broadly and deeply the malignancy had spread, and knew that it would require fast and decisive action to prevent an already frail American economy from succumbing. Bush didn't even wait until he was inaugurated to start working to address the issue. The remedies he would later implement, for both the S&L crisis and America's policy toward Latin America, had long-lasting and far-reaching positive effects.

LATIN AMERICA

Even before the election, George Bush and Jim Baker homed in on the deteriorating and complex situation in Central America. Relations between Congress and the White House, as well as with many of our allies around the world, had been soured by Reagan's aggressive tactics intended to unseat the Soviet- and

Cuban-backed communist government of Nicaragua. Providing military aid to the Contras, an insurgent group led by former Nicaraguan National Guardsmen trying to overthrow the Sandinistas, had undermined Reagan's capacity to do many other things. The foreign policy opportunities of the moment went far beyond Central America, Bush knew, and they could provide long-term stability in a nuclear world if addressed adeptly. He was ready to present a series of bold initiatives to hasten the historic changes then under way.

The Nicaraguan policy stood in the way of those initiatives. The Democratic-controlled Congress thought it had legislatively cut off financial support to the Contras, but the Reagan administration had devised a plan to funnel funds to them anyway via arms sales to Iran, thus the Iran-Contra affair. Democratic Speaker Jim Wright told Bush after the election that the Iran-Contra issue had been "the most implacable issue of the last eight years. Also the most politically polarizing and personally divisive question on the entire agenda."

To seize the wider opportunities open to him on the global stage and capitalize on the changes initiated by Soviet general secretary Mikhail Gorbachev, President Bush would first have to end this debilitating impasse with Congress and restore our credibility with the international community. Ending the United States' military support of the Contras was the only way to heal what James Baker called this "bleeding sore" that was destroying America's foreign policy efforts. For the United States to be effective abroad, at least some semblance of bipartisan cooperation between the Democratic Congress and the Republican White House had to be restored.

Bush knew that resolving the Contra issue would set the stage for an effective working relationship with the Democratic-controlled Congress on issues far beyond Central America. He understood very well the difficulties of operating with a divided government, and was smart enough to realize that the 260–175 majority the Democrats held in the House, and the 55–45 majority they held in the Senate, meant that he could achieve significant results as president only by nurturing a climate of cooperation. It was his only hope of getting his ambitious domestic legislative agenda through what would remain a very partisan Democratic congressional leadership.

Within a week of being named secretary of state, James Baker paid a visit to Jim Wright. Wright had served in the House for over thirty years and, like Bush and Baker, was from Texas. Bush had served with Wright in the U.S. House in the late 1960s; Baker had dealt with him as Reagan's chief of staff and later treasury secretary. Baker told Wright the president wanted to come to an accommodation with Congress. He wanted to reframe U.S. policy on Nicaragua, abandoning military support to the Contras in favor of humanitarian assistance to the insurgents and the people of Nicaragua. By providing American financial support to both sides, Bush hoped to create a peaceful environment for fair and open elections. Wright was supportive.

With the initial goodwill established by that meeting, the next step was to signal this commitment to cooperation in a more public way. The first opportunity to do so was during the confirmation hearings for Baker's appointment as secretary of state. During those hearings, Baker told the Senate that the new administration wanted to refocus its Latin America policy away from the internal conflicts in Central America and toward the broader issue of easing the burden of foreign debt crushing the economies of all of Latin America. In his testimony, he also made it clear that the administration was prepared to move quickly to improve the United States' relations with Mexico. He pledged to return to Congress with a new policy, making

good on his earlier promise to Wright about Nicaragua and the
Contras.

The public promises were followed by another formal meeting between Baker and Speaker Wright during the first week
of March, and yet another with key leaders of Congress shortly
afterward. Baker and Bush quickly put together an agreement
that came to be known as the Bipartisan Accord on Central
America. President Bush, Speaker Wright, Senate Majority
Leader George Mitchell, House Majority Leader Tom Foley,
Senate Republican Leader Bob Dole, and House Republican
Leader Bob Michel signed the accord at the White House within
the first two months of the Bush presidency. At the signing ceremony, the president noted, "Today, for the first time in many
years, the president and Congress, the Democratic and Republican leadership in the House and Senate are speaking with one
voice about Central America." Bush had made good on his promise. And he had done so without delay.

Legislation passed by the House and Senate on April 13, 1989,
and signed by the president five days later formalized the accord.
The legislation provided for humanitarian assistance to Nicaragua and incentives for the Contra insurgents to reintegrate into
the political process via elections scheduled for the following
year. The 1990 elections in Nicaragua proved pivotal. The Sandinistas were overwhelmingly voted out of office and a civil war
that had ravaged the country for ten years came to a peaceful
end. Even more significant, however, was that the agreement
repaired relations with Congress well enough for Bush to focus
his foreign policy on establishing a world-changing new relationship with the Soviet Union.

The agreement also allowed Bush to move on another major
initiative. Often referred to as the "lost decade," the 1980s were
a difficult period in Latin America. Dictatorships, civil wars, and

coups had given way to some surprising election results during the Reagan years. Suddenly, at the end of the decade, democratically elected governments held sway in virtually every country in the Western Hemisphere. That democratization came with serious economic strife, however, largely because of an estimated $500 billion debt load carried by these countries, which were unable to meet their payment obligations. The debt was beginning to imperil the new democratic governments by hampering any new investment in their countries. The debt was also a drag on the United States' economy because many Latin American countries were significant trading partners. One estimate pegged the loss of U.S. sales to Latin America at $100 billion during the 1980s alone.

To address the heavy burden of this debt, the president called a special meeting in his office in late February 1989. Led by Secretary of the Treasury Nicholas Brady, we discussed a variety of approaches to deal with the problem. Most, however, were constrained by the United States' own ballooning budget deficit.

In that conversation, Secretary Brady suggested that the only way to address the Latin American sovereign debt crisis would be to encourage the foreign banks holding the debts to "voluntarily" reduce those burdens. In exchange, he indicated, the Latin American countries would be asked to liberalize their own markets. They would have to allow more imports and eliminate high taxes on foreign goods. Such liberalization would benefit American producers, and when restrictions on investment were removed and profits were allowed to leave those countries, new investors would come in to expand business, add jobs, and stimulate the economy. The president liked the sound of such a market-based approach to the problem and asked Brady to come back with a more detailed recommendation.

A month later, Brady returned with a specific program to make that approach work. The plan was to convert the troubled commercial bank loans into bonds covering the principal sum and, in some cases, the unpaid interest. The new bonds would be tradable, and the United States and other Western nations would provide some level of guarantees to make them appealing to investors. The innovation of the Brady approach was that it effectively converted defaulted or near-defaulted bank debt into marketable bonds. Commercial banks could then get much of this bad debt off their balance sheets, and since they could sell these bonds, reduce their exposure to risk. Brady was confident that the approach would also help reenergize the economies of Latin America.

The president quickly agreed to try to implement the plan. He then joked that he was going to allow it to be called the "Brady Plan." If it turned out to be successful, he said, we would have to convert the name to the "Bush Plan."

The approach did turn out to be extremely successful and, of course, it continued to be called the Brady Plan. Once in place, it helped reinvigorate economies across Latin America and the Western Hemisphere. Its effectiveness is underscored by the fact that a similar approach was devised to deal with other sovereign debt problems surfacing in the 1990s and then into the twenty-first century in locales as diverse as Bulgaria, Jordan, and Vietnam. Ultimately the approach helped not only Latin America, but the world. In the following decade, virtually all of the Latin American countries that took advantage of the Brady Plan were able to repay and retire all of their Brady Bond debt.

The president's efforts to help restore the economies of the democracies in the Western Hemisphere did not stop with the Brady Plan. In June 1990, he announced the Enterprise for the Americas Initiative (EAI). By then, the dictatorships that had ruled many Latin American countries for decades had been replaced by democratically elected governments. Only

Cuba remained the outlier in this tide of democracy sweeping over the region. The president wanted to nurture and support these changes, so he announced this new EAI to provide additional support and incentives for the countries to accelerate the reform of their markets.

The plan focused on trade, investment, and debt. Its approach and implementation set the stage for all the Western Hemisphere free trade agreements that would be negotiated over the next decade. It established the economic environment that produced the North American Free Trade Agreement, known commonly as NAFTA, as well as the Central American Free Trade Agreement (CAFTA).

The EAI also helped stimulate the flow of capital throughout the hemisphere. The United States committed to work with the Inter-American Development Bank to create and invest in a new lending program providing funds to nations that removed barriers to direct investment of capital. This program would reward the Latin American nations that modernized their tax structures, allowed foreign ownership of businesses, and opened up their markets to outside businesses. The EAI also expanded on the Brady Plan by creating additional ways for countries to have their outstanding loans forgiven. One particular provision demonstrated the president's innovative commitment to environmental issues. So-called debt-for-nature swaps provided for in the EAI allowed countries to create new, protected nature reserves. In return for those set-asides, they would have some of their debt to the U.S. government forgiven. Under these programs, over the past twenty-five years, more than $1 billion of conservation and preservation has been achieved.

The president formally sent his Enterprise for the Americas Initiative to Congress in September 1990, and the legislation was approved as an amendment to the 1990 farm bill. The EAI

as signed by the president had three principal components, and
provided a high-powered boost to all the Latin American economies. The first component reduced the debt owed by Latin
American countries to the United States government. The United
States would accept some debt payments in local currency, which
would then be turned around to pay for environmental protection programs in those countries. The second created a development fund in the Inter-American Bank to which the United
States would contribute $100 million a year over five years as seed
money. The third component may have been the most important.
It created a process by which a Western Hemisphere free trade
regime could take hold and set the stage for the creation of the
North American Free Trade Agreement between Canada, the
United States, and Mexico sometime later, a gratifying achievement for the president.

In 1989 George Bush had reestablished a working relationship
between the White House and Congress by resolving the bitter
dispute over how to deal with a civil war in Nicaragua. He saw
the resolution of that impasse not as the end of a problem, but as
the beginning of an opportunity—a chance to reinvigorate the
hemisphere—and his initiatives certainly had a significant impact.

Within a short time after taking office, Bush had solidified the
democracies of our neighbors and put them on a path to prosperity with the Brady Plan and the Enterprise for the Americas Initiative. In doing so, he had also stimulated the United States' own
economy through trade with these neighbors, helping to make the
decade of the 1990s one of unprecedented growth throughout the
hemisphere. George Bush and his deeply experienced economic
and foreign policy team applied the principles of free markets and
used the strengths of capital markets and trade to benefit everyone. His commitment to practical, conservative solutions ushered
in a new era of trade and growth that lasted a quarter of a century.

THE SAVINGS AND LOAN PROBLEM

Surprises are a regular occurrence in Washington. Sometimes they are good surprises. More often, though, they are unpleasant. And so it was that we set out in those early days to frame an ambitious domestic agenda centered on reining in the huge budget deficits of the 1980s, only to be jolted by a problem that eventually looked as if it would require hundreds of billions of dollars to fix—the savings and loan crisis.

In the weeks between the election and the inauguration, I found myself serving in two roles: chief of staff and governor of New Hampshire. The chief of staff part of me was able to make a few one-day trips to Washington to help select staff and cabinet members for the new administration, as well as help the president define a good, constructive agenda. The governor part of me, though, had to stay on duty until my successor, former congressman Judd Gregg, was sworn in on January 5. That gave me only two weeks to focus exclusively on my new responsibilities as chief of staff.

The economic data that George Bush and our team were looking at indicated that 1989 would not be a very good year for the country. The rate of growth had slowed significantly, and the budget deficit loomed large. President Reagan's tax cuts had boosted government revenues for a while, but his spending to rebuild America's military strength had offset that boost, and required him to increase taxes. As a result, the economy was limping along and the deficit continued to expand.

Richard Darman, who understood government and budgets inside out, was charged with compiling economic information for the president-elect, and none of it was very encouraging. On December 5, George Bush gathered Darman and other members of his new economic team to discuss the details of what was happening and possible initiatives to improve the situation. I flew down to Washington to join the meeting.

Darman loved memos, so he had drafted a lengthy one outlining the key issues. It laid out, in detail, the growth of spending over the last few years and the resulting deficits. He mentioned only in passing that there was a problem in the savings and loan institutions across the nation. There was no discussion of the savings and loans, as none of us realized at the time just how serious a problem it really was.

The December 5 meeting was the first of many formal group discussions on budget strategy. The most urgent question facing us was whether the first budget Bush presented to Congress should be a multiyear one with radical departures from "business as usual" to fix the budget deficit, or whether we should just propose a basic, one-year package to give the new president more time to craft a long-term fix for the spending-revenue imbalance. It was clear to everyone that the deficit controls imposed by the Gramm-Rudman-Hollings budget rules (formally the Balanced Budget and Emergency Deficit Control Act of 1985) had not been slowing the growth of the deficits.

Just after the inauguration, on our second working day in the White House, Nick Brady asked Dick Darman and me to join him for a meeting at the Department of the Treasury. He didn't tell us what the agenda would be. When we arrived, Brady asked his assistant secretary David Mullins and undersecretary-to-be Robert Glauber to lay out what was happening in the thrift industry in the United States.

In the early 1980s, they explained, Congress had passed legislation regulating the savings structure of the country. Unbeknownst to many people involved in that legislation, a Democratic congressman from Rhode Island, Fernand St. Germain, the chairman of the subcommittee leading the process, added a provision to the bill that raised the size of savings accounts that would be insured by the federal government from $10,000 to $100,000.

That seemingly minor change in numbers sparked a huge growth in deposits to private savings accounts and significantly expanded the liability of the federal government via the Federal Savings and Loan Insurance Corporation (FSLIC). Taxpayers were subsequently on the hook by up to ten times as much as they were before in the event that a thrift should fail for any reason and require a federal bailout.

The resulting deposits inundated savings and loans with cash, which they then would need to invest. Traditionally, most thrifts had been conservative and disciplined in the manner in which they invested deposits. In a harbinger of the collapse of discipline and judgment we would later see during the subprime crisis of 2008, savings and loans began investing the new flood of cash in more speculative loan portfolios with significantly reduced requirements on the borrowers. More dangerous still was their shift to investments in major commercial and retail developments—even riskier areas. The banks that had historically helped financially sound families afford modest homes were lending money to build shopping centers, hotels, golf courses, and other recreation facilities that were significant business risks and had never been an important part of their loan portfolios in the past.

As the economy began to slow down in the late 1980s, some homeowners began finding it difficult to pay their mortgages. Under normal circumstances, the thrifts would have weathered such conditions easily because they had enough good loans to offset the bad ones. But this time was different. Besides the home mortgages, they now were saddled with those other, riskier loans to commercial operations that were also in trouble. For some thrifts, the combination was a knockout blow. Some began having trouble meeting their own interest payment obligations to depositors and, in many cases, saw their balance sheets drift below the levels required by banking regulations. They were becoming, in a word, insolvent—and taxpayers were on the hook.

The problem had been bubbling up quietly over the previous decade and had been virtually ignored, escaping any serious regulatory or congressional scrutiny. It was now about to become one of George Bush's surprise challenges. Unless the president acted expediently and effectively, it would be almost impossible for him to get much done on his domestic agenda.

In that first presentation at Treasury right after the inauguration, I was quite surprised to hear that although the problem was not trivial, it was portrayed as only an $8 billion to $10 billion problem. That was the message that Brady, Darman, and I took back to the president. When George Bush heard the details he understood enough about the fragile nature of the economy to know that even at the size currently being described, it was a problem he had to fix quickly.

The following day, the president gathered his economic team in his office once again to continue an overall review of the economy and budget. By then, we all knew the savings and loan problem had to be added to the list of difficult issues we faced. The hardest part was figuring out what actions might help, and what responses might actually make things worse.

In order to assure the industry that he was focusing on the problem, the president invited a number of banking and business leaders to weigh in with their concerns and to offer advice. Unfortunately, most of the meetings were only frustrating. The same financial leaders who had ignored the developing crisis would now tell him he needed to do something. When the presi-

dent asked them what they wanted to see done, he almost invariably got an answer equivalent to "I don't know, but you'd better
do something quickly." The few specific recommendations he got
from them often completely contradicted what had been said by
one of their colleagues just a few hours earlier.

After absorbing a lot of contradictory and largely unhelpful
input, President Bush accepted the fact that it would be best
to rely on his own team to solve the problem. We would need
to send a recommendation to Congress and work hard to get it
passed. His directive to us was simple: "Let's fix this and fix it
fast!" He had, he said, an obligation to the American people to
do so.

Darman and I met with Brady and Mullins again. After
discussing some of the options, Secretary Brady and his team
sorted out the problem and worked out a possible solution. Brady
directed Mullins to work with the legal staff at Treasury and craft
a package of legislation that the president could send to Congress. Amazingly, they did it in just two weeks. Their proposal
included a complete restructuring of the regulatory boards overseeing the industry, using federal funds to support the deposit
insurance obligations, and establishing a Resolution Trust Corporation (RTC) to acquire and dispose of the failed assets of the
thrift institutions that had to be taken over by the regulators.

Not everyone was quite so efficient, however. One of the few
things that genuinely surprised me about Washington was how
poor performers, or even downright incompetent people, could
enhance their status just by having a couple of friends in the
press to burnish their reputation.

Shortly after the severity of the savings and loan problem
became clear and the tools to resolve it were put in place, Nick
Brady came to brief the president on the situation. I was in the

Oval Office with Bush when Brady laid it out. By that point, every update Brady gave us put the cost at a few billion dollars more than the previous update.

This time, however, Brady had another problem. The chairman of the Federal Deposit Insurance Corporation, L. William Seidman, was dragging his feet. Seidman had been snubbing the treasury secretary ever since Brady panned a proposal of Seidman's on how to deal with third-world debt. Brady told the president that if Seidman stayed at FDIC, the savings and loan problem would get worse and last longer. Brady was worried that it would fester throughout Bush's entire first term. He said Seidman had to go. Bush agreed, and told him to figure out how to get it done.

When Seidman got that message, he decided to stay anyway. Brady, exasperated and with far more important things to deal with, came to me for help. When I saw what was happening, I wasn't sure whether it was because Seidman was still upset at Brady or whether this was just a petulant play by a power-hungry ego. Whatever the reason, the president wanted Seidman out. Brady and I both had our marching orders.

Brady tried a few more times to get Seidman to step down. Each time he tried, however, Seidman got more intransigent. Finally, Brady asked me to speak with Seidman directly. I went over to the FDIC and told him the president wanted him to step down. I explained it would be best for everyone not to let an interdepartmental squabble impede something as important as the successful resolution of the savings and loan crisis. Seidman was unmoved.

Seidman then tried another tack to justify his intransigence— one very attractive to the Beltway press. He turned it into a conflict between the chairman of the FDIC and the White House chief of staff. He told the press that I, not the president, wanted

him out. I really didn't care one way or the other about Bill Seidman personally. At the White House, we had already identified
several people who could do the job and do it well, in concert
with policies that would dovetail with Treasury. Seidman got a
lot of mileage out of claiming he was staying on only to spite the
chief of staff. He was able to make the rounds of the TV shows
and get good press in the banking newsletters as well as from a
couple of friendly Washington reporters.

George Bush had wanted the problem "fixed and fixed fast."
Seidman, however, took his time in order to prolong his tenure.
That delay in getting the assets acquired by RTC onto the market
and sold back to the private sector increased the overall cost of
the bailout. As they lingered in government hands, the assets
continued to deteriorate and lose value. After it was all over, I
saw estimates that his delays to the implementation of the new
legislation added $10 billion to $20 billion to the total cost of
solving the savings and loan problem. Only in Washington could
somebody be praised by his friends for costing taxpayers that
much money.

On February 7, just eighteen days after the inauguration, the
president sent a message to Congress. He outlined the initial steps
that he felt had to be taken and that needed to be supported with
legislation. They included tougher regulations and tighter standards, including increased reserve requirements, for savings and
loans. They also provided for funding to pursue those who had
been involved in illegal activities, and called for the creation of
the private entity, the Resolution Trust Corporation, to manage
the closing and disposition of insolvent banks. There also would
be an increase in premiums for deposit insurance, and the FDIC
would take on oversight of the FSLIC.

Congress passed virtually all of the president's proposals
in early summer, and Bush signed the Financial Institutions

Reform, Recovery, and Enforcement Act on August 9, 1989. Even after the president sent his bill to Congress, however, the magnitude of the problem grew. First it was an $8 billion to $10 billion problem. Then it was a $15 billion to $25 billion problem. Then $70 billion to $100 billion. The final estimate of what was actually spent by the federal government was $130 billion.

Sometimes in life you don't get proper credit, because you make things look too easy. That was George Bush's predicament with the savings and loan crisis. The fix was more efficient and more effective than the remedies applied to our financial woes in 1929 or even in 2008. In the long run, as expensive as it was, the solution cost much less than it might have, and stressed the economy for a much shorter period of time than the remedies for other similar bubbles and crashes.

The tab for the savings and loan crisis certainly made the subsequent budget negotiations more difficult, but by responding swiftly and taking hold of the budget crisis, the president put the American economy on the path toward growth and fiscal integrity. Bush got the government out of the problem as fast as possible. He pressed for the assets to be rotated back into the private sector as quickly as possible. He established the process in which, over time, the money shelled out by taxpayers to solve the problem would be paid back by those who caused the problem in the first place.

"Fix it right, and fix it fast," along with the budget package of 1990, set America on the path toward the great growth and economic success of the next decade.

4

The Disciplined Leader
Ending the Cold War

W hen George Bush took office in January 1989, the Cold War was still very much alive, despite the progress that had been made by President Reagan and Mikhail Gorbachev to reduce the tensions. The Soviet Union and the United States still had tens of thousands of medium- and long-range nuclear missiles pointed at each other. Reagan and Gorbachev had begun discussions aimed at mothballing many of those warheads, but the missiles still remained in place.

Bush understood the importance of personal relationships among leaders, and used them to great advantage. He developed those relationships first, then waited for the right moment to build on them. Relationships required cultivation. They required nurturing. Once they were solid, he believed the climate of trust would enable both parties to take chances and achieve real and dramatic breakthroughs. Bush's expertise was the art and the talent to frame the results of negotiations in such a way that there were no losers, only winners. The new reality of super-power cooperation that he coaxed from this successful style of diplomacy was evident in, among other instances, the resolution of the Gulf War, which was the only major conflict of the period.

When he was vice president, George Bush had seen Ronald Reagan initiate and nurture negotiations with Mikhail Gorbachev, the general secretary of the Soviet Union, and begin to lessen the nuclear tension. As president-elect, Bush set out to continue that engagement with Gorbachev and take advantage of what he believed was a once-in-a-lifetime opportunity to create a truly stable world. Ultimately, his handling of the collapse of the Soviet Union and the momentous changes in Eastern Europe offers us an extraordinary example of what a smart and disciplined American president can accomplish. Contrary to the superficial analysis of some media commentators and academics, the smooth and peaceful transition of those years was *not* predestined. It was achieved by an American president with the vision to recognize the opportunity before him, and the knowledge and experience to lead the world to capitalize on that and close the deal.

Bush recognized the need for a shift from the confrontational rhetoric of the Reagan years to a quieter, personal, and more humble diplomacy that would ease tensions as they arose—the sort of diplomacy of which he was a master. Step by step, meeting by meeting, he brought our European allies and the Soviet Union closer to rapprochement. Over the next three years the Cold War would come to a very gratifying end and we would witness the most significant, tranquil evolution toward peace in its history. The threat of a nuclear war virtually disappeared. With thoughtful, deliberate, focused, and disciplined action, Bush deftly used America's strategic and economic power to bring peace and stability to the world.

Bush would be the first to acknowledge that he had a very important and courageous negotiating partner in Mikhail Gorbachev. He had met Gorbachev for the first time in the spring of 1985 when President Reagan asked him to represent the United States at the funeral of Soviet general secretary Konstantin Chernenko in Moscow. After the funeral, the American delegation, led by the vice president and the secretary of state, George Shultz, returned to the Kremlin to meet with Gorbachev. Bush reported back to Reagan that the new Soviet leader seemed to have a more engaging personality and a capacity to communicate more effectively than was commonly assumed in the West at the time.

Bush came away from that visit sensing that the Soviet Union finally had a leader with whom the United States could engage in real discussions on the difficult issues facing the two superpowers. He met Gorbachev again during a U.S.-Soviet summit in Washington at the end of 1987 over a typical American breakfast at the Soviet embassy—a meeting I attended as well. They touched on a number of issues including the forthcoming presidential election. Bush made it clear to Gorbachev that if he became president, he was more than ready to build on the new relationship between the two superpowers.

Bush began to understand that Gorbachev was very "street smart," with great survivor instincts. He was quick in negotiations, and smart enough to see the real differences in the capacity and might between the United States and the Soviet Union. Gorbachev was a realist.

Bush's third significant meeting with Gorbachev took place a year later, in December 1988, at Governors Island in New York Bay, after he had won the election. Gorbachev was in New York to address the United Nations and deliver what many believe to be one of his most significant speeches as Soviet leader. He told the U.N. General Assembly that foreign policy should not be shaped by threats or the use of force, and said he would shift the stance of the Soviet military from an offensive to a defensive one. The size of the Soviet armed forces, he said, would be dramatically reduced. He also made what George Bush felt was a key statement: that several Soviet army divisions would be withdrawn from Eastern Europe. Bush believed if Gorbachev followed through on those statements, there would be a real opportunity for mutual steps leading to a more stable and peaceful world.

After that speech, Vice President Bush was waiting with President Reagan to greet General Secretary Gorbachev at Governors Island. Six weeks remained before George Bush would be inaugurated. President Reagan and Gorbachev had come to respect each other and had developed a real friendship, so the meeting was somewhat awkward for Vice President Bush. He remained supportive of all that President Reagan had done, but he was ready to go even further. He did make one diplomatic overture. Vice President Bush told Gorbachev that it would be very helpful to the United States if the Soviets would rein in their aid to Nicaragua, which had become a point of concern in the Western Hemisphere.

The next day Gorbachev was called back to Moscow suddenly because a strong earthquake had struck Soviet Armenia, killing tens of thousands of people and leaving nearly a million homeless. The tragedy was so devastating that the Soviet Union, for the first time in nearly fifty years, allowed outside help to come into the country. Some of that assistance was delivered by AmeriCares, a relief organization supported by Robert C. McCauley, a friend of the Bush family. McCauley asked Vice President Bush if any members of the Bush family would care to help in the relief efforts. Jeb Bush and his son, George, who was twelve at the time, agreed to go, even though it meant they would not be with their family at Christmas. Jeb and George flew in with the AmeriCares team to help distribute aid and visit a hospital in the devastated area. Their very emotional participation made a deep impression not only on the Soviet leaders, but on the people of the Soviet Union as well.

Two weeks before the Governors Island meeting, George Bush had asked Brent Scowcroft to be his national security advisor. The day after the summit Bush spent an hour with Scowcroft at the vice presidential residence in Washington reviewing his discussion with Gorbachev. Bush told Scowcroft of his sense that there was an opportunity for "significant breakthroughs" ahead of them. He asked Scowcroft to develop a set of proposals to take advantage of the opportunity, something "which would reaffirm American leadership in shaping the international agenda."

Bush also correctly sensed that those proposals should contain a substantive response to the initiatives Gorbachev had laid out in his United Nations speech. However, he knew his instinct for a direct, strong response had to be balanced against the need to craft a careful, measured set of steps. As much as the president-elect felt he could work with Gorbachev, he soon discovered that his national security advisor, along with a number of other advisors, was somewhat more skeptical. They were concerned that an overly forthcoming response to Gorbachev could be very risky for America and its allies. If we went too far in reducing our role in NATO, which was overwhelmingly reliant on the U.S. military machine, it might leave Europe at risk.

Reagan had focused on rebuilding America's defenses so that we could negotiate with the Soviets from a position of strength. He came into office concerned that post-Vietnam America was unwilling to invest in national security or our military, that the post-Vietnam malaise had sapped our strength and emboldened our enemies. Reagan was determined to rebuild our armed forces and was willing to spend billions on new technologies like the Strategic Defense Initiative, or "Star Wars," program. He wanted to make it clear that the United States was the world's undisputed military powerhouse and that it would be in everyone's best interest to develop a more peaceful, stable relationship. The buildup had the intended effect, as I was to learn very clearly later, and it was one of the reasons the Soviets were so eager to come to the table.

Gorbachev's initiatives created the cautious hope that, for the first time, the two nations had reached a juncture that could lead to an end of the Cold War. The Soviet leader hoped his policies of opening (glasnost) and restructuring (perestroika), would reenergize the Soviet economy and allow him to divert money and resources from the military to support domestic development. As general secretary of the Communist Party, Gorbachev had been working diligently to garner support for these changes. Not surprisingly, he was receiving some significant resistance from the Soviet military and other hard-liners in the entrenched Soviet leadership. He was making bold and personally risky moves, steps that would prove treacherous down the road.

For his part, George Bush's close involvement in international affairs as vice president provided an unusually well-informed perspective on the historic moment confronting him and the potentially dramatic and volatile changes ahead. Bush had been involved, in one way or another, in the administrations of the last three Republican presidents—Nixon, Ford, and Reagan. Those years of direct involvement taught him that the White House was fertile ground for personality conflicts and disputes over power and turf. He was determined to structure his own team and his own processes to minimize those potential pitfalls. His choice of Baker as secretary of state and Scowcroft as national security advisor was very much influenced by those concerns. He considered both of them trusted friends and talented advisors who were eager to work together.

There was one small setback in the process as Bush the president assembled his national security team. He wanted former senator John Tower of Texas, who had been a strong and leading voice on the Senate Armed Services Committee and who understood the nuances of defense policy as well as anyone who had been in the Senate since World War II, to be his secretary of defense. After nominating Tower, we were dismayed by the painful confirmation process. We had thought Tower's relationships with his colleagues in the Senate would help him get approved, but he was soon overwhelmed by a series of personal attacks, both open and leaked anonymously to the press.

The Tower nomination was defeated in a very partisan vote. When I brought this news to the president, I urged him to send a new nomination back to the Senate immediately. The president asked me to sit down with Vice President Quayle and come back with some recommendations. Quayle and I soon narrowed the choices. At the top of our list of recommendations to the president was Congressman Dick Cheney of Wyoming.

Although Cheney had not sat in any leadership positions on any of the House national security committees, he had been a part of the Republican congressional leadership and served on the Select Committee on Intelligence. He had a solid background in national security and defense. He had also been chief of staff to President Gerald Ford and understood the workings of the White House. Scowcroft also felt comfortable with Cheney. The president was pleased with the choice, and after a series of quick phone conversations with Cheney and a meeting in the Oval Office, Bush offered him the job. We sent his nomination to the Senate the next day, and he was confirmed immediately.

When Admiral William Crowe retired in September 1989

as chairman of the Joint Chiefs of Staff, Dick Cheney recommended Colin L. Powell to replace him. General Powell had been national security advisor to President Reagan, so the president was familiar with his talents and abilities. The president accepted Cheney's recommendation, and Powell became chairman of the Joint Chiefs of Staff on October 1, 1989.

President Bush's leadership style placed a priority on information. He encouraged the presentation and open discussion of all possible positions, facts, and details of an issue, but he was not a micromanager. He took advice from experts, his key staff members, and his cabinet, then made a decision and delegated its execution.

His style demonstrated the power of one-on-one diplomacy. Over the years, he had built up an extensive Rolodex of contacts, but they were more than just names and numbers in a file. They were close relationships nurtured by countless kind and generous acts over the years. He once told Condoleezza Rice that your first call or meeting with someone should never be to ask for something. Virtually every leader in the world at the time had received a handwritten note or a personal call from George Bush on one occasion or another. Many leaders had shared a meal or coffee with him and Mrs. Bush. Some even owed their own careers to the fact that they had a good relationship with George Bush. The amazing aspect of all of it was that the friendship was genuine. It was the real George Bush, and they all realized that.

Personal contact, which some leaders derided as unimportant or unnecessary, was an important part of the president's approach to diplomacy. "Henry Kissinger once told me there are no substitutes for deep national interest," Bush said once. "He pointed out that the leader of one country's not going to change a policy because he likes another leader. I suppose there is a danger that one can be naively lulled into complacency if one expects friendships will cause the other party to do things your way, but I thought that danger was remote. For me, personal diplomacy and leadership went hand in hand."

That was George Bush's style.

On January 9, 1989, the president-elect gathered a few of us to meet with Henry Kissinger. Jim Baker, Brent Scowcroft, and I listened as Kissinger, the distinguished old sage of international affairs of the time, laid out a broad historical view of what he saw as the opportunities of the moment. He spoke of what he believed would be needed to take advantage of the opportunities in Europe and the changes in the Soviet Union. Kissinger had a trip to Moscow scheduled in the days after the meeting, and Bush asked him to deliver a personal note to Gorbachev. In the note, Bush said he needed some time to reflect on U.S.-Soviet relations, but that he was fairly certain he wanted to go beyond simply arms control.

Upon his return, Kissinger offered a detailed account of his discussions in Moscow. Gorbachev had said how pleased he was that George Bush had initiated the process of contact and exchange of views even before being inaugurated. He said he hoped a dialogue could begin in the following two months. Gorbachev also indicated that he welcomed discussions on the changes occurring in Europe, but he underscored that any such changes must not threaten the security of either side.

The Soviet Union's occupation of Eastern Europe was Bush's highest priority. For the decades since World War II, the Soviets had dominated Eastern Europe through repression and intimidation. The Warsaw Pact was Moscow's answer to the West's NATO alliance. It was established in 1955 in response to West Germany's joining NATO, and it bound the nations of Albania, Bulgaria, Czechoslovakia, East Germany, Hungary, Poland, and Romania inextricably to the Soviet Union, both politically and

militarily. Now, Gorbachev's new policies were allowing things to
change dramatically in those countries. He was giving them more
and more control over their own affairs. He was even accepting
reform of their economic structures. All this change was presenting significant political challenges for the leaders of the Warsaw
Pact countries, many of whom had been handpicked by Moscow.

President Bush and his advisors concluded that Poland would
most likely be at the forefront of these changes in the region.
By word and deed, the Polish pope, John Paul II (Karol Jozef
Wojtyla)—first as a bishop and then as a cardinal—and the
Catholic Church were providing more than just moral support to
the efforts of the Poles to unshackle themselves from the Soviets. Poland's largest labor union, Solidarity, was in open dissent
against the existing government. Under the leadership of Lech
Walesa, it had pressed the government to hold real elections.
Finally, with Gorbachev's tacit approval, that was actually going
to happen. The United States provided support to these efforts.
In some cases, support was given via American labor unions and
in others through groups affiliated with the Catholic Church.

By the time Bush took office, there was real movement in
Poland. Laws were amended to allow for private ownership and
operation of businesses. The Soviet-sanctioned leader of Poland,
General Wojciech Jaruzelski, had opened the door to opposition
participation in the political process. Decades of communist mis-
management of the economy were beginning to take their toll
and Poland was distancing itself from Moscow.

Bush had met Polish leader General Jaruzelski in 1987. Even
then, he said, he found him to be "more reasonable and thoughtful than I had expected." He came away thinking Jaruzelski
was a true patriot, despite the fact that the Polish general had
declared martial law and unleashed tanks on his countrymen in

order to quash a Solidarity-led uprising in 1981. Bush hoped that he could eventually encourage the general to be a part of the solution as things changed.

The president also saw opportunity elsewhere in the Warsaw Pact. In Hungary, reformers had been allowed to move up the power ladder, and legislation had been adopted that loosened the constraints on political opposition. The streets of Czechoslovakia, too, were filled with demonstrators and this time, unlike in 1968, Soviet tanks were nowhere to be seen.

Bush believed the United States had to do more than just watch this all take place. In his mind, the substance of U.S. talks with the Soviet Union had to move beyond arms control and include the delicate steps of nurturing and supporting the changes taking place in Eastern Europe. The key, he believed, was to negotiate agreements on conventional forces that encouraged the withdrawal, or at least reduction, of Soviet forces in the region. Removing the military threat would give domestic reformers in those nations some breathing room.

The second imperative—which directly followed from the first—would be to modernize America's strategy as it applied to each of the individual Eastern European states. The existing strategy took a one-size-fits-all approach to the region. The policy hoped for a critical mass of change that would affect the entire region at once. Cognizant of the different culture and circumstances of each country, Bush believed in a more targeted, individually tailored approach. He wanted to give preferred treatment and support to the Soviet satellites that were most aggressive in their quest for economic and political reform. With this new approach, however, the president knew he had to be careful not to send mixed signals that might encourage violence. It was essential that he find just the right tone.

Surprisingly, the changes under way in Eastern Europe were occurring with the assistance of Mikhail Gorbachev. He was actually encouraging a loosening of top-down control in the belief that the communist regimes imposed upon those countries by the Soviets could reform themselves and gain enough real public support to remain in control. Bush, however, sensed that once the people of those countries realized they had some control in choosing their leaders, the communist regimes would quickly be replaced.

Bush also sensed that perhaps our own policy leaders did not understand exactly what was going on inside the Soviet Union. He addressed this knowledge gap by inviting to the Oval Office a series of experts—ambassadors and former ambassadors, academics, and intelligence officers—to discuss what might actually be happening in Gorbachev's USSR. That became the pattern for the president as he tackled one foreign policy issue after another. He absorbed information, suggestions, and recommendations from a variety of sources he believed credible before making any momentous decisions.

The president ordered a strategic review of Soviet policy, but wasn't satisfied with the first recommendations he received. It wasn't bold enough, he said. He directed Scowcroft and the NSC to take another crack at it, to come back with more specific, more imaginative, and more dynamic proposals that would quickly move the United States and the Soviet Union toward a real path to a constructive relationship.

Bush also knew he had to work with our European allies. There were critical differences to be resolved among the three most important ones—the United Kingdom, West Germany, and France—and only together, as a strong, credible NATO, could we effectively encourage reform in Eastern Europe. Modernization of NATO's nuclear capabilities coupled with conventional arms reductions on both sides of the Iron Curtain would provide that strength. He also recognized that even though the United States was having its own problems with budget deficits, economic assistance could be a formidable tool in ushering along the changes in Eastern Europe.

To encourage uninhibited discussion among his most trusted advisors, on March 30, 1989, the president gathered a select group of us in the Oval Office. Among those present were Vice President Quayle, Baker, Cheney, Scowcroft, Deputy Secretary of State Lawrence Eagleburger, CIA Director William Webster, and I. The session began with Scowcroft presenting the proposal Bush had asked him to develop. At its core, it called for the withdrawal of United States and Soviet ground forces in central Europe. It was a bold and unprecedented proposal, with the Western allies getting the better part of the bargain. NATO countries, even without U.S. troops, were very capable of defending themselves against any Warsaw Pact aggression that did not involve Soviet troops. If successful, such a mutual withdrawal could dramatically eliminate the destabilizing impact of the Soviet troops occupying Eastern Europe.

Secretary of Defense Dick Cheney thought the proposal premature. Jim Baker suggested that the initiative call for the elimination of tanks rather than personnel. Throughout the conversation, George Bush kept reminding the participants that the focus should be on developing a proposal that was bold, but still achievable, in order to regain the initiative in negotiations.

The president came out of this first meeting pleased with the results. It turned out to be a lively yet friendly exchange of ideas. Bush liked the tone and the seriousness this group brought to the discussion, and he was pleased by the frank, direct, yet cordial interaction among the participants. He felt confident that this approach would provide him with the best advice over the long haul, so he continued to use this "core group" structure through-out his administration. Although actual decisions were affirmed in formal NSC meetings, the president used this informal group to formulate and hone his decisions.

The meeting clarified in his mind that the first overture to the Soviets should be framed around troop reduction. The consensus from the core group to use a more targeted Eastern European strategy instead of the broad-brush approach also appealed to him. In his memoirs, Bush said that in hindsight he was very impressed that Scowcroft's initial presentation also addressed the possibility of German reunification: this was something few others considered even remotely possible at the time, but Scow-croft's idea turned out to be remarkably prescient.

As much as Scowcroft's strategy of troop withdrawal appealed to the president, however, Bush was smart enough to understand how complicated it would be to present such an approach to our allies. This new strategy would require frequent and personal consultation to explain both the short-term and the long-term objectives. On top of that, Bush had a summit meeting with Gor-bachev to think about.

Throughout the Reagan administration, the principal topic of discussion at U.S.-Soviet summits was nuclear arms control. Bush's new focus on the reduction of troops and of conventional arms made negotiations much more complex. The president and his team had to work out the nuances of an approach that would not create instability or escalate any crisis. NATO was embroiled in a debate over how to reduce conventional forces while at the same time reducing and/or modernizing its cache of short-range nuclear weapons. Our major NATO partners faced considerable domestic pressure on these topics, especially on the subject of nuclear weapons. Thousands of antinuclear demonstrators were taking to the streets of London, Paris, and Frankfurt calling for the complete removal of nuclear weapons from the Continent. All too often in the Reagan administration those pressures were not properly appreciated. Bush felt he could not truly succeed without taking those political problems into account.

The president, Scowcroft, and Baker recognized that the key to any successful summit was going to be proper preparation. There had to be a definable objective, supported by hard work on the part of the staff to clarify and facilitate a path to reach that objective. There needed to be a clear delineation of what was to be gained, and what could be offered in the negotiations to achieve that gain.

While the president was trying to be thoughtful and measured in choosing among the options, the inevitable criticism from the political opposition claimed that he was proceeding too slowly. He was accused of dragging his feet and of having no philosophy, design, or strategy. False rumors even surfaced about internal dissent. The editorial writers of *The New York Times* were especially self-flattering in their criticisms of the pace of progress and the capacity of the president and his foreign policy team to tackle the issues. They seemed to genuinely believe that they understood more than the Bush team how to deal with Gorbachev. Of course, they really had no clue.

At times, the criticism was just petty. The *Times* once complained that Bush should not have made his national security advisor Brent Scowcroft chairman of a policy committee that included the secretaries of state and defense because "there are few touchier relationships than that between the National Security Advisor and Secretary of State." Headlines such as "Early Bush, Early Folly" were not unusual. John Tower should not have been nominated as secretary of defense, wrote a former *Times* editorial page editor. There was "disarray" in the White House on foreign policy, this writer opined. Bush's Latin America policy was a folly, said some pundits. Barely three months later they were backpedaling. By then the headlines were different. "Mister Bush's Leap Towards Leadership" was soon followed by another, Anthony Lewis's *New York Times* column "Abroad at Home" titled "Bush Vindicated."

Meanwhile, momentous things were happening across the Atlantic. Gorbachev's perestroika was having an impact in Eastern Europe. Serious talks were under way in Poland between the Solidarity movement and the Soviet-backed government of General Jaruzelski. In early March 1989, after a decade when Solidarity leader Lech Walesa was ignored by state-controlled media, the first serious interview with him was published, and a month later, Solidarity was afforded legal status. The opposition would be permitted to run in upcoming elections.

Finally, President Bush was comfortable with the broad framework of his new foreign policy initiative. After much discussion, we decided to have the president lay out his strategy publicly in a series of four speeches.

A lot of thought and effort went into those speeches. They would define the president's policy on what would be one of the important initiatives of his administration. Bush was well aware of their significance. In his characteristically diplomatic manner, mindful of his inclination against unsportsmanlike gloating, he scrutinized every passage and turn of phrase.

"There are a number of points that I wished to make and several issues to avoid," he would later write. "For example I wanted to respond to a comment Gorbachev had made at Governors Island back in December. I asked that a statement be inserted specifically denying that some quarters in the United States hope to see Glasnost and Perestroika fail, and declaring that there should be no doubt that we saluted the changes made so far and encouraged reform. I also wanted to eliminate a passage reading that 'some regimes are testing the limits of Soviet tolerance' and was certain language giving some credit to Jaruzelski for what was happening in Poland was necessary. I also reworked the words, the kind of fiddling I always like to do and would sometimes drive speech writers crazy."

His first speech in the series of four was given in Hamtramck, Michigan, a small town near Detroit with a significant population of Polish immigrants. In the speech, the president said he wanted to "address the central questions of the Cold War." He outlined the policy, which recognized the reforms taking place in Poland, and announced some specific economic measures to encourage more movement toward a market economy there. He signaled to the Soviet Union that the United States was ready to engage in serious discussions on the changes put forward by Gorbachev.

Disappointingly, the speech received minimal press in the United States, but it was widely noted in Europe and the Soviet Union as significant in its "appraisal of Soviet reforms and the prospects for improved U.S.-Soviet relations."

It marked the beginning of what would become long-distance diplomacy between Bush and Gorbachev, played out at public podiums instead of over a bargaining table. At about the same time, Gorbachev was conducting a full-scale public relations blitz in Europe with similar speeches of his own, and at times the two leaders seemed to be addressing each other rather than the audiences before them.

When Bush spoke at Texas A&M University in College Station, Texas, on May 12, 1989, he urged the Russians to embrace Gorbachev's new principles. He indicated that the United States was ready to move beyond the strategy of containment, which had dominated American policy toward the Soviet Union since diplomat George Kennan first articulated it in 1947, and was prepared to help integrate the Soviet Union into the world community of nations. He emphasized that the United States would match constructive Soviet moves with moves of its own, and articulated how a reduction of Soviet conventional forces in Eastern Europe would benefit everyone. The president also underscored the importance of self-determination among the Warsaw Pact countries.

Bush's third and fourth speeches, at Boston University and at the Coast Guard Academy in New London, Connecticut, respectively, that same month, again applauded the changes under way in the Soviet Union and called for a "less militarized Europe." The president said his goal was "a real peace, a peace of shared optimism, not a peace of armed camps." The president indicated that although the United States intended to maintain an effective nuclear deterrent, it would seek serious reductions in nuclear arms to allow for a stable peace maintained with the lowest possible number of weapons. He again repeated his call to the Soviet Union to follow up on its rhetoric with more action, to move away from an offensive military strategy, and to restructure the Warsaw Pact as a defensive alliance instead of an offensive one.

The strategy laid out in those four speeches contained the message George Bush wanted to convey to the world. It put into the public domain a policy thoughtfully crafted by the president and his core team that would allow America and our allies to benefit from the opportunities presented by the changes under way in the Soviet Union. It was a strategy designed to increase stability and to improve the prospects for real peace. It was designed to encourage the Soviets, to give them the confidence that they could proceed full steam ahead with the West's full support and, if they succeeded, participate in a global economy to everyone's benefit.

Gorbachev responded within weeks, in a speech in July to the Council of Europe in Strasbourg that would be called one of the most momentous of his career. In it, he called for a "common European home" and acknowledged that the social and political order of some countries had changed and would probably change more. Such changes, he said, were matters to be decided by the citizens of those countries.

"It is time to deposit in the archives the postulates of the cold war period, when Europe was regarded as an arena of confrontation, divided into 'spheres of influence,' and somebody's 'outpost,' and as an object of military rivalry, a battlefield," Gorbachev said. "In today's interdependent world, the geopolitical notions born of another era turn out to be just as useless in real politics as the laws of classical mechanics in quantum theory."

Both men's speeches were well covered and reported in the press and in official circles in Europe and the Soviet Union. The press and the officials recognized the significance and the strategy that were linked in Bush's presentations and Gorbachev's responses. In the United States, however, the ever-critical press missed the seriousness of the messages.

The Washington Post highlighted its own lack of awareness with headlines like "Life After Containment—Muddling Through" and "NATO Arms Cut Proposal Faulted as Too Cautious." It even ran a column titled "Reagan Is Concerned About Bush's Indecision," based on nothing but conjecture. The most egregiously witless comment came from the *Post*'s diva, Mary McGrory, who penned a column titled "Witlessness as Foreign Policy." The other "newspaper of record" was no less off the mark. *The New York Times* ran editorials such as "Mr. Bush's Arms Control Blunders" and "What East-West Policy?"

All of these were great examples of how the partisan filter of the media was keeping them from understanding how George Bush was steering the process. The press was just reflecting the partisan news releases coming from its Democratic friends in DC.

Once President Bush had formulated and articulated the framework for his new strategy, the hard part followed: dealing with America's allies and adversaries to implement that vision. In order to make it happen, George Bush had to use his many talents as a leader, his personal relationships, the power of the presidency, and the leverage of America's economic might. He now had a strong sense of what a stable and peaceful world should look like. He just had to make it work.

Two important events lay ahead that would help President Bush implement the strategy he laid out. The first was a NATO summit at the end of May on the fortieth anniversary of the alliance, at which the topics of conventional forces and nuclear weapons were on the table. The second event was an economic summit of the Group of Seven (G-7) scheduled in July.

In our conversations at the White House preceding these two events, the president noted how complicated the discussions would be, given Gorbachev's very effective public campaigns in Europe on behalf of his domestic reforms. Gorbachev's charm offensive had convinced much of the European public that the Cold War was already over and that we could all go home. We knew better, and had to convince European leaders that they needed to maintain a strong strategic defense until we were 100 percent certain that the Soviet threat was gone.

The antinuclear movement was in full swing in Europe at the time, particularly in West Germany, and seriously affected the conversation about and development of NATO policy over the following year. There were two camps. The United States and the United Kingdom felt that until the Warsaw Pact's tremendous superiority in its conventional forces stationed in East Germany and in the occupied countries of Eastern Europe was diminished, the nuclear assets remained necessary. West Germany and some other members of the alliance, on the other hand, wanted to delay the nuclear question in light of Gorbachev's initiatives. The nuclear negotiations dealt with questions both on modernization and on significant reductions of short-range nuclear weapons. This issue would require George Bush's most artful personal diplomacy with Prime Minister Thatcher in the United Kingdom, Chancellor Helmut Kohl in West Germany, and President François Mitterrand in France. Bush arrived at the NATO meeting prepared to work out a solution they all could support.

The president used personal contact and personal telephone calls as very effective tools to build trust and understanding among the leaders with whom he had to deal. To produce dramatic changes in policy, comfort and confidence between the participants were critical. Brent Scowcroft once said that George Bush probably spent more time on the telephone with foreign leaders than all of his predecessors combined. I often joked that his dialing finger probably was an inch shorter at the end of his term than it was at the beginning. Those calls created a comfortable appreciation on the part of other leaders that there would be no surprises when the sides finally sat down to discuss these difficult issues. Ultimately, the one-on-one conversations allowed George Bush to get significantly more out of his negotiations than anyone could have expected.

This personal diplomacy was characteristic of his entire presidency. His previous service as U.S. representative to the United Nations and as vice president had brought him into contact with virtually everyone on the planet sitting in a position of power. At one point or another, he called nearly every one of them in Asia, Africa, Europe, Australia, and South America. By the end of his first year, he had spoken with virtually every leader in the Western Hemisphere and most of the rest of the world's leaders.

Bush's personal diplomacy strongly reinforced the diligent efforts of his advisors and of our diplomats around the globe as they worked on the details of these and other complicated issues. As Scowcroft put it in *A World Transformed,* "it was enormously helpful . . . that the various foreign ministries knew that if they were disposed to be negative or simply dragged their feet on an issue, they might receive an inquiry from their head of government—stimulated by a Bush phone call."

As George Bush prepared to meet with our NATO allies, the antinuclear protests were taking their political toll on Helmut Kohl. In April, President Bush and his advisors began a focused effort to help the German chancellor. The president spoke to Kohl on the phone a number of times, and even invited him to come to America for more detailed discussions. The president also had a number of chats with Margaret Thatcher on the issue. She was worried that West Germany's internal political issues could undermine NATO's capacity to regain the initiative with Gorbachev. Bush and Thatcher agreed to maintain a unified front.

Bush also sent Secretary of State Baker to Moscow in mid-May. While Baker was there, Gorbachev added to the allies' discomfort on the nuclear issue by announcing that he would withdraw five hundred short-range nuclear warheads from Eastern Europe. Even though the Soviets would still retain significantly more nuclear weapons in Europe than the allies, this announcement fueled the antinuclear opposition pressuring Kohl in West Germany.

On May 19, just before his third policy-defining speech, at Boston University, the president gathered his "core group" and some additional advisors at his residence in Kennebunkport, Maine. In those discussions, the president again heard serious concerns about the risks of pulling back in Europe from the military wing of his administration, including Cheney and the chairman of the Joint Chiefs of Staff, Admiral William Crowe. The day after this meeting, the most important test of George Bush's skills in personal diplomacy took place. François Mitterrand of France came to visit the president and Mrs. Bush at Kennebunkport.

During the prior few years, the relationship between the French socialist president Mitterrand and our conservative president Ronald Reagan was not exactly cordial. The two really did not like each other. Their personalities were studies in contrast, their styles clashed, and neither made any real effort to warm things up. They all but stopped speaking to each other. George Bush recognized that the personality mismatch had harmed U.S.-French relations, and he was determined to improve the situation. He knew that a recalcitrant France could slow any progress in Europe or block any policy initiative outright. He hoped that a private, cordial two days in Maine would help.

When I, and a few members of the staff, heard the president's plans, we were a bit apprehensive, to say the least. We knew that Mitterrand was a very formal, precise, almost academic individual. The Bush home in Maine, by contrast, was as informal as one could possibly get, with a horseshoe pit, a high-speed boat, tennis, fishing, and a generally homey feel. The accommodations were comfortable, but plain at best.

George Bush had known the French president since Mitterrand took office in 1981. He had developed a fairly good relationship with him, but he was determined to make it even better. One of President Bush's strongest assets was that he had no ego when it came to allowing the older, longer-serving president to be granted protocol deference in meetings. Bush almost always asked Mitterrand for his opinion before laying out his own positions.

When the Mitterrands arrived at Walker's Point, François Mitterrand was dressed just as one would imagine a French president to be attired for dinner—shoes shined to a high gloss, starched cuffs, and sharply pressed trousers. The Bushes,

meanwhile, looked as if they were ready for a backyard barbe-
cue. Soon, however, the relaxed atmosphere—purposefully set
by the Bushes from the first moment—proved contagious. The
Bushes cordially welcomed the French couple and treated them
like family. Almost from the outset, the savvy former diplomat
had Mitterrand eager to move things forward.

Displaying the deference that Mitterrand seemed to appreciate, Bush opened the conversations at Kennebunkport by asking
the French president what he thought about the Gorbachev initiatives. Then he asked him, "How should NATO respond to all
that is taking place?" Bush gave him the floor and Mitterrand
laid out his own views in detail.

Since Mitterrand had shown a willingness to tackle the issue
of conventional forces before moving on to negotiate nuclear
assets, Bush took advantage of this time to explain, in detail, how
he had evolved his own strategy. He said he was willing to fine-
tune and adjust it, if need be, to take into account Kohl's own
problems at home in Germany. Mitterrand explained at length
the finer points of European politics and, in particular, the politics in West Germany. As he always did, Mitterrand presented it
all within a grand historical context.

All of us who had the opportunity to be part of those discussions were somewhat surprised to hear Mitterrand's response to
a question about German reunification. Mitterrand, president of
a country that had been devastated by Germany in two world
wars during the twentieth century, said he would not oppose
unification if that was what the German people wished. Those
two days of personal diplomacy by Bush may have been the most
important two days in his determined efforts to refocus and redi-
rect NATO policy.

Brent Scowcroft described the conversations in *A World
Transformed* as follows: "The Kennebunkport meeting was the

president's personal style of diplomacy at its finest." Indeed. Mitterrand may have arrived with the same cool feelings he had toward Reagan, but by the time he left, George Bush and François Mitterrand had begun a constructive and personal relationship that made working together to change the face of Europe easier from that moment forward.

After Mitterrand's visit with Bush at Walker's Point, the two presidents continued to develop an amicable and effective working relationship. In December 1989, George Bush flew to a quiet Caribbean resort on Saint Martin, a French and Dutch territory in the Caribbean, for the second of many summits with the French president. That visit was the last of a handful of meetings between the two leaders during the president's first year in office. They also talked on the telephone nearly a dozen times throughout the year.

Over time it became obvious that these two strong personalities were working hard to accommodate each other's style. George Bush's natural approach was more informal and personal, while Mitterrand, as is typical of French diplomats schooled at Sciences Politiques in Paris, preferred to operate in a much more formal, protocol-driven manner. Within just a year, however, they developed a genuine, mutual respect and were comfortable deferring to each other.

Their improved working relationship produced a dividend for Bush when, in the last session of the G-7 Economic Summit in Paris in July 1989, Mitterrand endorsed President Bush's plea for financial assistance to Poland and Hungary. It was Mitterrand's support that moved the other European nations to support the Bush proposal.

Mitterrand's support was also crucial for the president as he worked to facilitate the reunification of Germany. Although France was for obvious reasons uncomfortable with the prospect of a unified Germany, Mitterrand acknowledged it as an inevitability and supported America's encouragement. In backing Bush, Mitterrand disappointed Margaret Thatcher, who shared his misgivings about a rejoining of East and West Germany.

Although Mitterrand may have been the most formal of all of the major allies Bush had to deal with as Europe was transformed by the collapse of the Soviet Union, I also found him to have a surprisingly strong, dry sense of humor, often shown by an unmistakable twinkle in his eyes. He was also a true scholar of history and extremely shrewd politically. Invariably, when Bush had to deal with François Mitterrand he knew he was going to get a constructive response, but it was always prefaced by a scholarly and detailed historical presentation of the context in which Mitterrand's strong support was being given.

The four years of George Bush's leadership may have been the period of the closest and most genuine bipartisan Franco-American cooperation since the early days of the American republic. That happened because both George Bush and François Mitterrand were world-class leaders.

The journey to the NATO alliance meeting set for May 29–30 in Brussels began with a stop in Rome. We all knew it was going to be a historic trip, but for me it was even more significant because I got to meet and speak with Pope John Paul II. As a Catholic, I was inspired personally, and as a member of the Bush team I was energized by meeting the man who had done so much to bring about the changes we were seeing in Poland and beyond.

John Paul was warm and welcoming during our private audience, thanking the president again for his hospitality when the pope visited Detroit in 1987, and for the leadership America was providing at this important moment in history. In public remarks a little later the pope noted that 1989 was the bicentennial of the first Constitutional Congress in Philadelphia as well as the two-hundredth anniversary of the establishment of the first Catholic diocese in the young republic of the United States. The world was witnessing another historic moment, the pope said: "The hour of international independence has come."

We left Rome on Sunday afternoon for Brussels. The first formal session of the summit began Monday morning. Even as the president was chatting informally with the heads of government and foreign ministers prior to the formal meeting, he was quietly working on his agenda. He paid particular attention to Prime Minister Thatcher, who seemed a bit concerned.

In the first formal session of the Brussels meeting, President Bush outlined his four-point proposal. Overall, he was proposing a process by which NATO and the Warsaw Pact nations would shift from a state of military confrontation to one of constructive give-and-take. The first step would establish a ceiling on the number of tanks, armored carriers, and artillery pieces maintained by each side. The equipment was not just to be withdrawn; it had to be destroyed to qualify as a reduction. The second step would be a reduction in the number of NATO helicopters and combat aircraft. The third was that both the United States and the Soviet Union would reduce to 275,000 the number of troops maintained in the region—a significant reduction in Soviet forces but only a moderate one of American troops. The fourth step was to accelerate the timetable for achieving steps one through three.

The president's proposals went over well. He had taken the time to let all the key leaders know what was coming, which made a real difference. Most of them came with speeches in support of the Bush proposal already in hand. The reaction from the Soviet Union was also positive. Gorbachev accepted the proposals as a serious response to his own initiatives on the Warsaw Pact, and even hinted that the president's plan could be put in place earlier than anticipated.

The second issue on the table in Brussels, a revision of the policy on nuclear forces, turned out to be much more complicated. Virtually no progress had been made by the staffs and experts ahead of the NATO meeting. In a last-ditch effort to come to some agreement on the issue before the end of the summit, the foreign ministers agreed to skip a scheduled banquet and worked through the night to develop an acceptable resolution.

George Bush kept in constant contact with his secretary of state, Jim Baker, who was part of those late-night discussions. Baker and Scowcroft worked with the European ministers to come up with language that balanced the antinuclear tendencies of West Germany with Bush and Thatcher's desire to maintain a strong hand. Around two in the morning Baker notified the president that they had reached an agreement.

With that agreement, the summit closed and was recognized as a major success for NATO and for George Bush personally. Even the president's most severe critics had to agree that his proposals had recaptured the initiative, and were truly reflective of a serious vision and a serious strategy.

Our trip through Europe continued. We flew directly from Brussels to Bonn, West Germany, to visit privately with Helmut Kohl. He was very gracious in his comments about the president. Bush laid out for Kohl in great detail his strategy for dealing with the opportunities presented by Gorbachev. In his public comments following the meeting, Bush deliberately avoided the topic of a reunified Germany. As a harbinger of what was to come, however, he did call for "a Europe whole and free."

The last stop on the trip was London, where the president had his first extended, private conversation with Prime Minister Thatcher.

Margaret Thatcher served as prime minister for all eight years of Ronald Reagan's term, and once called Reagan "the second

most important man in my life." The Thatcher-Reagan relationship has been described as the most important Anglo-American
relationship since that of Franklin Delano Roosevelt and Winston Churchill during World War II. Thatcher was proud of her
relationship with President Reagan, and I sensed that President
Bush was unsure of how effective a working relationship he
would have with her. He made sure it quickly morphed into one
of mutual respect.

As the president was developing his agenda and initiatives to
respond to Gorbachev's European actions in the early months
of 1989, he and Prime Minister Thatcher spoke on the phone a
number of times. And though they had spoken with each other
at the NATO summit, it was not until June 1 that the president
and Mrs. Thatcher had their first face-to-face meeting since his
inauguration.

"It was a fascinating discussion, and its relaxed atmosphere was
a welcome contrast to the worries of the past weeks—especially
the NATO meetings—where she had been very much on edge,"
Bush later wrote of the meeting in A World Transformed. "Margaret and I compared notes on the situation in various places
around the world—from economic reform and nationalism in
the Soviet Union to the Middle East and South Africa. She was
well-informed and insightful, and I discovered, as I was so often
to find, that our thoughts on these matters were quite similar."

My own first impression of Margaret Thatcher was even more
favorable than I had anticipated. She was as firm and direct as
her reputation led me to expect, but she also listened well and
was very willing to try to find a way to frame the discussion and
the decisions to accommodate both her needs and those of the
president. She proved, in the long run, to be as helpful to Bush
as she had been to Reagan.

Although Bush and Thatcher often disagreed on the nuances

of issues, there was only one subject on which they were clearly at odds: the reunification of Germany. The British, like the French, have unpleasant, even bitter memories associated with a powerful Germany. Like Mitterrand, Thatcher was a bit uneasy about the timing associated with the two Germanys' joining again as one, while Bush was much more supportive of West German chancellor Helmut Kohl's desire for an early reunification. Bush and Thatcher were determined to work out their differences, however, and they easily came to a compromise.

At the end of his June meeting with Thatcher in London, George Bush could look back on a very successful first six months in office. The president and his team had found a happy accommodation between Thatcher and Kohl on the issue of reunification. Bush also pushed through a significant proposal for the reduction of conventional forces in Europe and initiated the first steps toward getting Gorbachev to reduce the Soviet army presence in occupied Eastern Europe. Furthermore, Bush had reinvigorated NATO's commitment to a solid strategy of defense. None of this could have been accomplished without respectful and effective teamwork among Bush, Thatcher, and the other leaders of Europe.

The second major trip for 1989 was scheduled around a Group of Seven Summit in Paris, July 14–16. Bush thought it would be a perfect opportunity to put his more targeted approach to the region to work and visit the Eastern European countries where significant reforms were taking place. Of the dozens of trips I would take with President Bush, these stops in Eastern Europe were among the most memorable and inspiring. With the president, I witnessed history as it was happening.

In the months leading up to our trip, reform was changing the face of Eastern Europe. In Poland, the communist government and the opposition party, Solidarity, were layering economic reform and political liberalization into the national fabric. In Hungary, the government was even dismantling the fences that limited passage from that country to Austria—literally and symbolically removing significant parts of the Iron Curtain. Across the region, people were flocking to the ballot boxes for the first free and fair elections in four decades. Freedom was at hand.

Gorbachev continued to send signals of his approval in highly publicized trips through Europe, including West Germany, France, and Romania. Everywhere he went, he touted his own proposals to reduce nuclear weapons in Europe or even eliminate these weapons altogether. In Bucharest, Romania, at a Warsaw Pact meeting, Gorbachev hinted that Moscow would not intervene in the dramatic changes occurring in Poland and Hungary. He said Warsaw Pact countries should control the pace of their own reforms.

President Bush recognized that as he traveled through Eastern Europe, he would have to walk a fine line between supporting reform and saying anything that might encourage violence against those repressive regimes that had lorded it over the region for so many decades. He felt an obligation, he said, to be what he called a "responsible catalyst."

He later wrote, "We could support freedom and democracy, but we had to do so in a way that would not make us appear to be gloating over Gorbachev's political problems as he moved away from the ironfisted policies of his predecessors."

From the Soviet perspective, our trip was of serious concern because of its potential to either intentionally or unintentionally stimulate unrest or violence. Of course, there is no way the leaders in Moscow could have known at that time how sensitive the president was to those concerns. Bush was disciplined and curbed his public rhetoric accordingly.

By mid-1989, Poland was moving toward freedom at an almost

unbelievable pace. In June, Lech Walesa and his Solidarity movement won all 161 of the contested seats for the lower house of the
Polish parliament, the Sejm, and 99 of the 100 contested seats in
the senate. Since the executive branch was still controlled by the
communists, the legislative elections created such confusion that
the Poles decided to delay their upcoming elections for president.

George Bush was scheduled to visit Poland in the second week
of July. The president prepared carefully and extensively for what
he knew would be a tricky balancing act of dealing with both
Solidarity and the communists as they shared power. He was
intent on not disrupting the peaceful transformation that seemed
to be under way throughout the Iron Curtain satellite nations,
and sat through a round of very intense briefings before we left
Washington. When we did finally leave, it appeared to me that
we still did not have a definitive plan to deal with the situation.

We left Andrews Air Force Base on *Air Force One* in the early
morning of July 9 with a significant contingent of reporters and
staff—hundreds, in fact. By contrast, during Bush's previous trip
to Poland two years earlier when he was vice president, only a
handful of staff members and maybe a dozen journalists had
accompanied him. Now, en route, he told some of the assembled
writers that he felt "a little delicate" about the trip. Typically, he
downplayed his prospects, saying that he didn't want to over-
promise—he didn't want to "do too little or too much."

At one point during the journey, he made another decision
that took some of his staffers by surprise. "Set up a lunch," he
said. He told our ambassador in Warsaw, John Davis, to invite as
many members of the current Polish leadership from both sides
of the aisle as the embassy could hold.

It was a balmy midsummer evening when we landed in Warsaw.
On hand to greet us were a small official welcoming group and a
military band that played the national anthems of both nations.

The group included not only the communist leader, General Wojciech Jaruzelski, but also representatives from Solidarity— the first time members of the opposition had been included in such an official reception. On our trip into the city, the streets were lined with Poles waving and carrying welcoming signs.

The next day Bush had discussions with both Jaruzelski and Lech Walesa on how best to help guide Poland from its communist system toward a market economy, and do it in a way in which both perspectives were accommodated along the path to that goal.

His conversation with the colorful and earnest labor activist Walesa, who had only recently been released from jail, was very moving. Walesa described the approaching realization of a dream that he and other reformers had been working toward for decades. Bush was slightly taken aback when Walesa told him that Jaruzelski, his former jailer, could be helpful in navigating the transitional challenges Poland faced.

In his meeting with the president, Bush was impressed by General Jaruzelski's patriotism. The two men spent nearly two hours discussing in detail the situation in Poland at the time, and how it might evolve. President Bush, much to his own surprise, found himself urging Jaruzelski to run for reelection as president. Here sat Bush, an American president, encouraging a communist to run for office. In Bush's eyes, Jaruzelski's experience was what Poland needed at that time. He and Jaruzelski discussed how the upcoming elections could spawn a coalition government that could lead Poland through its transition and avoid instability or, worse, further bloodshed.

Bush kept his conversation with the once hard-line communist low-key, courteous, and positive. He complimented the general on how well he had, up until then, handled the changes. The genial and positive conversation made an impact on the Polish leader.

"Gorbachev believes that the Europeans are more encouraging of his reforms than the United States," Jaruzelski said. But after his conversation with Bush, he himself was convinced otherwise. He said he would reiterate that message to Gorbachev.

After those meetings, we went to the lunch at the embassy, and I saw almost immediately what George Bush had in mind when he asked for this lunch while aboard *Air Force One*. The crowd came together on the patio and under huge white canopies on the rear lawn of the ambassador's residence. The gathering was unprecedented in recent Polish history. As the president had suggested, it included leaders from the Communist Party, Solidarity, and the Catholic Church. In spite of the changes taking place in Poland, virtually none of these leaders had ever shared an informal meeting with anyone from an opposed group. However, under Bush's orchestration, that was now happening. Communist party jailers and former prisoners from the Solidarity movement strolled around the lawn in shirtsleeves and neckties, clinking champagne glasses and exchanging hesitant smiles in the summer humidity.

At the luncheon the president had his key advisors and staff members each chair a table—round tables in a deliberate nod to the so-called Round Table Agreements three months earlier that legalized trade unions and essentially ended Communist Party rule in Poland. I was assigned a table of ten that included the minister of the interior and a few of the recently elected Solidarity members of parliament. After a few moments of conversation, one of the guests pointed a finger at the communist minister sitting next to me and sternly told him, "I don't know if you remember me, but you put me in prison." Without missing a beat, the minister looked at him and smiled and replied, "Yes, but remember, I gave you a good cell." The rest of the table smiled sheepishly during the exchange, but as the conversation went on they soon discovered that all at the table were, first and foremost, patriotic Poles.

Shortly after 1:00 p.m., President Bush ad-libbed a toast that few in the room would ever forget. After praising his hosts and guests and marveling about how much had changed in Poland since his visit two years earlier, he promised that America would stand by Poland in its time of change. "We will support Poland's hopeful mission, unparalleled in your history," he told the crowd. Solidarity leader Bronislaw Geremek said it was exactly what they wanted to hear.

"Roughly two years ago, the vice president of the United States and Mrs. Barbara Bush talked with members of Solidarity right in this house," said Geremek, who wasn't even scheduled to speak at all, in his own impromptu toast. "None of us at that time expected that we would meet in two years in a situation like the present."

Clearly there was no way this amazing occasion would have happened had it not been for the vision of George Bush, a man committed to the simple idea that talking things out can yield surprising results. The last thing I remember about the event was Jaruzelski and the leaders of Solidarity huddled in a corner after lunch, deep in conversation, beginning negotiations on how to deal with their current concerns over the divided government and the upcoming presidential elections.

Later that day, President Bush spoke to the Polish National Assembly. He spoke again of the four-way approach he had laid out in his critical foreign policy speeches in America earlier that year. From Warsaw, we went to Gdansk in the north. There the president sat down again with Lech Walesa. In his earlier meeting with Bush, Walesa had suggested that Jaruzelski could be helpful in the transition. When Bush suggested he might even be a good choice for reelection as president in the same spirit of hopeful cooperation that seemed prevalent everywhere in Poland, Walesa agreed. Bush was pleased to hear that his own assessment of the Polish communist president matched Walesa's.

Following their meeting, President Bush, accompanied by Walesa, visited the Gdansk shipyard that had been the epicenter of the Solidarity opposition movement. There he spoke to a crowd of upwards of a quarter million people. It was by far the most emotional moment of the whole trip. All of us there during those two days with President Bush sensed how extraordinary it was to be in the middle of history as it was happening.

The amazing and unexpected outcome of all of this was that one week later, Jaruzelski was reelected president by the National Assembly with the support of Solidarity. The former foes had joined forces to ensure a peaceful and gradual succession of power, a unity partly forged over a meal at the American ambassador's residence. It was exactly what President Bush, a master at cultivating relationships and bringing people together for the kind of discussion that leads to effective solutions, had hoped would happen. Poland's march to democracy, and to real freedom, was well under way, not in small part because George Bush's instincts told him the way to make that happen was for former enemies to break bread and simply get to know each other as people.

The next day we flew to Budapest. The same feeling of hope and optimism prevailed in Hungary as in Poland. Interestingly, in Hungary, most of the pressure for change was coming from within the Communist Party itself. Our conversations there focused on how the leaders planned to make a smooth and orderly transition in both the political and the economic structures of the country. Although the Hungarians were not as far along with reform as the Poles, it was clear that most of their former communist leaders were determined to be instrumental in realizing effective change.

In Budapest, I was fortunate to witness one of those remarkable moments that illustrate the character of George Bush. We landed in the middle of a heavy rainstorm. The president was scheduled to speak in the center of the city, where a crowd of 100,000 had gathered in the pouring rain. On the way to the podium, the president noticed an older woman standing in the front row, soaking wet. He removed the raincoat he was wearing and draped it over her shoulders. The crowd roared and applauded.

After an overly long introduction, the president stepped to the microphone, pulled out his speech, raised it to eye level, and tore it up in front of the crowd. Again, the applause and the cheers from the soaked audience were thunderous. Instead, as he put it, he "spoke from the heart."

"You've been standing here too long," he told the soggy crowd. "Barbara and I feel the warmth of this welcome, and the rain doesn't make a darn bit of difference. . . . I salute the leaders of Hungary; I salute the reforms and change taking place in this wonderful country." The United States and its people, he said, would continue to work with Hungary to continue that progress.

The next day the president met with the Hungarian communist leadership and then with opposition leaders. All his conversations with both government officials and opposition leaders were marked by a mood of optimism and ambition. One of our last meetings offered another extraordinary moment as Prime Minister Miklos Nemeth presented George Bush with a plaque containing a section of barbed wire the Hungarians had cut the night before from the border fence between Austria and Hungary. Later, the Hungarians gave each of us a similar memento of this beginning of the end of the Iron Curtain.

That afternoon, the president spoke to the students and faculty of Karl Marx University of Economics. He outlined his broad strategy for Eastern Europe and offered some incentives specific to Hungary, including a private enterprise fund and most favored nation trading status. Scowcroft felt the speech was the best the president made on the trip, both in content and in delivery. He noted that although, in keeping with Hungarian custom, there was no applause while the president spoke, at the conclusion the president received a long, standing ovation.

Energized and encouraged by the stops in Eastern Europe, we then made our way to Paris for the G-7 Summit. Bush had just one nagging regret from the first part of the trip. Because of the tight fiscal conditions the United States faced domestically at that time, he could make only limited offers of financial support to the emerging democracies in Eastern Europe. He vowed that one goal of the G-7 meeting would be to convince our partners at the summit to carry some of the economic obligations to support the financial and political reforms taking place in their backyard.

Our visit to Paris coincided with the gigantic two-hundredth anniversary celebration of Bastille Day, France's independence day. We then proceeded to the three-day economic summit (July 14–16), at which Bush was able to convince our partners to relax Poland's payment schedule on its foreign debt and begin coordinating a financial aid package for the new democracy. Interestingly, Gorbachev had sent a letter to François Mitterrand as chairman of the summit asking the group to consider letting the Soviet Union join the group of industrialized nations. It was taken under consideration.

On our return flight to Andrews Air Force Base, we all were much more relaxed than we had been on the way over. Once back at the White House, in the wake of two truly historic meetings in two months, the president gathered his team to review what had taken place, to assess where things stood, and to decide what to do to keep things moving forward. In that meeting, President Bush let the team know that it was now an appropriate time to arrange for a meeting with Mikhail Gorbachev.

Again, ever mindful of the personal touch, Bush drafted a letter to Gorbachev suggesting they meet, but avoiding the word "summit" in the description of arrangements. The Soviet marshal Sergey Akhromeyev, who had been in Washington at the end of July to discuss arms control, delivered the letter, and about a week later, Foreign Minister Eduard Shevardnadze's first deputy, Alexander Bessmertnykh, returned to Washington with Gorbachev's answer. Gorbachev recommended meeting near Italy, where he had scheduled a visit at the end of November. After mulling a number of options, the two sides finally agreed on a shipboard meeting on the Mediterranean island of Malta off the southern tip of the Italian peninsula.

The meeting was eventually scheduled for the first three days of December. While the president prepared, events were progressing even further in Europe as a result of his two successful trips that summer. In the middle of July, Jaruzelski had run for reelection as president of Poland with the support of Lech Walesa and Solidarity. Following the election, after a few fits and starts, a new government was formed, headed by Solidarity. Nearby, Hungary opened its entire border and it became a conduit for escape for people from other Warsaw Pact countries such as East Germany, Romania, and Czechoslovakia.

As ecstatic as Bush was with the result in Poland—the events in Hungary were more a cause for concern than celebration at that point—he admonished all of us in his administration to maintain a public posture that was subdued and restrained. George Bush decided that the best way to maximize the chances of success in the region was to avoid embarrassing the Soviets and Mikhail Gorbachev every time the Soviets lost a former satellite. Gorbachev's response was also quite subdued. He publicly stated that the composition of the new government in Poland was an issue that had to be decided entirely by the Poles. It was the clearest and most significant signal yet of the level of change that the Soviets would permit to take place within those countries.

In the run-up to the December meeting in Malta there were a number of minor challenges. Boris Yeltsin, a former mayor of Moscow and now a member of the new Soviet parliament and one of Gorbachev's loudest critics, was coming to Washington in September as part of a speaking tour across America. When Yeltsin asked to meet with Bush, Brent Scowcroft had to decide on the protocol for such a visit. Bush wanted to see Yeltsin, but he needed to do it without seeming to endorse Yeltsin's attacks on Gorbachev. The choices ranged from a formal meeting in the Oval Office with the president to a meeting with just Scow-croft. Finally the president and Scowcroft split the difference and decided on what was termed a "drop by" visit in Scowcroft's office. Yeltsin would meet with Scowcroft in the national secu-rity advisor's office and the president would "drop by" for a chat with them. Yeltsin also managed to secure a photo op with Vice President Quayle. And, to nobody's surprise, on his way out of the White House, the notoriously attention-hungry Yeltsin made sure reporters saw him and interviewed him. His visit came off with much more visibility than the president had hoped for, but Gorbachev did not seem to be offended by it.

East Germany, and in particular East Berlin, presented one of the most complex challenges of the period. The president and his advisors were uncertain how Gorbachev would react to change there. Protesters in East Germany were completely disillusioned with their own communist government—led by hard-liner Erich Honecker—but, curiously, had great affection for President Gor-bachev. Gorbachev's visit to the country in October was marked by angry antigovernment demonstrators actually chanting, favorably, "Gorby, Gorby, Gorby." Soon afterward, Honecker and his government were forced to resign, and real change began. The weeks leading up to the Malta meeting, in mid-November, were a historic period for the East Germans and the world.

The president's critics, mostly on a partisan basis, again suggested that he was not doing enough to foster change in Europe, although all one had to do was look at the results to see that such was not the case. Dramatic changes had already occurred in Poland and Hungary, and East Germany was next.

On November 9 the East German government announced that it would relax controls on its borders with West Germany. There was no mention that the East Berlin–West Berlin border—symbolized by the famous wall that East Germans had been shot for attempting to cross in earlier days—was excluded from that policy change. Crowds in East Berlin began to accumulate at the border, and the East German guards, unsure of what the policy really was, allowed the assembled crowd to cross into West Berlin. In one confusing and momentous instant, the Berlin Wall came down. Crowds of jubilant young Germans took it apart piece by piece with chisels and sledgehammers, carting off chunks as souvenirs. Beer steins were clinked and champagne corks were popped all over the city. A long oppressive era ended, abruptly, peacefully, and, in fact, in a party atmosphere.

At the White House, when we heard what was happening, Scowcroft and I went quickly to the president's office, where he was working at his desk. The three of us moved into the small office adjacent to the Oval Office and turned on the television to watch live coverage of the events unfolding in Berlin. We watched in fascination as the primary symbol of Soviet control in Germany was being chipped away by dozens of Germans on both sides of the wall under the eyes of the East German guards, who appeared to be as fascinated as we were. Bush was clearly happy to see the wall go, but he also understood the possible impact this climactic event could have on Gorbachev's capacity to keep the hard-liners in Moscow under check.

The White House press clamored for a statement from the president. Mindful that the best way to maximize good results was to maintain a disciplined, low-key response, we decided to allow the press to come into the Oval Office for a short photo op and a few questions.

For such events, coverage by the press is on a pool basis: representatives of print, television, and radio come in and then share the sights and sounds they gather with the rest of their colleagues in the press room. The press hoped to capture the president jubilantly proclaiming a Cold War victory over Gorbachev and the Soviet Union. The president, however, maintained a cautious and measured response.

As expected, the president's critics in both the press and government had a field day. They said he did not understand the significance of what had happened, or perhaps was indifferent. But George Bush was simply disciplined enough not to impede the successful movement that he had helped initiate. Some of his strongest partisan critics, such as Senate Majority Leader George Mitchell, said the president should have gone to Berlin to "dance" on pieces of the fallen wall. But as Bush noted in his memoirs, Chancellor Kohl told him that this would have been "outrageously stupid." Gorbachev himself was extremely concerned that what was happening in Berlin might spin out of control with "unforeseen consequences." Until that moment, Gorbachev had not expressed such anxiety about what had taken place anywhere else in the region. It was a far tenser moment than most of the president's critics could have hoped to understand.

Inside the White House we certainly understood the significance of the events in East Germany. What happened in Poland

and Hungary was a peaceful revolution with the cooperation and consent of communist governments moving into reform mode. In East Germany, however, the communist government had been virtually overthrown by a population emboldened by changes occurring in neighboring countries. It was apparent that dramatic changes in all of Eastern Europe were certain, but it was not certain that those changes would happen as peacefully as they did in Poland and Hungary.

The wave of uprisings next swept over Czechoslovakia. Anti-government demonstrations began there in late August. In late November, Vaclav Havel, the dissident playwright who had been imprisoned by the communists, reappeared to join the protests. Czechoslovakia, which had seen its protests severely put down by Soviet troops in 1968, much as the Soviets had suppressed the Hungarian uprising in 1956, was ready to join the march to freedom. We all hoped it would happen peacefully.

In the face of all this, George Bush continued his intense schedule, prepping for the meeting with Gorbachev in Malta. Scowcroft and the National Security Council took the lead in preparing materials and gathering experts to brief the president. The president sorted through differing opinions from his team about the prospects for a successful meeting with Gorbachev, but everyone recognized that it was a chance we had to take. George Bush was the most optimistic of all of us. He had a good feeling about Gorbachev's chances of surviving the political backlash he faced at home, and the president felt that Gorbachev genuinely believed his reforms were critical to the survival of the Soviet Union. The president was concerned, however, that Gorbachev might have to resort to "cracking down" somewhere in order to placate hard-liners at home and keep perestroika alive. Bush knew that he had to do everything he could to dissuade Gorbachev from taking such measures.

In his preparations for Malta, George Bush was mindful of the importance of consulting with his principal allies in Europe. He invited Margaret Thatcher to visit and had a long meeting with her at Camp David. As always, Prime Minister Thatcher steadfastly reminded the president that America's military strength, and the pressure it put on the Soviets, furthered the reforms under way in the USSR. She encouraged him to maintain the strong defensive posture started under Reagan.

Bush also met with Brian Mulroney, the prime minister of Canada, with whom he had developed an extremely close relationship. It was clear from the tone and frankness of their conversations that they had a deep trust in each other's judgment. Mulroney encouraged the president to try to create the same kind of relationship with Gorbachev.

Brian Mulroney became one of George Bush's closest friends and confidants. Although they had met while Bush was vice president, the relationship blossomed during the president's first trip to Canada early in 1989. Bush's commitment to address the environmental issues associated with pollution emanating from American manufacturing and coal-fired power plants across the border helped considerably. Acid rain had become a very important issue for Mulroney, and Bush described in detail to the Canadian leader his aggressive efforts in Congress to solve the problem via the Clean Air Act. Mulroney was pleased to hear it.

I also was fortunate to develop a good close personal relationship with Prime Minister Mulroney. This happened even though in that first meeting, it was I who, at the president's prompting, was the "bad cop" and had to point out that Canada had more polluting emissions per capita and per unit of industrial output than the United States. We nevertheless became good friends, and during my last couple of months as chief of staff the prime minister was kind enough to write and call a few times with encouraging words.

As Bush was preparing for Malta, Mulroney came to Washington and provided some extremely important input. He had recently met with Gorbachev and, over dinner in the president's residence, Mulroney conveyed Gorbachev's concerns about German reunification. Mulroney put it in the context of Russia's "hatred for the Germans." It was a deep-seated animosity traceable in part to the death of twenty-four million Soviet citizens during World War II—the highest mortality rate of the war by far of any Allied country. Bush asked Mulroney to convey to Gorbachev his promise not to "posture at the wall," for he knew how such an act might embolden the hard-liners in the Soviet Union and intensify their efforts to block Gorbachev.

Additionally, Mulroney expressed his concern to Bush that the incentives for unification of West Germany and East Germany seem to be "fueled by the total collapse of the economy of one state and the economic strength of another." Mulroney also put it more succinctly when he said, "You are not really talking about a merger here. This is a takeover." Unless it was handled properly, what would surely begin as a happy reunion could become a strained partnership if West Germany was not able to provide financial and economic support to East Germany.

One concern in our preparations for the Malta Summit, scheduled for December 2–3, was how to brief the allies after the meeting. This became the subject of a couple of our early-morning meetings at the White House. We finally decided to ask NATO to set up a meeting of its members so that immediately after Malta the president could visit and brief them together.

We spent a great deal of time discussing the tone and tactics the president should take into the meeting with Gorbachev. Jim Baker suggested that the president open the meeting by laying everything on the table—a full list of initiatives covering every possible component of cooperation and improvement in the relationship. Then, the president and Gorbachev would address the particulars of each topic. The president liked the approach because he wanted to maintain the initiative.

Finally, the time came to actually go to Malta. *Air Force One* took off on the evening of November 30 and, after a light dinner, virtually everyone else had found a place to sleep. Scowcroft and I were awake reviewing some of the details for the meeting when we received a call from his deputy (later CIA director), Bob Gates, who told us the military in the Philippines appeared to be attempting to overthrow President Corazon Aquino.

Gates convened a meeting of the Deputies Committee to discuss potential options. Vice President Quayle suggested it be treated as a formal NSC meeting with the legal authority that this implied. Secretary of Defense Dick Cheney was at home and chose not to attend. He felt he needed to protect the protocol associated with the chain of command—that any orders for military action should come directly from the president to the secretary of defense and not through a meeting chaired by the vice president. Deputy Secretary of State Lawrence Eagleburger was there on behalf of Baker.

Scowcroft and I were getting frequent updates by phone. We learned that the rebels had seized some facilities and were threatening to attack the Philippine presidential palace. We were fielding calls from Gates, Quayle, and Cheney, who were trying to formulate a reasonable response. Eventually, the recommendation from the deputies' meeting was to fly American fighter jets over the rebel forces and the palace to demonstrate U.S. support for Aquino.

The president and Jim Baker were both asleep. After Scowcroft and I were confident that the group had finally committed to a course of action, I woke up the president and asked him to approve the recommendation. After thinking about it for a few moments, Bush agreed. Then he went right back to sleep. The strategy turned out to work well, and it nipped the uprising in the bud without requiring any serious intervention.

We arrived in Malta to atrocious weather—the worst in decades, or so some locals said. We landed around 10:00 a.m. After a couple of welcoming meetings and a visit to the aircraft carrier USS *Forrestal*, we boarded the cruiser USS *Belknap*, which, at that time, was the flagship of the U.S. Sixth Fleet. The Soviets also had two ships in Valletta Harbor. One was a smaller naval cruiser, the *Slava*; the other was a very large civilian cruise ship, the *Maxim Gorky*, which was berthed at the dock. It turned out that the protected berthing of the *Maxim Gorky* saved the day, shielding the summit from the worst impacts of the inclement weather.

Our White House team spent the night on the *Belknap*. The weather began to get even meaner during the overnight hours. The winds blew harder. The rain grew more intense, and waves pounded the ship mercilessly. We actually had to delay the start of the meeting, originally set to take place on the Soviet ship *Slava*, because Gorbachev was leery of the heavy seas. We moved the meeting to the *Maxim Gorky*, which meant we had to tackle a trip through those treacherous waters. The young seaman who handled the launch must have felt a great deal of pressure since he had in his hands the lives of the president of the United States, the secretary of state, the president's national security advisor, and the president's chief of staff. He did a magnificent job in getting us back and forth.

The *Maxim Gorky* had been recently refurbished, and it was a very impressive sight. Originally, it was intended to house only the Soviet team, but it ended up being the meeting place for all of our sessions. Although the meetings were laid out with the usual protocol—the Soviets on one side of the table and the five of us as the president's team on the other—there was ample room and opportunity for the two staffs to support their principals and engage in conversations with each other.

The first meeting began with a formal welcome from Gorbachev, who then asked Bush to make the first presentation. Bush went through his long list of initiatives. He outlined every point of difference between the United States and the Soviet Union, and then suggested ways to resolve those differences. He laid out a fairly complete agenda of topics and put enough constructive proposals on the table that his presentation clearly impressed Gorbachev. Then the president, in a signal of his serious intent, suggested another meeting, a real summit, at the end of June.

Gorbachev hesitated for a moment and then responded by complimenting the president on his presentation. He outlined how he envisioned the Americans and the Soviets should approach the problems before them. He said we lived in a changing world, and admitted that an integrated Europe might have to be part of that New World Order. He talked of the emerging economic powers of Asia—Japan and China—and acknowledged the rapid pace of development in India. His key message was that since the United States and the Soviets would have to cooperate well into the future, "we have to abandon the images of ourselves as enemies."

In his response, Bush said he hoped the Soviets had noticed how the United States had reacted to the changes in Eastern Europe in a very temperate manner. Our response, he told Gorbachev, had been intentional so as "not to complicate your life.

"That's why I have not jumped up and down on the Berlin Wall," Bush told the Soviet leader.

It was a good start to the meeting.

The president and Gorbachev then went into a private meeting of their own. In it, they discussed Bush's concerns about Soviet assistance to insurgents in Latin America. Gorbachev spoke about Eastern Europe and Germany. The reason he was permitting the reforms, he said, was to bring the United States and the Soviets closer. He wanted those changes, including European unity, if that was where the chips fell, to take place without America's trying to impose its own values on the newly democratic countries. His next point may have been his most important one. Gorbachev said, "Mr. Kohl is in too much of a hurry on the German question. That is not good."

We met for five hours on the *Maxim Gorky* that morning. During that time the weather had continued to worsen, and, unbelievably, the wind was even stronger, but we had to make our way back to the *Belknap*. Again, the skill of the young helmsman was challenged and again he did an amazing job. In our first pass, we actually damaged the starboard boarding platform and had to circle around to the port platform. Because of the weather, Gorbachev was never able to get to the *Belknap* to join us for a dinner scheduled for that evening. Those of us who were already on board enjoyed a fantastic state dinner without him. That night's sleep on the *Belknap* was a different story, however. The surging waves tossed the ship back and forth to the point where I wondered if I was going to be rolled out of bed.

By the next morning, the weather had eased a bit and we went back to the *Maxim Gorky*. The second session started, and this time Gorbachev seemed more relaxed. He remained direct and tough, but on a number of occasions let his tremendous sense of humor show through.

This second day's meetings began, after some pleasantries, with what was clearly an important and carefully prepared message from Gorbachev. He began by saying that the Soviet

Union "will under no circumstances start a war." He said the Soviet Union had switched to a defensive military doctrine, and he accused the United States and NATO of not reciprocating. At the end of his comments, Gorbachev handed the president a map prepared by his defense and military team. It showed the world with the Soviet Union in the center surrounded by U.S. bases indicated by blue flags, literally "encircling" it. The president accepted the map and said he would have his defense team review it. When Bush asked why the Panama Canal was marked as a site "encircling" the Soviet Union, Gorbachev grinned and, acknowledging a bit of embellishment in his demonstration, quipped mischievously, "Never mind the Panama Canal."

After we returned to the United States our intelligence and defense teams classified the map even though it had been prepared by the Soviet Union. Nearly a year later, President Bush had it declassified and made four copies. He presented them, with a very kind comment on each, to Vice President Quayle, Jim Baker, Brent Scowcroft, and me.

Bush then returned the topic of conversation to Germany. He told Gorbachev he understood how sensitive the issue was to the Russians, but added that the United States could not stand in the way of German reunification. He asked Gorbachev what his own opinions were. Gorbachev replied that he felt that all the countries of Europe would develop closer relationships. He even went so far as to suggest that NATO and the Soviet Warsaw Pact should act as political rather than military entities.

The president then raised one of the most difficult issues the two superpowers were to face in the coming months, that of the Baltic states of Lithuania, Latvia, and Estonia. These countries had actually been annexed by the Soviet Union; the Soviets believed them to be part of the USSR, not just occupied territories like the countries of Eastern Europe. We and our allies disagreed. Bush and Gorbachev went back and forth on the topic in very reasoned terms, eventually coming to an understanding of how complicated the subject was but with a feeling that over time it could be settled without the need for coercion.

With that exchange and a bit more general conversation, the Malta meeting came to a close. Although both sides sensed that they could have continued to cover more of the items on the agenda, everyone felt good about the way the meeting had progressed. The United States and the Soviet Union had found they could deal with tough issues in a reasoned way, and the leaders agreed to let Baker and Shevardnadze continue the discussions in the near future.

As the meeting was winding down, Bush asked Gorbachev if he could make one last request of the second most powerful man in the world. Just before the Malta meeting the United States and the Soviet Union had agreed to a joint issue of postage stamps. I was a longtime stamp collector, and had obtained a couple of first-day covers of those stamps with both the U.S. and the Soviet postmarks on them. As we were flying to Malta, I asked President Bush if it would be OK if I asked Gorbachev to sign those envelopes. The president simply said that if there was an opportunity, it would be fine with him. As the meeting ended the president said, "Mr. Sununu has a question for you."

I explained the joint issue of stamps to Mr. Gorbachev and asked him if he would kindly sign my two envelopes. He reached over with a big smile and signed them and then asked if I had anything else I wanted him to sign. "No, thank you," was the only obvious reply. From then on at the end of every meeting we had with Mikhail Gorbachev, the very last thing he did was turn to me and ask if I had brought anything for him to sign. On a couple of those occasions I took full advantage of his very kind generosity.

George Bush felt the Malta meeting was a great success. There were no significant formal agreements, but such agreements had never been the intention of the meeting. The intention, one that Gorbachev appeared to share, was to establish a personal working relationship between the leaders that would allow frank and direct discussion on any serious issue in the future. That had clearly been achieved. There were fruitful discussions on bilateral economic issues and trade normalization, but the most important single result was the development of that personal bond.

They held a joint press conference afterward, the first joint U.S.-Soviet news conference in history. It was a clear demonstration of the relationship that had developed and the openness and willingness both sides now seemed to have to work through tough issues in a public manner. The changes that had been going on in Eastern Europe would continue, but now the changes would take place in a climate of quiet cooperation between the two superpowers. The European political landscape was changing dramatically. The fall of the Berlin Wall and the Malta meeting between George Bush and Mikhail Gorbachev were undeniably the most important, dramatic events in the unwinding of the Cold War. Gorbachev would later put it even more succinctly. "Malta," he said, "marked the end of the Cold War."

The president knew that his two most important allies in NATO, Great Britain and France, had strong historical reasons to be suspicious and concerned about the unification of West and East Germany. It was a bitter topic for everyone in Europe, in fact, as well as in the Soviet Union.

Germany was divided into communist East and democratic West after World War II, when the prevailing Allies—Britain, France, the United States, and the Soviet Union—divided the conquered Nazi nation into four "temporary" zones, each to be managed by one of them. The three NATO partners eventually allowed their zones to be merged into a single entity known as the Federal Republic of Germany. The Soviets held sway over the east, ironically named the German Democratic Republic. Until the end of 1989, reuniting the two entities did not seem even remotely possible. Now it was.

From the start, everyone involved knew how complicated this would be. There were enormous differences in the economies of the two countries, and any merger would require a huge influx of financial support from west to east. Everyone also was extremely mindful that the conflicts between Germany and its neighbors not only extended throughout the twentieth century, but, in some cases, were rooted in centuries-old border disagreements.

George Bush knew that if his hope of "a Europe whole and free" was to be realized, he would have to work hard to get a disparate cast of nations on the same page. Over the previous four decades West Germany had rebuilt itself, not only economically, but ideologically as well. It was now a robust democracy with an extremely powerful economic engine that could be a tremendous asset as Europe worked through the integration of its markets and political structures.

The president also appreciated that Margaret Thatcher and François Mitterrand were not completely comfortable with the idea of rapid German reunification. Bush worked hard, usually one-on-one with the leaders of Europe, so that they all had a chance to be frank about their concerns and reservations. He also spent a great deal of time with Helmut Kohl, encouraging him to understand the commitments and the posture the Germans themselves must take to help ease tensions. George Bush's personal diplomacy was clearly going to be the catalyst for whatever results lay ahead.

With Bush's encouragement, Kohl agreed to provide financial assistance to East Germany. The president signaled to the
German leader that he heard his earlier warning about the fool-
hardiness of dancing on the fallen Berlin Wall loud and clear,
and reiterated his commitment to encourage change without
posturing or public celebration. Bush spoke with Prime Minister Thatcher, who at the time was teaming with President Mitterrand of France to try to slow down the process of German
reunification. She insisted that too much haste might destabilize
Gorbachev's position at home. George Bush reassured her that
he too was intent on making sure nothing would cause problems
for Gorbachev.

When his great Malta Summit with Gorbachev had ended,
George Bush knew that he had to quickly harmonize his positions on the pace of German reunification with Chancellor Kohl.
We flew from Malta to Brussels, as planned, to brief our European allies on the Malta meetings, landing in Brussels early on
the evening of December 3. The president went right to a short
meeting with the Belgian prime minister, then arranged to have
dinner with Kohl at the Château du Stuyvenberg. It was a three-
on-three meeting: the president, Brent Scowcroft, and I dined
with Kohl, his foreign policy advisor, and his chief of staff.

The conversation at dinner was all business. Bush described
what had happened at Malta and laid out for the Germans his
support for reunification, but Bush warned them that Gorbachev
was uncomfortable with a fast pace. Kohl spent a great deal of
time dwelling on the crisis he saw developing in East Germany,
which he sensed was now a land without leadership. He clearly
was sensitive to Gorbachev's apprehension.

Kohl confirmed for Bush his belief that a unified Germany
would need to be integrated with Western Europe and join the
NATO alliance. Bush was pleased to hear that, but emphasized

that NATO had to tread a fine line on that topic and not create problems for Gorbachev. At the dinner, the president strengthened his personal relationship with Kohl. That would serve both sides well in the coming difficult weeks. Just as the main course ended, Bush and Kohl agreed that they were close to being in sync on reunification.

As we moved on to dessert and coffee, the waiters brought out a huge bowl of ice cream–filled profiteroles, each about the size of a golf ball. With the intense conversation on Malta and reunification over, the six of us now had a very lighthearted conversation about how amazing the preceding year had been. Through it all, Kohl, a giant of a man standing six feet four inches tall, kept reaching over and popping one profiterole after another into his mouth. Scowcroft and I couldn't help exchanging subtle looks of amazement as we watched him plow through at least two dozen of those pastries.

It was in the relaxed atmosphere of this dinner that George Bush, building on the trust he had nurtured over the previous year, moved a long way toward resolving the reunification problem, one of the most intractable issues of the twilight of the Cold War.

The next morning the president met with all his NATO partners to brief them on the Malta Summit. He addressed the basic purpose of NATO, with particular emphasis on its role in undoing the division of Europe that occurred in the aftermath of World War II and during the Cold War. He then laid out some very specific principles, which he felt had to be considered as they reviewed the possibility of German reunification. Kohl then asked to speak, and after complimenting the president, tried to limit further discussion, but it was clear that the gathered allies wanted to have their say. In general, however, the comments that followed supported the position of President Bush.

Bush continued his consultations on these tough issues, broaching this subject and others during his December meeting with Mitterrand in Saint Martin in the Caribbean as a follow-up to their fruitful weekend at Kennebunkport in May. In their conversations in Saint Martin the president discovered Mitterrand was now resigned to the eventual unification of Germany, though Mitterrand continued to be uncomfortable with the rapid pace.

The Soviets also continued to express their wariness through Shevardnadze in his meetings with Baker. Their principal priority was Soviet security, and for them the question was whether Germany would be part of NATO and whether it would be armed or neutral. Shevardnadze made these concerns very public in a speech to the European Parliament.

As 1989 came to a close, President Bush realized it had been a momentous and historic year, but one whose events were only a prelude to the significant and difficult work still to be accomplished.

Six months after Malta, Mikhail Gorbachev came to Washington for another summit meeting with George Bush. Gorbachev's primary goal was to try to get some financial help for his country's economy, including a trade agreement to allow the sale of Soviet goods and products to America. He also came to discuss the details of how German reunification should take place and how reunification would affect the balance of conventional forces in Europe.

On May 31, 1990, as the drama of the budget battle was escalating, we welcomed the Soviets with all the flourish of a White House arrival ceremony for a head of state, including the Old Guard Fife and Drums. When the South Lawn show was over, the president and Gorbachev went to the Oval Office for a private meeting. Bush has described the conversations there as "largely philosophical, the kind each of us had hoped to have at Malta."

Both were confident that they had, in a very constructive way, brought their two superpowers to a "watershed in history." They discussed arms control and German reunification. They reviewed the history of U.S.-Soviet confrontation. They talked about the changes in Europe since Malta. And they spoke about the Baltics, especially the pressures in Lithuania for independence. Their conversation went past the allotted time, but Gorbachev wanted to continue. In his presentation on the progress of perestroika in the Soviet Union, he explained the difficulties he was encountering and how complicated it was to move from a centralized economy to a market economy. He suggested that he would need financial help to get through the difficult transition.

Gorbachev left the White House to host a lunch at the Soviet Embassy, but returned around 4:00 p.m. He and the president then chaired a meeting in the Cabinet Room for about two dozen officials representing both countries. As I looked around the room I realized that Gorbachev had brought all the key players from the Soviet hierarchy, including some of the tough old guard who were not thrilled with his makeover of the Soviet Union.

The meeting turned out to be one of those extraordinary events that provided a rare inner glimpse of the fine line Gorbachev was walking in his steps toward change. Bush opened it up by recognizing the Soviet concerns on the reunification of Germany. He argued that Europe would be stabilized if a unified Germany joined NATO. Gorbachev responded with a long analysis of alternatives for the future of Europe. At the end of the analysis, Bush asked whether Gorbachev accepted that the Helsinki Final Act (aka Helsinki Accords, 1975) gave countries the right to choose their alliances, and whether he believed that this meant Germany should be able to choose whether it wanted to join NATO. Gorbachev said yes. His answer stunned our side and the Soviets. There was dead silence and then suddenly among the Soviets there was a flurry of loud whispers, which slowly built in volume and intensity. Gorbachev's advisors were openly opposing the position of the leader of the Soviet Union.

In the midst of all the commotion, foreign minister Shevardnadze slid over and whispered into Gorbachev's ear. Then Gorbachev turned to Valentin Falin, who was a leader of the Central Committee, and asked him to comment. Falin unabashedly argued that Germany in NATO was unacceptable. When Falin finished, Gorbachev spoke again. This time he backtracked a bit by saying that even though he felt Germany could choose, there had to be an extremely long transition before that could happen. He was obviously trying to undo the fuss he had caused. He closed by saying we should "let our foreign ministers pursue these issues."

For all of us, seeing firsthand the reality of the tension in those discussions was truly amazing. As Scowcroft put it, "It was obvious Gorbachev had created a firestorm in his delegation and faced bitter opposition." The day was capped with more ceremony as the president and Mrs. Bush hosted Mikhail and Raisa Gorbachev at a state dinner.

The next day, the Bushes brought the Gorbachevs to Camp David. By the time they left for that trip, Gorbachev was very pleased. He had closed the trade agreement, which was, in fact, his highest priority. He had been able to make progress on the chemical weapons issue, and on the Treaty on Conventional Armed Forces in Europe. He had also been able to resolve a few tough issues on START, the Strategic Arms Reduction Treaty. For his part, Bush felt he had pressured Gorbachev hard on all those issues, but had left the Soviet leader knowing that he "was not out to drive him against the wall."

They flew to Camp David together on *Marine One*, the presidential helicopter. Even in the noisy helicopter, the conversation was comfortable and friendly. Bush later wrote about the flight:

"Ironically, we were accompanied by military aides carrying the nuclear codes that allowed each of us to destroy the other's country. Yet we were sitting there talking about peace."

The flight from Washington northwest to Camp David is about sixty miles and takes only about thirty minutes by helicopter, but traverses an entire range of American landscape in that short time—the grandeur of urban Washington; the beautifully arrayed suburban neighborhoods of Bethesda and Gaithersburg, Maryland; and the rural farms and densely wooded state parks around Frederick. As we flew over those changing landscapes, Gorbachev, a former minister of agriculture, was full of questions. What do they grow on these farms? Are they irrigated? How do people buy and sell a house? Who lends the money? How much does this or that house cost? He seemed genuinely surprised at the apparent prosperity, efficiency, and natural beauty spread beneath him.

When Bush told us later about those questions, I concluded it was that sort of experience—whether this one with Bush or another similar trip elsewhere in the country—that convinced Gorbachev the game was over. I believe that as he looked out over the rich and diverse American landscape, he came to the undeniable conclusion that the inefficient and ineffective socialist system of central planning could not compete with the marvel that is free-market capitalism. The Soviet Union would never catch up.

Once they arrived at Camp David, the Bushes convinced the Gorbachevs that it was time to relax and be casual. They even managed to get the Soviet president to take off his tie. Eventually, they loosened up and drifted into low-key conversation. Again, Gorbachev expressed the nature of the problems he was facing as he tried to reform the Soviet Union. He also talked about the difficulties of dealing with the other republics and the great variety of nationalities within the Soviet Union.

Those conversations were followed by a dinner attended by most of us who had been in that Cabinet Room meeting. Just before dinner Gorbachev had strolled past the horseshoe pit and picked up a shoe and thrown. He hit a ringer on the first try. The president's assistant Tim McBride had the horseshoe mounted on a plaque with a notation commemorating the visit and Bush gave it to Gorbachev at the dinner.

After dinner the president and Gorbachev helicoptered back to the White House. Bush took Gorbachev inside the residence for a tour, showing him the copy of the Gettysburg Address that was in the Lincoln Bedroom. The president also took him around the residence and spoke to him about some of the history associated with each of the rooms.

After the tour, they headed down to the Oval Office, where they became engrossed in a discussion of how the days in the White House were organized. Gorbachev was very interested in the organization and inner workings of the White House. He noticed, he said, that the president operated from a prearranged daily schedule. He noted the visible structure and staff that seemed designed to make it easy for the president to access information, reach key advisors, and have directives implemented. He told the president that he suspected he probably would have to change the way the Kremlin operated.

Finally, Gorbachev asked Bush, "Would you be willing to send Sununu to visit with my chief of staff and our administrators in the Kremlin to show them how you do this because I believe we are going to have to operate differently under democracy than we did under our old system." Bush responded in the affirmative with a smile, "Sununu can run it either way."

We were able to make arrangements fairly quickly, and at the end of August 1990 I took about a dozen White House staffers with me to Moscow. It was my own most fascinating personal interaction with the Russians. We traveled to the Kremlin at the very cusp of the transition from a totalitarian government to a democracy. It was a unique moment in history, and the week we spent discussing that transition with the Soviet leaders feeling their way through their changing system only enhanced my already tremendous respect for the American constitutional system of government.

It was a wonderful trip, not only for me and my wife, Nancy, but for all of the key White House staffers I brought along. Joining us were my deputy, Andy Card; and key staffers Ed Rogers and Jackie Kennedy. Roger Porter was there to discuss how we framed domestic policy, Jim Cicconi was there to explain how he managed the very complex flow of paper in the White House, and Fred McClure was there to talk about how we dealt with Congress. Condoleezza Rice, an expert on Russia who spoke Russian fluently, came in her role as a deputy to Brent Scowcroft to discuss how the national security operations were handled in the White House.

In Moscow we met with President Gorbachev, who by then had been elected president by the Congress of People's Deputies in March 1990, and his chief of staff, Mikhail Shkabardnya. We also met with a number of ministers such as Yevgeny Primakov and Dmitri Yazov, who would prove to be key players in the Gulf War saga unfolding at the time. We also met with many members of the new legislative body that had been formed as part of the transition in the Soviet Union.

Everyone was interested not only in White House procedures but also in the overall political and democratic processes in the United States. Most of the people we spoke with sought effective solutions for managing the changes they were going through; others, mainly old hard-liners, just grumbled about everything.

The Soviet Union was undergoing this monumental transition without a real master blueprint or clear sense of what the final destination might look like. In preparation for our trip, I had asked our intelligence community to prepare a Russian translation of *The Federalist Papers*—essays written in 1787 and 1788 by Alexander Hamilton, James Madison, and John Jay on the proposed new Constitution of the United States and the federal system of government—and had about five hundred copies printed and bound. We gave them to almost everyone we talked to, and the response was amazing. The recipients all seemed to have devoured it overnight, because the next day in our conversations they were invariably full of questions about what they had read.

They were pleasantly surprised by the fact that when America was formed more than two hundred years ago, our founding fathers had struggled with the same problems they were facing. They sought comfort in our own earlier tussles over sharing power among the executive, legislative, and judicial branches. They were also curious about how we delegated powers between the central government and regional governments—in our case, the American states. They had even more departments, or ministries, than we did, and some novel ways of dealing with them.

In one of the rooms of the Kremlin there was a table, about the size of an average dining table, covered with more than two dozen yellow telephones. Instead of having a single phone with multiple buttons, the staff had a different phone as a direct line to each specific department. Remember, this was 1990, and they were operating with a phone system that looked like something out of an episode of *I Love Lucy*. "When you hear a ring, how do you know which phone is ringing?" I asked the Kremlin staffers. That talent, they said, was part of the secret of their job security.

They also took us on a tour of some of the Kremlin museums and inner chambers. One was a room maintained under the authority of the USSR Diamond Fund. I had not realized until then that the Soviet Union was a major producer of diamonds, and the room they showed us was unbelievable. It had glass aquarium–like cases filled with diamonds encircling three sides of the room. Tens of thousands of diamonds. And not just small ones. Most of them were about as big around as a dime.

We spent three days in Moscow and then flew to Leningrad, which was soon to be rechristened with its historical name, St. Petersburg. In Leningrad, we spent two days with Mayor Anatoly Sobchak and his staff discussing the relationship between the Kremlin and its regions and cities. Mayor Sobchak's chief of staff at the time was a man named Vladimir Putin.

I was extremely impressed with Mayor Sobchak. He was by far the strongest and most astute of the Soviet leaders we encountered on the trip besides Gorbachev himself. I left feeling that someday this man would end up in Moscow in a very significant position. He was a staunch ally of Gorbachev and came to Washington a couple of months later. Unfortunately, his career ended too soon—Sobchak died in 2000 at the age of sixty-two.

As I was preparing to leave Moscow after mentoring Mikhail Gorbachev's staff, a secure cable arrived at the U.S. Embassy asking me to deliver a highly classified message to Margaret Thatcher on the return trip home. The instructions were emphatic that the message was for her ears only. We took off from Russia and landed in England a few hours later. After a brief stop at the residence of the U.S. ambassador, I was taken to 10 Downing Street to meet with the prime minister.

Mrs. Thatcher and her senior foreign policy advisor Charles Powell were waiting. We went over a few items that I had been asked to present to her, and as the meeting drew to a conclusion

I let her know that I had an additional message for her alone. She asked Powell to leave, and I repeated my instructions, reminding her that the information was for her ears only, and that she should not share it with anyone, including her staff. I repeated the instructions to make sure there was no misunderstanding, then communicated the message.

A few months later, when she came to Washington to visit the president, I was standing in the Oval Office with Bush and Scowcroft to receive her. After she had been greeted by Bush and they had exchanged some quick pleasantries, she came over to me, and, with a twinkle in her eye, told me that she "deserved excellent marks, because to this day," she had "not told a single soul," just as I had instructed.

Although Margaret Thatcher was known as the "Iron Lady" and was often characterized as tough and not the warmest of people, I found her to be extremely pleasant, with the dry sense of humor so characteristic of the English. That assessment was more than confirmed in another light moment I had shared with her just one month before our meeting at 10 Downing Street. It was the day after Saddam Hussein's army invaded Kuwait. Coincidentally, she and President Bush had committed to be at the Aspen Institute to discuss global strategies in a post–Cold War world. That evening, I may have tested the limits of her good humor. She was staying in a residence not far from the president and in between the two residences there was an inn that catered to tourists visiting the Rocky Mountains village.

The entrepreneurial owner of that inn, hearing that both Bush and Thatcher would be staying nearby, had printed a large batch of T-shirts saying "Margaret Thatcher and George Bush almost slept here," along with a logo and picture of his inn. At a reception that evening I asked the prime minister if she would autograph one of the shirts for me. She looked at me and said drily,

"Oh, John, I'm not sure I want to have my signature on that." I promised her that it would be sealed in a plastic bag and kept in a bottom bureau drawer inaccessible to anyone. She finally relented and said, "If George signs then I'll sign it."

I quickly took the T-shirt over to President Bush, who autographed it immediately, and brought it back to the prime minister. True to her word, she signed it, and it remains one of my more cherished mementos from my years in the White House. True to my word, I have let no one outside my family ever see it.

When she had to step down from her post as prime minister, I was as saddened as Bush to see her go.

The last summit for Bush and Gorbachev together was in May 1991, seven months before Gorbachev resigned and the Soviet Union was officially dissolved. Bush traveled to Moscow to sign the Strategic Arms Reduction Treaty (START). By then, Gorbachev had been named the first, and, as it turned out, the only president of the Soviet Union, but it was a Soviet Union unraveling beneath him. Nationalists were attempting to break away from the union in the Baltic states, the Caucasus, and elsewhere. Boris Yeltsin had been elected president of the newly formed Russian Federation. Those in the Soviet defense and military structure were not happy about the turn of events.

We landed in Moscow and President Bush attended a day of meetings and presentations with Gorbachev, then met separately with Yeltsin. While he was working the diplomacy side, Barbara Bush spent much of the day with Gorbachev's wife, Raisa. The two first ladies, like their husbands, had developed a warm friendship.

While her husband was in Washington and at Camp David the previous year, Raisa Gorbachev came along and took several side trips, one of them to Boston. While there, Raisa became enamored with a sculpture by artist Nancy Schön in Boston Public

Garden of a mother mallard and her eight ducklings erected in commemoration of the 1941 children's book by Robert McCloskey, *Make Way for Ducklings*, which was set in Boston.

Before departing for Moscow, Barbara decided to have an exact replica of the statues made for Raisa as a gift from the children of the United States to those of Moscow. Making it all happen was something of a monumental undertaking for Barbara's chief of staff, Susan Porter Rose. In addition to coordinating with the artist, she organized the installation. The equipment, sculptures, and cobblestones and even the workers from an Acton, Massachusetts, landscape and construction company were all flown to the Soviet Union for the job.

The trail of ducklings was placed in Novodevichy Park in Moscow, adjacent to a feeding station for live ducks, posed on cobblestones brought from Boston and surrounded by the native black basalt consistent with the rest of the park. A special edition of the best-selling book was produced in Russian, and hundreds of copies of those books were distributed in Moscow. To this day the *Make Way for Ducklings* sculpture is a much-loved and visited tourist attraction in Moscow, and in that small way to me represents a symbol of the Bush-Gorbachev relationship that helped end the Cold War.

That evening Gorbachev hosted a state dinner in the Hall of Facets in the Kremlin. It should have been a completely upbeat event in celebration of the START signing the next day. As is the custom for these events, we were all seated at various tables hosted by senior Soviet officials. I was seated at a table with Defense Minister Dmitri Yazov.

As we sat down to dinner, Yazov almost immediately began downing shots of vodka, in spite of Gorbachev's standing directive to promote more temperate consumption of alcohol throughout the country. Yazov kept trying to convince me to match him shot for shot, but I could tell he was well practiced in the art, so I prudently traded him only sip for shot. Yazov did not seem like a happy man despite the copious consumption of alcohol. Finally, after downing more shots than I could count, he began to complain that START was one more step in the undermining of the Soviet military. He complained that Gorbachev had cut off funding for new equipment for the military. He said that troops returning from abroad were not receiving the respect they deserved. I tried to respond to all of this in a positive tone, suggesting that what Bush and Gorbachev were doing was working toward a lasting peace that would keep soldiers from both sides out of harm's way.

Toward the end of the dinner, Yazov began blaming everything on Ronald Reagan and his Strategic Defense Initiative. This surprised me greatly, since I recalled our American critics of the program complaining that SDI was a waste of money. Yazov proved to me that evening that it was money well spent. He said one of the principal reasons the Soviet Union was being pushed into reform mode was that the Soviets felt they did not have the economic resources to compete against Reagan's investment in SDI. The Soviets were afraid that SDI would leave America in a position of permanent military superiority.

Yazov's final rants were the most disturbing yet. He said, "All this [will] change soon. . . . The military [is] no longer going to sit by and let it all happen. The reforms [will] soon be reversed."

When we got back to the embassy, I quickly went to President Bush and Brent Scowcroft and recounted as best I could, word for word, what I had heard from Yazov. Scowcroft then said he had had a slightly similar conversation at his table with General Sergey Akhromeyev.

The next day the president hosted a reciprocal state dinner for Gorbachev at Spaso House, the residence of the U.S. ambassador in Moscow. This time Scowcroft was seated with Yazov. His dinner conversation, also replete with vodka shots, was almost a word-for-word repeat of what I had heard the night before at the Kremlin dinner. Scowcroft later boasted to us that by the end of his dinner he was able to get Yazov to join him in a toast to NATO.

When we got back to Washington, we reported those conversations to our intelligence community. They added the information to snippets they were receiving from other sources and came to the conclusion that Gorbachev was truly at risk of a coup. The president tried to convey these concerns to Gorbachev, but the Soviet leader did not seem overly worried. A little more than two weeks later, while Gorbachev was at his summer home in the Crimea, there was such an attempt to overthrow his government by the Soviet armed forces and a handful of military leaders. It was a failed attempt, put down in less than three days, but it did confirm that George Bush was right in maintaining his disciplined demeanor as the modern "world transformed."

When George Bush came to the White House as vice president, Ronald Reagan's objective was to maintain a stable and peaceful world through strength. Reagan made the investments to bolster our already strong arsenal to the point where the Soviet Union could see it could not keep up with America's economic might. When Bush succeeded Reagan, he leveraged that strong position with quiet, smart diplomacy to end the Cold War. By temperament and example Bush shaped a team to craft a win-win strategy in the global arena. America's quiet leader managed to harmonize our allies, earn the trust of our foe, and end the superpower confrontation without ever firing a shot.

5

"Read My Lips"
The Budget Agreement of 1990

═══════════

Read my lips. No new taxes."

Those six infamous words, uttered by George Bush at the Republican National Convention in New Orleans in August 1988, dogged him throughout his presidency.

I was uncomfortable when I heard him deliver them because as a former governor I knew that at the very least there always were fees and taxes that had to be ratcheted up for inflation. It was a promise that I knew would be difficult, if not impossible, to keep. I later found out Dick Darman, a man intimately familiar with the financial workings of the federal government, didn't like the line either. He was part of the team drafting the speech, and had crossed it out in a few of the early drafts.

Peggy Noonan, who had been brought in to write the speech, liked it, as did the vice president's communications guru, Roger Ailes—so it stayed. Noonan had done a commendable job on the speech overall, filling it—not an easy task—with strong phrases that Bush found comfortable to deliver, and the "read my lips" line hit an oratorical home run that ended up making a huge difference in the campaign.

Bush gave one of the best speeches of his life that night in the Crescent City. I knew how reluctant he was to talk about himself or to chase rhetorical highs, so I was well aware of how hard he must have pushed himself to get it just right. I was really proud of him and, in spite of my unease over the tax line, very happy for him.

The art of the presidency can be demonstrated in historic crises and world-altering events, but more frequently it is executed in the challenging circumstances and decisions of the everyday operations of government. Even in prosperous times, the unglamorous and predictably controversial work of shaping a budget is a process full of political pitfalls. When economic realities demand a rethinking of the status quo, a shrinking of habitual spending, or an increase in revenue, it rarely ends in political success for those who have to make the hard decisions.

The Reagan administration and Congress had drifted through the last few years without any serious effort at preventing a budget crisis. Reagan succeeded in holding down some of the growth of domestic spending, but he spent a lot of money building the military might that pushed the Soviets onto the path of reform.

As important as that defense spending was, it did not make it any easier to bring the budget under control—both domestic and defense spending had to be cut, especially now that the Soviet military threat was behind us. The deficits had to be reduced. The dollar had to be strengthened. George Bush was never one to shrink from formidable challenges—even when confronting them meant great personal cost.

When in early 1989 the economy developed problems that few had predicted, the Democrats were determined to make George

Bush eat the words he had uttered in New Orleans. They held a very strong majority in both houses of Congress, and that gave them the upper hand in the fight. When some of our Republican colleagues defected for purposes of their own, making fiscal matters even worse, it made the eventual sour compromise that much more difficult for the president to swallow.

Still, as the president made clear, he was willing to roll up his sleeves and do the hard work, to master the details of the problem, to negotiate with both allies and opponents alike, and to lead unwilling parties from stalemate to the difficult land of compromise. In doing so, he ultimately placed the good of the country above his own political interest.

Once the 1988 election was over, I knew the president-elect would have to focus on this growing budget problem and work through the major items on his domestic and foreign policy agendas at the same time. All the conversations I had with George Bush over the previous two years convinced me that one of his highest priorities was to reduce federal spending. Bush genuinely believed government had gotten too big, was inefficient, and was not managed well. He was sure cuts could be made without really hurting the needy or compromising our national security.

I was sure that my experience in putting together surplus budgets each year as governor of New Hampshire—the no-personal-income-tax and no-sales-tax state—would be of use as we tackled this complicated problem. There, I had been able to immediately eliminate a deficit I inherited when I took over by putting a balanced budget together without undoing our no-broad-base-tax tradition. I had become convinced that there was not a single public budget that couldn't be cut by 5 percent, and in public budgets a 5 percent cut was huge. In Washington it was unheard of to even try to hold a budget flat.

I was also sure the Democrats would be more partisan than George Bush expected them to be. The president was always expecting others to be as fair, rational, and cooperative as he was. He had not yet had to negotiate with a partisan legislature, and I felt he was underestimating how disappointed and even angry some of the Democrats were that "read my lips" had helped him win.

Around Thanksgiving 1988, I found out that Dick Darman would be his nominee for director of the Office of Management and Budget. I immediately called Dick and arranged to meet with him in Washington. Our first meeting was fairly short. He outlined the budget problem in broad and general terms: current spending levels were still more than 22 percent of the gross domestic product, and federal revenues were lagging significantly behind at only 19 percent of GDP. This difference of 3 percentage points was huge and generated an annual deficit of hundreds of billions of dollars. He also gave me a rundown on most of the key players in Congress who would be dealing with the budget.

He also went over the details of the Gramm-Rudman-Hollings Budget Law. Passed by Congress in 1985 and renewed in 1987, the law was designed to impose some discipline on a budget process that had gotten completely out of hand. It imposed a series of decreasing annual deficit targets that eventually led to a balanced budget. If Congress and the president did not produce a budget that achieved those targets in any given year, the act provided for large automatic spending cuts under a process known as sequester. Even a cursory analysis made clear that sequester-imposed spending cuts would hobble our defense forces and create serious national security problems for the president.

Darman and I agreed to touch base every couple of days, if not in person then at least by phone. From the start I was pleased to find out that he and I could get directly to the heart of an issue, then settle quickly on what had to be done, and we usually agreed on what action should be taken. During the six weeks before the inauguration I got to know Darman very well. He was one of the most talented public officials I ever met, and one of the hardest working. We soon found we had a lot in common, including a commitment to family and to making government work well. We also shared an irreverent sense of humor.

Dick Darman was quick and smooth. His presentations were always backed up by a pile of data, so it was difficult for people less prepared than he was to refute his arguments. When they ended up on the losing side, they would often feel sheepishly defensive. That style and personality led many conservative Republican members of Congress to conclude that Darman snookered George Bush into raising taxes. This was wrong on several counts. First, I never caught Darman cooking the books or misrepresenting any information he provided to the president or anyone else. Nor did he present the arguments in a way in which the only choice was taxes. He always responded quickly and effectively every time the president or I asked him to put together material in support of any agenda the president laid out.

George Bush invariably set the agenda and made the decisions. He might listen to a full spectrum of advisors, but the decisions on policy were always his own. On controversial social issues like abortion, on the budget, on clean air, on dealing with Gorbachev, on the liberation of Kuwait, on the question of whether to invade Iraq—all the final decisions were made by George Bush.

Once when we were discussing some of the characters in Congress, I asked Darman, "Where do you think you fall on the curve—liberal to conservative?" He answered without hesitation, "I'm a New England conservative." Then, remembering that I was a strong New England conservative from New Hampshire myself, he laughed and said, "I may be less conservative than you or Reagan or Bush, but I don't have an agenda. Get me a decision from the president and that's the track I ride."

The economy and the budget crisis came up in virtually every meeting I had with George Bush between the election and his inauguration. One of the most intense meetings was early on the evening of Sunday, December 4, at the vice presidential residence on the grounds of the U.S. Naval Observatory. I had flown down to Washington at Bush's request to join him, Vice President–elect Dan Quayle, Secretary of the Treasury Nick Brady, and Darman. Bush also invited Secretary of State Jim Baker. Baker was one of George Bush's closest friends. Although Baker was not at Treasury anymore—he had served there as secretary under Reagan—Bush still had a lot of confidence in his judgment on budget issues.

The vice president's residence in Washington is not grand at all. A three-story home on Massachusetts Avenue that used to house the chief of naval operations, it was designated by Congress as the vice president's residence in 1974. When I arrived that Sunday, I chuckled as I recalled the first time I had been there—in 1988, when I came to DC for a meeting of the National Governors Association. Vice President Bush had invited Nancy and me to stay overnight in the residence with him and Barbara. That evening we had to go to a black-tie event for the NGA. We got back after the Bushes had gone to sleep, so we took off our shoes and tiptoed up the stairs, in the dark, in tuxedo and gown, to our bedroom. Now, with the budget team, I was there for more serious business.

Before Darman arrived, we were chatting about the budget problem in general when Bob Teeter, who had been the pollster and a political advisor in the campaign, turned to the president-elect and said, "In the end, you will have no choice. You will have to raise taxes." Nick Brady seemed to agree, but Baker pushed back. "We don't need to do that this year," he said. Quayle nodded in agreement with Baker, and I added, "There's no public budget that can't easily be cut five percent." After I said that, Quayle gave me a thumbs-up.

During the transition, I discovered that Quayle and I shared a disdain for new taxes. We first met at a small dinner party about a year and a half before the election, and ran into each other only infrequently during the campaign. After the election, however, we spent quite a bit of time together discussing the opportunities and problems our new administration would face. I quickly discovered that he was very well versed in national security issues, and that we were almost totally in sync on social and domestic policy. He also was very smart on framing issues politically and on political strategy. We soon became close friends and have remained so to this day.

Darman arrived at the vice president's home with a detailed presentation on the harsh truths of the budget problem and the pitfalls of the budget process. The reality of the budget irresponsibility he outlined didn't surprise me, but the complete loss of fiscal control in Washington was a disappointment to the patriot in me.

The meeting lasted at least three hours and we covered a lot of ground. Darman repeated what he had told me in our first meeting: the initial estimate for the budget deficit in the coming year was a couple of hundred billion dollars, well above what was allowed under the Gramm-Rudman-Hollings law. In order to meet the targets, it looked as though nonentitlement spending increases had to be held under $15 billion if—and only if—we could maintain defense spending at current levels.

As Bush listened to Darman's presentation, I could see that he was beginning to appreciate the political bind he faced in

Congress. The Democrats controlled the house 260–175. They controlled the Senate 55–45. "Read my lips" was their target. Much of federal spending was on automatic pilot: that is, already part of legislation because of locked-in increases. With the economy looking as if it might collapse and reduce federal revenue even further, the Democrats would have added ammunition for their demand for new taxes. There was also the horrific impact of a sequester on defense spending to worry about.

We discussed a variety of options, including the wisdom of trying to get a one-year budget with no tax increase passed first, and working later with key congressional leaders on the much more complicated challenge of a multiyear package.

Bush asked Baker, "Does a one-year fix get this going?"

"We need to get budget negotiations started early," Baker replied, "and then take it step by step."

Bush then looked at Darman and me and said, "Get me a good proposal without any taxes. Right now I don't want to look at any package that calls for any tax increases at all."

As we were making our way out of the meeting, I stopped and spoke with President Bush. Relations between the White House and Congress had deteriorated over the previous two years, and we both knew how important it would be to rebuild a climate of trust and cooperation. He asked me to think about how to get that process started.

"Congress is in a really foul mood," he said. "They are really wound up over the Contras. For the past year, they didn't want to work with us on anything."

"You're really going to have to spend some serious face time with the Dems at the top," I warned him.

Bush told me he was going to have lunch soon with the chairman of the House Ways and Means Committee, his old friend Dan Rostenkowski. Bush and Rostenkowski had been friends since they both served on the committee as young congressmen in 1967. Bush even urged President Reagan to go out of his way to be extra friendly with Rosty. By 1989, Rostenkowski was the powerful chairman of that committee.

That lunch meeting two days later would prove to be the first of more than two dozen face-to-face conversations they would share over the next twenty months. Person-to-person contact would be an important part of repairing the strained relations between the two branches of government. Rostenkowski appeared to try to be helpful throughout the process, but in the end he joined with the rest of the Democratic leaders in opposing the 1990 budget agreement after Georgia congressman Newt Gingrich destroyed the deal.

The same core budget group met again a few days before Christmas. By then, Bush had just about decided to tee up a one-year budget for the coming fiscal year and buy some time to develop a working relationship with the Democratic leadership before engaging in the more divisive multiyear budget negotiations that would eventually have to be fought. After the others had left the meeting, I reminded him that negotiations with Congress in 1990 would be much more political than negotiations in 1989. Midterm congressional elections loomed in November 1990.

"There's so much other stuff we've got to get done," Bush answered, so the big budget battle just might have to wait. I agreed, but felt I had to at least remind him of the real political seasons built into the calendar and the pitfalls they presented.

By January, Bush had made his decision. Although he understood that a "big fix" would eventually be needed to rein in the deficits and protect the credibility of the dollar around the world, he told Darman, Brady, and me that he would settle for a one-year package with no new taxes at first and hope an improved economy would make for smoother sailing on a multi-year package later.

"Let's go with one year," he said. "Then we'll figure out how to get them into honest give-and-take."

In our meetings between New Year's Day and the inauguration, we all focused on sequencing the agenda—including what legislation to send to Congress first and what meetings and travel would have priority—and deciding what the president should highlight in his inaugural address. Preparations for the speech started right after the election, although Peggy Noonan didn't agree to write it until sometime in December. Peggy is a very good speechwriter, and a meticulous fact-checker. Bush appreciated that discipline, and he felt comfortable delivering the words she put to paper.

I gathered a couple of memos from the core group and from a few of Bush's friends among the Republican governors with whom we had consulted so extensively before the election. Everyone had recommendations regarding the things he might want to touch upon in his speech, but what Noonan ended up producing was primarily a collaboration between her and George Bush. She eloquently captured the very points that Bush himself wanted to make.

In the speech, the president offered an olive branch to Democratic congressional leaders:

> To my friends, in the loyal opposition, I put out my hand. . . . I am putting out my hand to you, Mr. Speaker. I am putting out my hand to you, Mr. Majority Leader. When our mothers were young . . . the Congress and the Executive were capable of working together to produce a budget on which this nation could live.

Let us negotiate soon and hard. But in the end, let us produce. The American people await action. They didn't send us here to bicker. They ask us to rise above the merely partisan.

From the moment the president was sworn in, the budget challenges that seemed so manageable in 1988 became more complicated and more difficult. Suddenly and unexpectedly, we discovered that a bailout of the savings and loan industry was going to cost tens of billions. Starting early in 1989, the economy began to weaken. Revenues slowed and the deficit ballooned. In 1989, the growth rate fell from 4.2 percent to just over 3 percent, and the deficit grew from $152 billion to $221 billion. In 1990, the GDP growth rate would fall to 1.9 percent. In 1991 it hovered just above zero at 0.1 percent.

Michael Boskin, who was chairman of the president's Council of Economic Advisers, had a knack for knowing what was going on in the economy and sensing economic trends. Early in the spring, Boskin sent the president a very downbeat memo expressing his concern that the Federal Reserve was tightening the economy to the point where it was starting to hurt businesses and families—people were starting to lose their jobs—and it was going to get worse over the following six to nine months. Federal Reserve Chairman Alan Greenspan was forcing the country into a slow-growth economy that would morph into a full-blown recession the following year. Greenspan was also sending signals to Secretary of the Treasury Nick Brady that he would not ease up on interest rates until a good multiyear deficit-cutting budget was passed and signed.

When it became clear that there was going to be no significant economic growth that year, Darman told the president that the assumptions we originally used when preparing the first one-year budget were turning out to be excessively optimistic. They had not anticipated the serious economic slowdown, nor the added costs of the savings and loan bailout.

The president's own cabinet was not much help, either. Virtually all the members had requested increases in their departments' budgets. The Department of Agriculture insisted that farm subsidies protected the "heartland of America." The Department of Transportation reminded us that our highways and bridges serve as "the arteries of commerce." The Department of Defense made sure the president heard, loud and clear, that "it was still a dangerous world" out there.

Even the two most conservative members of Bush's leadership team—Jack Kemp, the secretary of housing and urban development; and drug czar Bill Bennett—were lobbying for more money. Bennett had been secretary of education in the Reagan administration and, like Kemp, was a darling of our hard-line conservative friends. Kemp was a former congressman and a champion of tax cuts as a driver of growth, coauthor of the Kemp-Roth tax bill (aka the Economic Recovery Tax Act of 1981) credited with getting the economy moving half a decade earlier. Quayle and I lobbied hard to get Kemp and Bennett into the Bush cabinet. They were both good friends of mine, but each in his own way gave me heartburn on occasion.

Bennett was great at moving a wonderfully aggressive education and information program forward to cut drug use, and Kemp had brought some needed energy and conservatism to HUD. Kemp had, however, perfected what I came to call the "99 percent speech." He would make a public speech in which 99 percent of what he said was solidly supportive of the Bush program and agenda, but there was sometimes 1 percent that was not, and that 1 percent would, of course, be the only part reported by the press. I would end up having to call him, usually early in the morning after I glanced at the newspapers, to remind him that he wasn't being helpful. He always promised to be more careful.

Kemp wanted more money for HUD "empowerment zones," and Bennett for drug education programs. The president asked me to deal with their requests, so I sat them down together in my office one afternoon. There was only so much money to go around, and I had to decide who would get it. I listened to each make a pretty animated argument for his case.

"I wish I had a videotape of my two favorite conservatives whining for bigger spending," I jokingly told them when they finished.

There were about ten seconds of silence as Kemp and Bennett looked at each other. They were both startled to hear that they were sounding like a pair of big-government, liberal spenders!

"Let's split the difference," I suggested.

They both nodded sheepishly, and that brought the meeting to an end.

Over the years, I occasionally reminded them of that scene, and every time we shared a good laugh.

As we were tying down the rest of the numbers in a budget suitable to send to Congress, the president asked Darman and me to work with each cabinet department head to pare down the requests for money. I called the cabinet secretaries and heads of the major departments to tell them Dick Darman would be calling on them and their budget teams to work on the kind of budget the president wanted. When Darman sat down with each of them, he said his role was to help them find the easiest ways to achieve the required reductions. Then he made sure they understood that if they couldn't get down to the right number, they would have to join him in a budget session in my office. Almost no one opted to visit with me—a good example of the power of a chief of staff with warmth and charm! Eventually those negotiations worked out pretty well, and we had a well-honed blade to send to the Hill and into battle with the Democratic-controlled Congress.

In those efforts to reduce spending by our own agencies, one of the most challenging negotiations was with the Department of Defense. That department had enjoyed virtual carte blanche for eight years and wanted to stay on that course. The economic team believed that, in the face of the Soviet military retrenchment, it was time to slow things down. The defense budget had actually doubled as Ronald Reagan effectively rebuilt America's military might with a bigger and more modern navy and air force, and a tougher and more agile army and marine corps.

Now, Bush himself felt there should be some savings available there. As far back as our first defense budget discussions, the president asked me, "If Gorbachev's pulling back in Europe and moving on arms control, can't we slow down at least a little bit on our own defense spending?"

The struggle settled into a debate over the specific rates of increase in the defense budget over the next four years. The budget hawks, the president and I among them, hoped we could hold defense spending steady—to zero growth—over the following four years. The defense hawks—including Scowcroft and Cheney—were arguing for 2 percent growth compounded each year over the same period.

There was a lot of back-and-forth on the issue, including a long meeting at Camp David, in an effort to reconcile the differences. One day, Dick Darman spent two hours in Brent Scowcroft's office with the chairman of the Joint Chiefs of Staff, Admiral William Crowe, discussing the pros and cons of both approaches. Crowe had been appointed chairman by Ronald Reagan. His term was scheduled to run out that September, and President Bush chose to keep him on until then. I always felt, however, that Crowe never really bought into George Bush's agenda. My suspicions proved to be correct when he came out and endorsed Bill Clinton in the 1992 election.

I understood the pressure Darman was under to try to cut the deficit without increasing taxes, so while he was in with Crowe, I went down to the Oval Office to see if I could get a decision from the president that would settle the issue once and for all. Since we wanted to hold down defense spending over four years, my recommendation to the president emphasized how important it was, because of compounding, that at least the first two years be held at zero growth.

"Every percentage point we give in year one is carried through and compounded," I reminded the president. "If we give two percent in year one, that automatically raises the budgets for years two, three, and four by two percent as well . . . and so on."

The president nodded as he thought about it for a moment and said, "Let's start flat and increase the out-years."

In short order he had settled on what we referred to as a zero, zero, two, two compromise: zero percent growth in the defense budget for the first two years; 2 percent growth each of the following years.

As I was walking back to my office, Darman was leaving Brent Scowcroft's office. He looked worn out. Even before I could ask what had happened, he ran through a short summary of the two exasperating hours he spent trying to convince Crowe that the Soviet reductions gave us the breathing room to help the president out a little. Surely, he told Crowe, in light of the deficits, the Defense Department could get by with a little less than it had over the previous eight years.

When Dick finished, I said, "Relax, the president is on board."

Darman looked puzzled. "What do you mean?"

"The president's OK with zero, zero, two, two."

Darman breathed an only slightly exaggerated sigh of relief.

But it wasn't over just yet. There was another long-drawn-out defense budget discussion, this one in the Oval Office. Admiral Crowe and the four service chiefs were there, joined by the secretary of state and the defense secretary–designate, John Tower. Acting secretary of defense Will Taft was there, along with CIA Director Bill Webster, National Security Advisor Scowcroft, and Deputy National Security Advisor Bob Gates. They had all come prepared to urge the president once more to be a bit more generous on the defense budget.

"The reason Gorbachev is doing what he's doing is because he sees the strength in our defense structures," Scowcroft said. "We don't want him to think we can't keep it up."

John Tower supported him. "There's a lot more fat in other parts of the budget instead of defense."

It was a well-tuned chorus. Admiral Crowe did what most chairmen of the Joint Chiefs of Staff should do—he lobbied the president on behalf of the armed forces. But Crowe lobbied too hard. Even after the president made a decision, Crowe continued to rally his allies and wore the president down. When Bush suggested significant troop cuts in Europe as a response to Gorbachev's initiatives, Crowe reacted with real alarm. It was quite clear that the admiral and his fellow chiefs were adamantly against any cuts at all.

At the end of the barrage from the national security establishment, the president asked me to stay for a few moments. He asked a few more questions about the budget, then said, "Inflation is running at four percent. Let's give them just a little bit more. If we can keep things going with the Soviets maybe we can come back next year and take it down another notch."

Bush had now settled on 0, 1, 1, 2 percent growth for the defense budget. Compounded out, it added considerably to the deficit that we now had to deal with.

Somehow Darman, Porter, and Boskin made it all work out, and we were able to send Congress a one-year budget that met the Gramm-Rudman-Hollings requirements and avoided a sequester for the time being. With some help from President Bush's old friends in Congress, especially from Rostenkowski, we were able to get our one-year budget passed by the middle of 1989.

After we got our first budget through Congress, I met with Darman in early August to talk about the coming political battle over a longer-term budget. We talked about how partisan we could expect Democratic Senate majority leader George Mitchell and Speaker of the House Tom Foley to be. Mitchell, from Maine, was very partisan, but clever enough to conceal it under a benign veneer. He often directed one or more of his committee chairmen to execute the partisan attacks, but it was always clearly Mitchell doing the strategizing and coordinating.

Tom Foley, from Washington state, also was partisan, but not nearly as much as Mitchell. Foley also had to cope with 260 Democratic House members who were a bit more diverse philosophically than Mitchell's 55 senators, so Foley was more likely to seek compromise when he could.

Darman and I started to outline the real spending needs, then asked Boskin and Porter to join us to discuss what a responsible, multiyear budget would look like. As 1989 came to a close, I scheduled a meeting with the president to lay out our possible approach. Nick Brady joined us. Darman told us how difficult the process would be under the even tighter new confines of the Gramm-Rudman rules. Dick was very direct: "If a fiscal year 1991 budget is to be presented without relaxing any of the key constraints, it will have to be a genuinely radical budget," he said. In other words, it would have to include taxes.

We had tapped virtually all the available onetime savings for our 1990 budget. The Democratic-controlled Congress was going to be difficult enough during an election year, and there existed the very real possibility that it could get worse. Republicans would be likely to lose a further handful of seats in November, so the odds against us would climb after that. Now was the time to act, Darman said.

Pressure on the president was coming from all sides. The Soviet Union. Eastern Europe. Although I diligently scheduled opportunities for him to hear all the important pros and cons on budget questions, I tried to make sure the demands on his time were not overwhelming. Bush committed himself to be available whenever major budget decisions had to be made, and despite the foreign policy demands on his time he still managed to fulfill that commitment.

Even the presentation of the budget became an issue. Republicans did not want the budget as proposed by their president to include any cuts in entitlements. They wanted any reductions in Medicare or Social Security to be Democratic initiatives. It was dogma in Washington that touching those entitlements was the "third rail of politics." We heard that concern from even our closest allies.

Republican congressmen were also protective of farm programs, veterans' benefits, and many other subsidies enjoyed by strong constituencies. The same old malady evident in negotiations between the lifelong conservatives Kemp and Bennett was pervasive among all the Republicans in Congress: in public they demanded serious cuts in spending, but in private they lobbied to protect their pet programs.

Water projects, new highways, defense projects, expansion of entitlements, support for the cities and states—the individual members of Congress had a long list of noble causes they wanted to shield from the budget ax. Outnumbered already, Republicans saw the budget struggle as a losing battle anyway and did not want to face the heat for any unpopular measures during an election year.

Democrats in Congress had their own predictable set of partisan responses to Bush's proposed budget. They were wedded to unchecked expansion of their own favorite social programs and even more entitlement spending than their Republican colleagues. They obviously did not like the disciplined spending priorities built into the president's proposal.

The trend in budgeting over the previous two decades had been to expand entitlements. Even as Social Security and Medicare ate up bigger and bigger chunks of the budget, Congress expanded costly welfare programs, farm subsidies, and Medicaid programs. Those became permanent budget items making it even harder to cut spending. Predictably, the philosophical differences of the two parties were reflected in their virtually inflexible strategies, with the Republicans opposed to increases in taxes and the Democrats resisting spending cuts. It seemed all but impossible for the president to strike a big budget deal with the Democratic-dominated Congress *and* fix the very real crisis faced by the nation.

But Bush felt he had to get it done. He let me know: "We shouldn't—we can't—dodge it." It wasn't going to be easy, but he sincerely believed that the amazing international changes under way offered a once-in-a-generation opportunity for the country. If he could just get the economy and the budget under control, he thought, America would begin to enjoy a new era of surpluses, growth, and prosperity—and peace.

As the president had told Congress in his State of the Union address that year, "The American people did not send us here to bicker. There is work to do, and they sent us here to get it done. And once again, in the spirit of cooperation, I offer my hand to all of you. Let's work together to do the will of the people."

Another lobby group complicated things even further. During one of the annual Washington meetings of the world's financial community, Nick Brady had arranged for Bush to hold a small reception for central bankers and finance ministers from around the world. They all had different tones, but the unanimity of their basic positions and the almost overdone use of the same phrases led me to believe that we were being subjected to a coordinated barrage of arguments. These ministers told the president that if the United States did not produce a multiyear budget that included genuine cuts to the deficit, both the dollar and America's capacity to borrow would suffer greatly.

The one ray of hope was that George Bush had kept in close touch with his old colleagues in Congress. We continued to meet behind the scenes with Ways and Means Chairman Dan Rostenkowski. Rostenkowski had supported our earlier one-year budget with no new taxes, and now he too was seeing the reality of the economic data. Early in March 1990, Rostenkowski asked to meet with Darman and me. He told us he planned to unilaterally put forward a major plan for reducing the deficit, one that included both an attack on spending and an increase in taxes.

Over the course of an hour, we discussed Rostenkowski's approach with him in my office. His willingness to break with his fellow Democrats and include serious spending cuts in his proposal impressed both of us—so much so that I suggested we move our meeting down to the Oval Office so Rostenkowski could make his pitch to the president as well. The proposal was so bold it could not be ignored. And the Ways and Means chairman was too savvy a politician to propose something publicly unless he was serious about it.

We all recognized that because Rostenkowski was taking the lead in suggesting unpopular measures, his proposal was a politically difficult one. The president appreciated this, and when the congressman asked that we not "dump all over his plan," Bush assured him that he would not publicly criticize his proposals.

Rostenkowski put forward his proposal on March 11, and, as promised, it included a number of politically perilous features. It would impose a freeze on all cost-of-living increases, including Social Security, and it would raise the gasoline tax by fifteen cents per gallon. As easy a target as these would have been to attack, the president, true to his word, did not criticize the proposal. I reinforced the president's statesmanship by going on television and praising Rostenkowski for his "serious and comprehensive proposals." The proposal even got favorable reviews from the Senate Republican leader, Bob Dole; and from Bill Frenzel, the ranking House Republican on the Budget Committee.

The president wanted to take advantage of Rostenkowski's initiative with some serious steps of his own. He directed us to meet with the House Democratic Budget Group. But even these early bipartisan overtures hit some snags. The Senate Democratic majority leader, Mitchell, continued his broadsides against the president. Mitchell saw political advantage in attacking even the president's constructive comments about Rostenkowski's proposal. He tried to use the president's own words to blame the harsher components of the proposal on Bush, saying the president "opposed every single position in the Rostenkowski plan while appearing to be conciliatory. . . . The president is the cause of the budget deadlock."

Ignoring Mitchell, the president soldiered on. "What would our budget look like if we laid out the details on the package, keeping what we like and getting rid of what we don't in Rosty's proposal?" he suggested. "This might get things rolling." The president wanted the public to see there could be a responsible Republican budget without any increase in taxes.

Darman did so in short order. He outlined what could be done on the spending side, including restructuring programs like Social Security and Medicare, reducing funding for new projects and programs, and capping discretionary spending. On the revenue side, he put forth a list of potential new taxes—carefully avoiding any increase in the income tax rates. Most of those he included were the same consumption taxes as in Rostenkowski's proposal.

The president asked all of us for input on Darman's proposals.

"It's a good combination of spending cuts and taxes to get $500 billion worth of deficit reduction," I told him. "But inside of that I see an even better package of just spending cuts to get a reduction of almost $400 billion. If we had any chance of getting that passed, I'd go with just the spending cuts—but Mitchell and Foley aren't going to let that happen."

"I'd love to get the $400 billion package and hold off on taxes," Bush said.

He asked Darman whether there was any chance at all to get such a proposal through Congress.

Dick said he doubted it. "We could try, but I don't know any of our folks in Congress who think it could have a chance," he said.

Later, I was with Bush in the Oval Office when he told Darman and me, "This proposal may be good policy but it isn't good politics . . . but that's what I get the big bucks for."

It was clear that George Bush, who had campaigned on not raising taxes, understood the implications of the proposal. He asked us to develop and refine the details, and come back in two weeks for another meeting of the budget group.

Bush asked me to pull together a meeting of our core economic team to examine our new proposal. Before we gathered, I made sure everyone understood both the general budget frame-work and the political climate we faced.

The meeting took place in the White House residence in the early evening of March 20, 1990, and lasted nearly two and a half hours. It included the president and vice president, the secretary of the treasury, Chairman of the Council of Economic Advisors Michael Boskin, Domestic and Economic Policy Advisor Roger Porter, Darman, and me.

Darman laid it all out, and suggested that the president try to convene all of the congressional participants to begin serious negotiations. Boskin reminded us that the economy was slowing down. Quayle said it looked to him as if the tax part was "only there for the Democrats." Roger Porter and Nick Brady insisted that the "economy need[s] a budget." I told the president, "I know we have to get this started, but we need to do it right. . . . Foley and Mitchell are ready to pounce."

Before we engaged the Democrats, the president and our budget team had some tough choices to make. Bush wanted to hear all sides. In light of his read-my-lips pledge, the tax matter was the most difficult for the president to come to a final decision on. He encouraged those in his core budget group to be direct in their comments.

Brady felt that the need for a deal outweighed almost all other considerations, including any political downside of a tax increase. Quayle was strongly antitax, but the former congress-man in him understood the difficulties of negotiating with the Democrats. Darman said he could put together a good budget without raising taxes, but the Democrats had said they wouldn't even begin discussing such a package. Boskin kept reminding us of how debilitating any increase in corporate or personal income tax rates would be on the economy. He did not, however, seem to be particularly agitated by the possibility of a consumption tax.

My own position—since I came from New Hampshire, where "Ax the Tax" was a mantra of the Republican Party, and understood the benefits of no or low taxes—was that we should fight long and hard to preserve the president's no-tax commitment. However, since I had dealt with the legislature as governor, I also knew that the arithmetic of the Democratic majority in Congress was going to make that difficult if not impossible. In spite of my own personal perspectives, I was absolutely committed to support whatever decision the president made. It was critically important, for him and for the country, to get a credible multi-year budget in place.

The day after that session, at our morning meeting, the president asked me how I thought we could get serious negotiations started with the Democrats.

"Don't those guys feel any responsibility on getting this done?" he asked. "Is there any way to even get them started?"

"They want both a budget deal and a political win," I told him. "They are determined not to give you another budget without taxes."

The president again referred to the need for avoiding a sequester.

"We can't crunch the defense budget while we're trying to keep the changes in Europe and Russia moving," he said.

I then suggested we meet first with our own Republican congressional leaders so they would not feel left out of the process.

"The guys that know best how to move Mitchell and Foley are Dole and Michel," I told him.

The president agreed. "They've done a good job with the press for us. Let's get them in as soon as you can."

In the midst of all this jockeying over the budget, we had one of those trivial but memorable distractions—the great broccoli flap. *The New York Times* had reported a presidential off-the-cuff remark: "President Bush today declared that he never, ever, wants to see another sprig of broccoli on his plate, whether he is on *Air Force One* or at the White House or anywhere else in the land."

A couple of days later, the bruised broccoli producers delivered two truckloads of the produce to the White House. They were met by Barbara Bush and her ever-present dog Millie. She thanked the president of the United Fresh Fruit and Vegetable Association for the gift, but politely pointed out that there was no way it was going to be served at the presidential meal. "If his own blessed mother can't make him eat broccoli, I give up."

She then told the full contingent of the White House press corps, who had assembled to cover the arrival of the vegetables, "We are going to give it to the homeless." I couldn't resist commenting to her, in a private aside, "Why do you think they left home in the first place?"

As much as the flap seemed disconnected from the policy struggles of the day, it actually was helpful in that it gave the president a chuckle as he moved into the most hectic months of his presidency.

On March 28 we gathered the Republican congressmen in the Cabinet Room to discuss the situation. At that meeting, Bill Frenzel, the ranking Republican on the Budget Committee, spoke at the request of Minority Leader Bob Michel and Minority Whip Newt Gingrich. Frenzel said what we needed was a "heroic product" that could only "come from a summit." The Republican leaders told the president he would have to herd the budget players from both sides toward a joint package.

Bush tried to act on that advice. Over the next couple of weeks, Darman, Brady, and I tried to coax the Democrats into just starting to talk seriously. Our efforts were unsuccessful. George Bush now began to understand that he himself would have to lead the way and in doing so would be likely to take serious political heat.

On the afternoon of April 17, in a fairly long meeting with him, we reviewed where we were on our entire legislative agenda, and I told him, "I am sure the Democrats will not move on the budget without extracting a political pound of flesh from you."

Bush said he understood they were being "very political" and would continue.

That night, the president wrote in his diary, "[This] might be the first day I've really felt an accumulation of problems: the Middle East, the deficit, environment, Lithuania—but that's what I get paid to do."

The next afternoon, Senator Dole came to the White House with a delegation of senators who were en route to the Middle East. He stayed a few moments after the group meeting and told the president that the sequester clock was ticking and something had to be initiated before the summer congressional slowdown.

The president and I also met with Vice President Quayle to discuss how to get Mitchell and Foley moving on the budget. At the end of that meeting, Bush told Quayle and me, "They're hoping we get crunched by the clock. I have to put something on the table, and if they reject it at least everyone will see that they are the ones saying no." He then asked me to get the Office of Management and Budget to finish up the details of our budget, which would serve as the starting point for bipartisan negotiations.

A couple of weeks later, Darman, Brady, and I met with the president in the residence. It was the evening of Sunday, April 29, and by then long-term interest rates had begun inching up and the capital markets were getting queasy. The team quickly reached a consensus that the economic risks did not permit much more of a delay. The president had to take the lead and put pressure on the Democrats to follow along. We recommended that he meet with the four Democratic leaders to define a working procedure. He said, "Let's get them in here. Let them come in. They can propose, and we'll talk. They've got to be willing to negotiate." We suggested a major summit session on the budget, a one-day Camp David retreat, to include the key budget team from the administration and twenty-four congressional leaders from both parties.

The Republican leaders had deliberately recommended the relatively large number of twenty-four to allow the party leaders and their key committee chairmen to come, and to bring "leadership selections" to the table as well. That way, the Republican contingent could include Senator Phil Gramm and House whip Newt Gingrich. Not only did Gramm and Gingrich understand the arcane details of the budget, but they carried weight with the most conservative Republicans, who would be extremely important politically.

Phil Gramm was a well-respected, conservative senator from Texas, a professor of economics. Coauthor of the Gramm-Rudman-Hollings Act (officially the Balanced Budget and Emergency Deficit Control Act of 1985), he was analytical and understood the process of creating budgets. As conservative as he was, he wanted to make the system work and knew how important it was to get a budget done.

Gingrich was a glib and emotional congressman from Georgia. He first came to Congress in 1979 and had only recently been elected whip of the Republican membership in the House. He was extremely volatile and often seemed as if he was more concerned about his own agenda than dealing with the problems facing the White House, Congress, and the nation as a whole.

Throughout 1989, I considered Gingrich an ally as we tried to work the one-year budget and the rest of the president's domestic agenda through Congress. He had on occasion been quite helpful. But as we moved into 1990, with the November elections just a few months ahead of us, I began to get the uneasy feeling that the Gingrich agenda and the Bush agenda were not completely aligned. By that point, I simply did not trust Newt Gingrich.

Dan Quayle later told me that Gingrich actually wanted Bush not to be reelected, so a Gingrich-led Republican House delegation would have a better shot at becoming a majority under a Democratic president. Anyway, in spite of my misgivings about Gingrich, getting the support of these two conservatives would improve the chances of getting broad Republican support for our approach.

We hoped a Camp David retreat could produce a consensus. Then the twenty-four participants could return one month later to work out the details of a comprehensive agreement. We also recommended that the president, along with Secretary of the Treasury Brady, OMB Director Darman, and me, meet with the four congressional leaders—senators Mitchell and Dole, and congressmen Foley and Michel—to work out an agenda for the one-day meeting.

As our Sunday night meeting wound down, the president reviewed our recommendations and suggested two changes. He preferred not to use Camp David—it was not the place for meetings with huge groups of congressional leaders, Bush believed—deciding to do it at the White House instead. He also said he wanted to meet alone—privately and secretly—with each of the four congressional leaders before that preliminary meeting.

"I need them to see this is more important than just who wins politically," Bush said.

George Bush had very strong views about how Camp David should and should not be used. He used it to great advantage with foreign leaders, for whom the informality and intimacy of the setting created a relaxed atmosphere conducive to working out international differences. We would also have a few meetings of the Gulf War core group and key military leaders at Camp David as we were preparing for hostilities in the Gulf. The informal environment, away from the daily commotion of Washington, allowed everyone to focus better and hash out bothersome details, leading to clear policy positions and solutions that were difficult to achieve almost anywhere else.

The president was also very much aware of what a treat it was for his staff to visit Camp David. On a few occasions, he was kind enough to invite Nancy and me to spend a day or two with him and Barbara there. It's hard to describe how special those days seemed, but the setting and warm Bush hospitality made them very memorable occasions for us.

When the Sunday night meeting finally ended, the president thanked the participants for their efforts and reminded us that the road ahead was going to be a tough one.

"We're on the right track," Bush said, and then, to point out the political difficulty of our circumstances, he added wryly, "from a good government standpoint, that is!"

I couldn't resist adding my own bit of gallows humor: "Remember, there have been a lot of great one-term presidents!"

George Bush responded with a smile, "I can assure you that is not, in any way, on my mind."

But I knew he understood that he was taking a risk and doing what a president needed to do.

I arranged for the president to have his one-on-one meetings with the four congressional leaders. They came in individually on May 1 and May 2, and the president told us later that all of the meetings went well. We were all impressed and surprised that they remained secret—no small feat in Washington. That little victory alone encouraged George Bush and buoyed our hopes. The president also arranged for a private lunch with

Rostenkowski. At a social event after that meeting, Rostenkowski confided to Darman that he now felt that a big budget agreement was possible.

The joint meeting with the four congressional leaders—senators Mitchell and Dole, and congressmen Foley and Michel—took place on Sunday, May 6, immediately after a David McCullough presentation called "The Presidency," part of the Presidential Lecture Series. Appropriately, McCullough talked about how fortunate the country was to have had good presidential leadership at some of its most critical moments. It was a great presentation, but McCullough went on a bit longer than expected and I could see his audience getting a bit restless toward the end.

When McCullough finally concluded, the seven of us—the four congressional leaders along with Darman, Brady, and me—joined the president in his study at the residence. Bush asked Darman to brief us all on the sequester situation, and on the other fiscal and economic impacts of a stalemate. The briefing lasted nearly two hours, during which Darman also described the calamitous growth of entitlement programs, and proposed some ways to restore discipline to the budgetary process.

At that meeting we agreed on the "rules of the game" for the larger gatherings to come. We also expanded the group to twenty-six, and agreed to a second follow-up meeting with more intensive negotiations. The president would chair the meetings anytime the eight or the twenty-six met; House Majority Leader Dick Gephardt would coordinate the meetings when the president was not available. We also agreed to begin the process publicly with a meeting of the same group of eight who were in the room that evening on May 9 at the White House.

The May 9 meeting demonstrated just how difficult Democrat George Mitchell was going to be. Mitchell made it clear that there would be "no preconditions" to the discussions. He told us there was no way the president was going to get a deal and still keep his "read my lips" promise. The president listened very carefully. He pursed his lips and squinted a bit and nodded a couple of times while Mitchell was talking. When the Democratic leader was done, Bush said, "OK. Let's see if we can get this done." That was it. The group agreed to go forward with "no preconditions."

The next day's papers carried a picture of the "Group of Eight" and, as Darman noted, surprisingly, "we were all smiling."

Unfortunately, I inadvertently caused a bit of a flap by being quoted in a *Washington Post* story as saying, "The Democrats could propose tax increases, but the White House could veto them." The source was identified as "a senior White House official traveling on a plane from Costa Rica to Washington." Since I was the only senior White House official on that plane, the quote was obviously correctly attributed to me. The comment was to Ann Devroy. I didn't actually use the word "veto." I said the White House could say "no." But Devroy never let accuracy get in the way of jazzing up a story. She had it in her head that the May 9 meeting guaranteed that new taxes were inevitable in the new budget. I had only been trying to make it clear to Devroy that long, hard negotiations were still ahead and neither the White House nor the Democratic leadership agreed on any specifics.

I made that comment to Devroy on "deep background," trying to explain to her what "no preconditions" meant. In Washington journalism circles, "deep background" means the information can be used only without attribution. The source speaking on deep background is not to be identified in any way whatsoever. Nor can the reporter say how the information was obtained. Devroy's reference to "a White House official traveling on a plane from Costa Rica" was a blatant violation of the ground rules of the interview.

The Democrats pounced on the comment. Their leadership team and six major committee chairmen put out a joint statement. "We reject the statements made yesterday by the president's chief of staff. . . . It is a question of trust, of whether or not agreements are to be honored, of whether or not the Administration is prepared to negotiate in good faith on this important matter." We tried to point out that there was no such thing as a veto in negotiations: either you get an agreement or you don't. But they were enjoying their little victory of getting taxes on the table too much to notice.

The next day, on *Air Force One*, the president spoke to the press in the back of the plane and assured everyone that he was entering the negotiations in good faith, and that they would take place with no preconditions. When the press asked him about a possible tax increase, Bush said, "I'm not going to show you my hand, and I haven't seen a lot of hands laid down on the Hill.

"We're not dealing in a crisis mentality," he told the group, "but we've got a major deficit problem and we've got a law that says where the deficit has to be." He said he was trying to follow the sage advice of his mother: "Do your best. Do your best." He told the press he was going to be "trying hard" and he was going to "stay calm."

That was, in fact, what he would do.

The president chaired the first meeting of the group of twenty-six in the Cabinet Room of the White House on May 14. It was crowded around the table, but we managed to wedge everyone in cheek-to-cheek. The president laid out the difficult task the group faced, but emphasized that, individually and collectively, we had an obligation to succeed. The congressional leaders were given a chance to comment, and all of them offered congratulations to the president for having taken the lead. But beyond those tepid remarks, the discussions were all general and noncommittal.

Three days later, on May 17, the meetings continued on Capitol Hill without the president and chaired this time by, as agreed, Majority Leader Dick Gephardt. Unfortunately, the bipartisan tone of the Cabinet Room meeting dissipated, and both sides retreated to their bunkers. The Democrats were now fixated on a demand that the president make a televised national address explaining the depth of the crisis. Most of the rest of the conversation served merely to state the obvious—that there was a crisis at hand. Neither side put any constructive proposals forward. The stalemate would last for more than a month.

On June 20, Dick Gephardt convened a meeting at which he asked everyone except the twenty-six principals to leave the room. He urged us all to get down to business. I said the president was prepared to do whatever was necessary to reach a quick solution. Then, Senator Wyche Fowler of Georgia, who seemed to be present only to advance the most partisan Democratic perspective, suggested yet again that the president take the issue to the public via a televised address.

Then Phil Gramm surprised everyone by saying he recognized that any agreement would of necessity have to contain provisions with which each of us individually might disagree. The fact that this was coming from Gramm, a conservative antitax hawk, suggested to the Democrats how serious the Republicans were. Gingrich, the other archconservative in the room, confided that he could "imagine a five-year package where I tried to sell taxes." With those comments from both Gramm and Gingrich it finally appeared that the group might be ready to get down to business.

Rostenkowski, still the only member of the group who had put a serious proposal in play, stressed the importance of Gingrich's statement. To encourage the group to follow his lead, Rostenkowski promised he would not publicly criticize any suggestions or proposals put forward. The group members seemed to be ready to negotiate among themselves without any staff present and to establish tight channels for communicating any progress.

At that point, Senator Jim Sasser threw a wrench into all the progress that seemed to have been made. Sasser, despite being chairman of the Senate Budget Committee, really knew very little about actually crafting a budget. *The New York Times* called him the Democratic "mouthpiece" in the party's war with the White House over the budget. "As the keeper of the party line before the cameras, his partisan swipes helped build the pressure that led Mr. Bush to renounce his no new taxes campaign pledge," the *Times* said.

Fowler also attacked the president and snidely noted that the only staff people in the room were from the White House— meaning the secretary of the treasury, the OMB director, and me. Republican Bill Archer and Democratic senator Lloyd Bentsen tried to bring the discussion back on track, but Fowler's and Sasser's partisan rants on behalf of Senator Mitchell effectively killed the moment.

The next day we tried to move things forward by offering a specific proposal, with the president's approval, that would have reduced the deficit by $450 billion over the subsequent five years. Again, however, the Mitchell-Fowler-Sasser team attacked it, this time publicly.

Through all the bickering, Federal Reserve Chairman Alan Greenspan publicly lamented the lack of progress and continued to maintain the tight monetary policy that was dragging down the economy. He told Brady he could not relax that policy until a serious multiyear budget agreement had been reached.

I reviewed the dismal results in a phone call with the president. I told him, "It went worse than even I had expected." He said he wanted to meet with our core team.

Brady, Darman, and I gathered in the Oval Office the next day to review where we were. It was now clear that with elections only a couple of months away, the timetable for any constructive action was getting tight. There was one positive piece of news. Brady reported that he and Darman had lunch with Lloyd Bentsen and Dan Rostenkowski in the treasury secretary's private dining room a day earlier. The lawmakers said they were prepared to negotiate a private deal with the president and then help sell it to the congressional leadership.

It was a constructive approach to put something together before Congress left in August. They said they would accept a broad-based energy tax such as a gasoline tax increase as the only new tax, as well as serious reform of entitlement growth and a reduction in the taxes on capital gains. Obviously, getting this approach to work would depend on the president's getting support from Mitchell and Foley.

July 15 was G-day. That was the date under the Gramm-Rudman-Hollings Act when the president was required to spell out, in detail, the specific budget cuts that would reduce the deficit enough to avoid a sequester. With the date rapidly approaching, the president said he thought he had to go to the public with a plan and challenge Congress to accept. I argued the importance of trying once more to get a bipartisan agreement before July 15 so the president wouldn't have to stick his own neck out and suffer alone the political consequences of the bad news.

The president stalled a bit by deciding to meet yet again with the four leaders of Congress. Brady and Darman contacted Foley to arrange the meeting. The president approved my suggestion of trying to get a framework deal out of the Group of Eight before the July 15 deadline. That would allow a detailed agreement to be implemented before Congress left in August.

The president said he would try to work with Mitchell on a one-on-one basis.

To make sure he understood exactly where the Republican members of Congress stood, the president asked to meet with the Republican negotiators. I arranged that meeting to take place in the Cabinet Room on Monday, June 25. We reviewed where we were and addressed the key points that could mean the difference between an acceptable deal and an unacceptable one.

After we finished our presentation, Senator Dole reminded everyone present that "July 15 is a real decision date. If we don't get it going by then" it would send the process into an unproductive lame-duck session after the election. Bob Michel and Senator Pete Domenici of New Mexico made the same point. Domenici was particularly emotional. If the issue was not resolved soon, he said, "all hell is going to break loose."

There was unanimity in this Republican meeting that the country needed a big five-year agreement and needed it soon. We all knew how difficult it would be to get the controlling Democrats to accept any real spending cuts without including taxes in the package. Although philosophically they were all tax-cutters, the Republicans in the room all understood that the Democratic majority in Congress made taxes inevitable. They said they were ready to support the White House. They understood that in order to get any Republican policies in place, they had to stick together. That, of course, had been true in the past, was true at that time, and is still true today.

The president—his instincts right on target—focused carefully on what the two key conservative members of the group had to say.

Phil Gramm made it clear that it was in the best interest of the country and the Republican Party to avoid a post-sequester negotiation. "If we can get a deal, we ought to take it," Gramm said. "If we've got to do a little bit in taxes to get a deal, do it. I cannot vote to change marginal rates, but if the deal includes non-incentive-crushing taxes, I'm willing to take it."

Gingrich was a little less direct and a lot less forceful than he had been in my one-on-one meetings with him. With me he had been very consistent in saying that any increase in personal income taxes was a deal breaker, but he could accept an increase in the gas tax or other consumption taxes. In this meeting he said, "There is no way you can deal with income tax rates." He did say, however, that increases in other forms of taxes, including consumption taxes, would be acceptable. Gingrich also objected to any cuts that limited the cost-of-living increases for Social Security recipients.

Gingrich was carefully avoiding that third rail for reasons that would become obvious later. The outspoken, ex-Rockefeller Republican was now leading the antitax caucus of Republicans in the House but avoided publicly associating himself with the necessary, but politically unpopular, cuts that had to be made to keep taxes in check. He was unabashedly working on an agenda intended to get him elected Speaker of the House. In these meetings with the Republican leadership, he seemed to be the only one not focused on the greater good—fixing the country's fiscal and economic problems. It seemed to me as if Gingrich was inserting comments in the conversation like bread crumbs that he could later tell some biographer or historian to follow.

In spite of Gingrich's obfuscations, George Bush was generally pleased with the discussion, so a breakfast meeting of bipartisan leaders was convened the next day, June 26, at 7:00 in the White House Residential Dining Room. The guest list included the president, Speaker Foley, Senator Mitchell, Senator Dole, Congressman Michel, Congressman Gephardt, Secretary Brady, Director Darman, and me. It was a timely gathering because

Congress was scheduled to leave three days later, on June 29, for its two-week Fourth of July break, and the president was scheduled to leave on July 4 for a NATO meeting and an economic summit in Europe.

At 6:40 a.m., I met Brady and Darman at the White House and we walked over to the residence together. The president opened the meeting and then turned it over to Darman, who summarized the few areas of agreement and then tabulated all that remained up in the air. He starkly noted the need to act within the constraints of the calendar.

When Darman finished, the president looked at the three Democratic leaders and asked them directly, "What do you propose?"

Speaker Foley chimed in first. He said the problem was so big and so critical that both sides should put out a statement that a bipartisan solution had to include the following elements: entitlement reform, reductions in defense and discretionary spending, reform of the budget process, and tax increases. The president answered immediately, saying, "We can do that if you all agree."

We then turned to the process and timing. Everyone agreed that two groups would meet in parallel. The bigger group of twenty-six would continue to meet, and there would be parallel meetings of the Group of Eight. The Group of Eight would be joined by the committee chairmen from Ways and Means and Finance, if necessary, to deal with some of the more complicated specifics after general agreements had been achieved.

What happened next complicated things for everyone. Nick Brady suggested that the group affirm what the president and Foley had agreed to, and for some unexplainable reason, Darman suggested that they draft a public statement saying as much. Mitchell jumped on that, and urged him to do it. Once Darman drafted it, he realized that, although it accurately reflected what

Foley and the president had agreed to, it would create a political firestorm if released that way.

Darman handed it to me, and although my preference was to crumple it up and swallow it on the spot, we were boxed in at that point. I needed to try to soften the consequences. It was one thing for the president to have to accept taxes in a deal, but that change in his position needed to be presented to the public as part of a good, deficit-fixing, complete budget package. The real benefit of the president's sacrifice had to be spelled out loud and clear. I tried to change the statement to make it clear that we were just starting a negotiation. I added "growth incentives" to Foley's list, and also "the need for a package that can be enacted." I then changed Foley's "tax increases" to "tax revenue increases."

These minor tweaks were not enough, I knew, to insulate the president from the charge of having abandoned his "read my lips" pledge, but once Brady and Darman were trapped by Mitchell into producing a statement, the best I could do was to try to soften the blow as much as possible. In retrospect, I wish I had argued that the statement might inhibit free negotiations, or perhaps had found some other way to try to get out of releasing any statement at all. But there didn't seem to be any way to reverse course.

Mitchell then proposed changing "It is clear" to "It is clear to me." Those two words turned a sideswipe into an uppercut. It then became a statement by the president alone instead of a bipartisan statement by both the president and the leaders of Congress. But before any of us could object, Bush quickly agreed to accept the change and to release the draft to the press.

With that statement, as Rostenkowski later put it, "'read my lips' was history."

As much as I regret not having figured out how to prevent that statement from being released, it probably did not make much difference in the long run. The agreement was going to be whatever the agreement was going to be. There simply was no other way, with the schedule squeezed by the November election, to get anything else approved in time to avoid sequester. The consequences of inaction, in terms of both national security and the health of the financial markets, were just too dire.

George Bush was committed to do whatever would help the country, even if he had to pay a political price. The release of the statement didn't change the reality, but it did affect the way the president's compromise was communicated to the public. There might have been less outcry had it been communicated within the context of a completed agreement. Then, it might have been perceived for what it was—an exercise in leadership on the part of the president.

When the meeting broke up, I went into the Oval Office with Bush. He walked to his seat behind the desk and said, "I think we could get a good deal with Foley, but Mitchell wants his pound of flesh."

"He's going to hold any budget back until you pay the ransom in taxes," I said.

With a consensus framework now in place, the negotiators turned to the process of working out the details of "the deal." The venue was changed to Andrews Air Force Base. On September 7 we gathered there, and the negotiations were "locked up." Even with the framework we had so painfully negotiated, getting to a final agreement was not easy. But by the end of September the details had been worked out.

The agreement that emerged from Andrews reduced the growth of Medicare, and the growth of entitlements for federal employees, agriculture, students, and veterans. It cut subsidies in dozens of programs. It put real and enforceable limits on discretionary spending. It closed many loopholes, and cut back on programs that relied on federal credit to back them up.

The most important feature of the agreement, in my opinion, was that it added a "pay-as-you-go" system requiring any new entitlement programs to be paid for by specific revenues defined in the legislation that enacted them. This put some discipline back into the budget process. No longer could members of Congress dream up expensive new programs without putting forward practical, and sometimes politically painful, ways of paying for them.

It is important to understand exactly what was, and what was not, included in the tax side of the Andrews agreement. The tax increase did not include any increase in personal income tax rates. The bulk of it was in the form of an increase in the gasoline tax, a consumption tax that fell clearly into the category of taxes that Newt Gingrich had assured us he "could swallow." Although we could not get the Democrats to agree to a reduction in the capital gains tax, we did get a package of tax incentives for investment in entrepreneurial ventures. There were approximately three dollars in reductions of spending for each dollar of revenue increase in that five-year budget deal, a stronger ratio than in any other major budget package in history.

It is also important to recognize that all the key participants on the Republican side were part of the negotiation process from the beginning, and were kept informed of progress on the agreement at every point. As the president insisted, both Darman and I made sure that both Senator Gramm and Congressman Gingrich understood what was being negotiated at every stage, especially when taxes were being discussed. Both Gramm and Gingrich made it clear that they could not accept an increase in personal tax rates, so we refused to accept any increase in personal or business tax rates.

On July 23, Gingrich presented Darman with his own list of conditions that had to be met before he could accept any agreement. Those nine conditions specifically excluded accepting any "marginal tax rate increases," but did not rule out tax increases in general. Another condition was that "increased taxes and user fees cannot be greater than half the package in the first year." The agreement that came out of Andrews met every one of those conditions.

Before I took the message to the president that an agreement had been reached, I personally checked with both Gramm and Gingrich individually on whether they could accept the agreement. I took the time to review all the details with them. Phil Gramm made it clear that he thought it was a good agreement, and he would accept it. He said, "This is a good deal. We're getting away with just a gas tax and that's better than I thought the Democrats would let us have. Tell the president I'm with him all the way."

When I called Gingrich, he said, "It's a good package on the spending side, but I just wish we could've figured out how to keep the taxes out of it. . . . The gas tax is a lot better than a bump in the personal rates. . . . If that's what we got, go ahead with it."

I also spoke to Republican minority leader Bob Michel and asked him whether he saw any problems. He assured me that he had checked with Gramm and Gingrich and they accepted the package. "That will go a long way in holding the support of our guys," Michel told me.

With that, I went to the president and told him that an agreement had been reached at Andrews Air Force Base.

Throughout the process, Alan Greenspan made it clear that the president needed to get a "credible multiyear budget" passed. He told Brady that the president would have to, and should, accept some taxes in order to do so. In June, Greenspan testified before Congress that interest rates could fall "significantly" if and when a budget deal was reached. *The New York Times* quoted him as saying that he would not budge on interest rates until then "despite administration pressure," a mantra he repeated throughout the summer and into September, even as the economy was easing into a recession.

A couple of days before the vote on the budget package, Greenspan visited the White House and Congress and he put his stamp of approval on the package as agreed to at Andrews. "They have crafted what appears to be a credible, enforceable reduction in the budget deficit stretching over a number of years," he said.

On October 1, the president met with the bipartisan group of congressional negotiators in the Cabinet Room to thank them for their hard work. All the participants, including Newt Gingrich, were there. The group then went from the Cabinet Room to the Rose Garden to formally announce the agreement.

Gingrich, however, did not follow us into the Rose Garden. Republican leader Bob Michel later said that when he saw Gingrich quietly slink away, it was "the first inkling" he had that Gingrich would do an about-face. I also was blindsided by his reversal. As uneasy as Gingrich had made me during the prior few months, I trusted that he was sincere when he said he could support the package. I couldn't believe at that late date he wouldn't have been honest about his position.

Gingrich led us all to believe that if we delivered a package meeting his ground rules, he would support it. Never, during a full year of discussions and negotiations in which he was a principal participant, did he indicate otherwise. Bob Michel felt the same way. His fellow Republicans and White House staffers on the negotiating team, some of whom had known Gingrich since the Reagan administration, believed the Georgia congressman as well. Perhaps the most generous analysis of what happened is that while perhaps Gingrich wasn't blatantly lying to us, he was lying to himself until the deal was done, and then decided after the fact that it presented a great opportunity to lift himself up as leader of the opposition.

George Bush spoke to the nation about the budget package on October 3, 1990. His opening sentence laid out the issue: "Tonight I want to talk to you about a problem that has lingered and not been fixed in this country for far too long—the federal budget deficit," he said.

"As we speak, our nation is standing together against Saddam Hussein's aggression," he continued. "But here at home, there's another threat—a cancer gnawing away at our nation's health. That cancer is the budget deficit."

He explained the problem in detail and the bipartisan solution that the White House and Congress had agreed upon. He made it clear that neither personal nor corporate tax rates would rise as a result of it. It did not tamper with Social Security. It did not put America's national security at risk, and it would prevent the economy from slipping even further out of control, he said.

Over the next four days, Gingrich and his allies worked to organize tax hawks to vote against the agreement so painstakingly crafted over the previous months. We initially tried to reason with the congressman and his allies, explaining that it was a good deal for both Republicans and America. But once the fire was lit, it was impossible to put out. It wasn't like trying to extinguish a pile of burning leaves. It was as if a match had been put to a can of gasoline. Gingrich was eventually joined by far left Democrats in Congress who hated the spending cuts in the package. The House voted 254–179 to defeat the package.

The president and the Republican leadership had lost their leverage, and now had to negotiate all over again from a much weakened position. In the following round of talks, Democrats removed most of the growth incentives hard-won during the earlier negotiations. They also removed many of the reforms in entitlement growth, and increased the top income tax rate from 28 percent to 31 percent instead of passing the gasoline tax included in the original agreement. The negotiations lasted until October 26. On October 27, the House passed a revised five-year budget agreement by a vote of 228–200; the Senate passed the bill 54–45.

Ironically, Newt Gingrich, who like most Republicans was opposed to any increase in personal income tax rates, was the principal reason why the income tax rate was increased from 28 percent to 31 percent in 1990.

George Bush had done what we should all want our presidents to do. He placed the good of the country above his own best interests. In fact, in the spring of 2014, the John F. Kennedy Library Foundation presented him with the John F. Kennedy Profiles in Courage Award in recognition of the political valor he demonstrated by negotiating the 1990 budget agreement. Many members of the Kennedy family attended, along with the political professionals who had worked with John F. Kennedy and Senator Edward Kennedy.

It was very gratifying to see President Bush recognized for what he had done, but the day also brought a personally gratifying gift to me. Vicki Kennedy, Ted's widow, and a few of Senator Kennedy's family and staff, told me that Ted often spoke fondly of our frequently adversarial meetings, always saying how we both were battling intensely to get it "our way" and how we finally worked it out in the end. Each told me how Ted felt us better friends through it all, and he always made the point of reminding whoever he spoke with: "Two parties, two perspectives, the same commitment, we worked it all out."

Bush's agreement, however reviled at the time, has since been recognized as a very effective and successful policy initiative. Although it did contribute to Bush's loss in the 1992 election, the budget immediately began reducing the deficits and enabled the surpluses the country enjoyed during the 1990s. It also allowed the Federal Reserve to reduce interest rates. The increased availability of credit and loans sparked a blaze of economic growth. The spring of 1991 saw the beginning of a decade-long spurt of prosperity and the creation of millions of new jobs.

Not too bad for a bill no one really loved, but that bill had been passed by a president who really cared. George Bush, in agreeing to the Democrats' demands for new taxes, did what was required for the good of the country instead of what was politically expedient for him personally. The quiet man had made a courageous decision and America would be all the better for it.

6

Free-Market Policies for the Environment and Energy

<hr>

On November 30, 1988, seven weeks before taking office, at a breakfast meeting in the White House, George Bush met with a group of thirty activists from the very strong environmentalist lobby; among them were representatives of the Sierra Club, the Environmental Defense Fund, and the National Wildlife Federation. The Reagan administration had been somewhat dismissive of such groups, so the earnest men and women had not met with a president in nearly a decade. The depth of pent-up ambition was apparent in their presentations. They wanted more money for their favorite agency, the Environmental Protection Agency, and another $5 billion or so for other programs.

Bush had extensive experience in the energy sector and a personal commitment to environmental issues. In the campaign, he made it clear that energy and the environment were two of his highest domestic priorities. He knew, however, that trade-offs would have to be made in both of these areas, and he was keenly aware of the financial bind facing the country. Bush believed that market incentives could encourage sound environmental decisions and that a healthy, productive American energy sector would give the nation greater leverage in foreign affairs.

The environmentalists had to be realistic, Bush told the gathered group. He understood the complexity of the issues and they, in turn, needed to understand that there could be, and probably would be, some disagreements between his administration and many aspects of their own environmental agenda. He left them with an upbeat message, though. "I know there is some skepticism about my commitment, but it is real and I'm going to surprise you in a good way," he said.

The president surprised more than just the environmentalists in the subsequent years. With his Clean Air Act (1990) he deftly broke up a twelve-year legislative logjam that had prevented any progress toward cleaning the nation's air; then he implemented a national energy policy that is still reaping rewards to this day. The act and the policy were underappreciated at the time, but together they were among his greatest domestic legislative accomplishments.

THE CLEAN AIR ACT

During one of his many visits to New Hampshire in 1987, Vice President Bush had a long conversation with me about what a Republican agenda for environmental policy might look like. We both felt that the power of the marketplace could create incentives for the private sector to make the investments needed to protect the environment. Bush knew that a policy based only on prohibition could kill job creation and hold back economic development. The Reagan administration had similar concerns, but instead of proactively seeking solutions it just let the Democrats who were blocking legislation have their way.

On behalf of Yale University, baseball captain George Bush accepts *The Babe Ruth Story* autobiography from Babe Ruth.

George Bush, U.S. ambassador to the United Nations, meets with President Nixon in the Oval Office.

During his Texas Senate race, George Bush rides with his friend Will Farish in a parade.

Candidate George Bush drives himself to a hamburger fry in Marshall, Texas, during the 1970 Senate race.

As part of his governors strategy, Vice President Bush and a few Republican governors meet in Kennebunkport to discuss domestic issues.

Vice President Bush attends the campaign-kickoff event for the New Hampshire primary at the annual Gregg family-day picnic in Greenfield, New Hampshire.

In the first of their three debates during the 1988 presidential campaign, Vice President Bush responds to Democratic nominee Massachusetts governor Michael Dukakis in Los Angeles, California.

The president and Lee Atwater play the guitar at the Celebration for Young Americans at the D.C. Armory during the inaugural festivities.

President Ronald Reagan and his chief of staff Ken Duberstein meet with the incoming president and his chief of staff, Governor John Sununu, on the colonnade at the White House on the day before the inauguration of President Bush.

President and Mrs. Bush walk in the Inaugural Parade.

Supreme Court Chief Justice Rehnquist administers the oath of office to President George Herbert Walker Bush, the forty-first president of the United States.

Preparing for a speech before a Joint Session of Congress, in the family theater with Chief of Staff Governor Sununu, media consultant Roger Ailes, and OMB associate director Bob Grady.

On April 28, 1989, President Bush signs an executive order on Historically Black Colleges and Universities, in the Rose Garden of the White House.

President Bush meets with the House Republican Whip organization in the cabinet room to discuss budget issues. Pictured with the president are Bob Michel and Newt Gingrich.

The president and Mrs. Bush meet with His Holiness Pope John Paul II at the Vatican with Governor Sununu and other members of the president's staff.

George Bush and Solidarity leader Lech Walesa speak to an enormous crowd at the shipyard in Gdansk, Poland.

General Brent Scowcroft, Robert Gates, and Governor Sununu advise "President Skippy" in a spoof on the then-popular Garry Trudeau comic strip character from *Doonesbury*. President Bush's sense of humor set the tone for his White House team, and he was never too proud to poke fun at himself.

President Bush chairs the Education Summit at the University of Virginia in Charlottesville with Governor Gerald Baliles of Virginia, Governor Garrey Carruthers of New Mexico, and Governor William Clinton of Arkansas.

President Bush arrives at the USS *Forrestal* off the coast of
Malta. He is met by Commanding Officer Louis E. Thomassy
Jr., Rear Admiral Richard Allen, Vice Admiral J. D. Williams,
and Admiral Jonathan T. Howe.

At the Malta summit on the *Maxim Gorky*, President Bush and Soviet
president Gorbachev shake hands to open the meetings.

President Bush speaks on the phone to Secretary Cheney from the Oval Office study with Vice President Dan Quayle, Andy Card, and Governor Sununu regarding the situation in Panama.

Alan Greenspan, chairman of the Federal Reserve, visits the White House to meet with the president to review the economy. They are joined by Secretary Nicholas Brady and Governor Sununu in the Oval Office.

The U.S.–Soviet Union START Treaty is signed in the East Room of the White House by Presidents Bush and Gorbachev.

President Bush signs the Americans with Disabilities Act on the South Lawn of the White House.

President Bush takes a moment from playing tennis to visit with his mother, Dorothy Walker Bush, at Walker's Point in Kennebunkport, Maine.

From the Catto residence in Aspen, Colorado, President Bush talks on the phone to King Fahd of Saudi Arabia regarding Iraq's invasion of Kuwait.

On the patio at Walker's Point, President Bush discusses the Iraqi invasion of Kuwait with the Saudi foreign minister Prince Saud, Prince Bandar, Secretary Jim Baker, Governor Sununu, Robert Gates, and Richard Haas.

Supreme Court justice nominee David Souter meets with President Bush, Governor Sununu, and Fred McClure in the Oval Office, in preparation for his Senate confirmation hearings.

Breaking a twelve-year legislative logjam, President Bush signs the Clean Air Act Amendments while Secretary Watkins, William Reilly, and Vice President Quayle applaud.

President and Mrs. Bush greet the troops and enjoy Thanksgiving dinner with the First Division Marine Command Post, Saudi Arabia.

In a historic bilateral meeting with Syrian president Assad in the Le Rebat room of the Holiday Inn Crowne Plaza in Geneva, Switzerland, President Bush discusses the Iraqi invasion of Kuwait.

The core team for Desert Storm meets with President Bush in the Oval Office the day before the air war begins. *Left to right:* Robert Gates, Governor Sununu, Secretary Cheney, Vice President Quayle, President Bush, Secretary Baker, General Scowcroft, and General Powell.

George Bush takes a solo walk on the south grounds of the White House during the day of January 16, 1991, just hours before the air war will begin in Iraq.

CNN correspondent Bernard Shaw visits with President Bush in his residence office, with Marlin Fitzwater, General Scowcroft, and Governor Sununu, just after Shaw had reported live from Baghdad, Iraq, as the United States and her allies started operation Desert Storm.

President Bush confers by phone with British prime minister John Major while General Colin Powell gets a status report from General Norman Schwarzkopf during a meeting on Desert Storm with Secretary Dick Cheney, Governor Sununu, and Robert Gates in the Oval Office.

President Bush announces Clarence Thomas as his nominee for associate
Supreme Court justice in front of the Plate House at Walker's Point.

In commemoration of the fiftieth anniversary of their record-setting
1941 baseball seasons, President Bush honors Ted Williams and Joe
DiMaggio at the White House.

In a working luncheon, President Bush and Soviet president Mikhail Gorbachev discuss details of the final agreement on the SALT Treaty.

Just two weeks before the coup attempt in the Soviet Union, President Bush and Soviet president Mikhail Gorbachev hold a joint press conference in the Press Theatre, Ministry of Foreign Affairs Press Center, in Moscow to announce the START Treaty agreements.

Participants of the Middle East Peace Conference descend the stairs of the Royal Palace, Madrid, Spain. The conference ultimately led to the Oslo Accords.

Governor Sununu talks to the press on the tarmac at Key Field Airport in Meridian, Mississippi, where he had landed while traveling with the president, just after the governor announced his resignation.

The North American Free Trade Agreement (NAFTA) is signed by President Bush with Ambassador Derek H. Burney of Canada, U.S. Trade Representative Carla A. Hills, and Ambassador Gustavo Petricioli of Mexico looking on.

President Bush and Governor Sununu disembark Air Force One at Andrews Air Force Base after returning from the National Convention of the U.S. Hispanic Chamber of Commerce in Chicago.

President Bush participates in the town hall–style presidential debate in the 1992 campaign with H. Ross Perot and Governor William Clinton. This was the debate in which Bush inauspiciously looked at his watch.

We also talked during that visit about how Republicans could recapture the initiative on the environment as a political issue. In New Hampshire I had proposed legislation to cap the release of acid rain–producing emissions. That legislation passed without major modifications, and our Acid Rain Control Act of 1985 made New Hampshire the first state in the nation to enact legislation addressing the problem. I gave the president a copy of an article I had written for the National Academy of Sciences journal *Issues in Science and Technology* titled "Acid Rain: Sharing the Costs," and emphasized that breaking the decade-long political deadlock on clean air legislation would require sacrifice by both sides—the polluters and the rest of the nation.

Throughout the early months of the primaries, Congress was debating amendments to the 1970 Clean Air Act. The legislation had been stalemated in Congress for more than a dozen years. The environmental agenda faced two major opponents in Congress: Democratic senator Robert Byrd from coal-producing West Virginia, and Democratic congressman John Dingell from auto-manufacturing Michigan. Together they took advantage of a sharply divided Congress to prevent any serious legislation on clean air amendments from coming out of committee.

Byrd was a very senior senator and chairman of the Senate Appropriations Committee. His influence lay not only in his seniority, but even more in his control of the appropriations process. Any senators who wanted funding for projects in their states had to go to Byrd, hat in hand, to get the money, and Byrd knew how to wield that power. Dingell was chairman of the House Energy and Commerce Committee, which had significant influence over energy and environmental legislation.

During the long series of meetings Bush had with Republican governors in the year leading up to the presidential election, environmental issues were very much a part of the conversation.

Governors in the Northeast were concerned that sulfur diox-
ide emissions from the power plants in the Midwest could drift
east with the prevailing winds and create acid rain in their own
states. Midwestern governors were worried that strong legislation to curb those emissions would kill jobs and wreck the economies of their states.

Similar region-specific concerns applied to other issues, from
clean water and overfishing to the preservation of forests and
wetlands. In every case George Bush took note of how each issue
was viewed in the individual states and came to the conclusion
that, despite any differences, the American public as a whole was
ready to accept a solid environmental agenda.

Right after he was elected and soon after I had been named
chief of staff, the president and I sat down to generate a list of his
domestic priorities. Near the top of the list, right after dealing
with the budget deficits and education, was the environment.

Breaking the clean air stalemate in Congress seemed a good
place to start. Bush asked me and Boyden Gray, who had a very
strong interest in environmental affairs, to come back to him
quickly after the inauguration with some specific proposals to
get the legislation moving again.

As soon as Roger Porter joined the White House as assistant to
the president for domestic and economic policy, I met with him
and Boyden Gray to review environmental options that we could
present to the president. The three of us quickly agreed that air
emissions could best be dealt with by building a policy around
the concept of emission trading, or "cap and trade" as it is known
today. I asked Roger and Boyden to work out the details of a
package palatable to the president.

By late spring, after meeting several times to tweak the proposal to meet concerns expressed by Bush, we were ready to
send his proposed legislation to Congress.

I believed that an emissions trading scheme offered the best possible solution, minimizing costs and maximizing flexibility in the application of any new regulations. Our New Hampshire legislation allowed companies whose overall emissions were capped to trade their pollution allotments among the various facilities they owned. Even more flexible emission trading would be the key component of the president's proposals.

We sought support for our approach from external groups. One that proved especially helpful was the Environmental Defense Fund, which recognized the value of emissions trading policies and was quite visible in its support of the president's proposals. We also worked with ICF International, a well-respected consulting group in Virginia with experience in modeling and analyzing the cost and effectiveness of legislative provisions. ICF analyzed a variety of options and estimated that the emission trading approach would cost half as much to implement as the command-and-control strategies of the past.

In the week after the president sent his proposal to Congress, the Environmental Defense Fund supplemented our own efforts by explaining to various media outlets how an emissions trading process would function. Having such a strong, independent ally in the lobbying process helped our cause.

On June 12, 1989, George Bush convened a meeting of congressional leaders from both sides of the aisle, governors, conservationists, and business executives at the White House. He told the gathering there that with the leadership present, "we can break the stalemate that has hindered progress on clean air for the past decade." He laid out his proposal "to curb acid rain and cut urban smog and clean up air toxics," and reminded those assembled of the significant benefits that had already accrued from the 1970 Clean Air Act. He said his proposal provided solid environmental protection with cost-effective solutions and would, in the long run, enhance economic growth. "This legislation will be comprehensive. It will be cost-effective. But above all it will work," he said.

Prior to that meeting with congressional leaders, in February 1989, the president had met in Ottawa with Canadian prime minister Brian Mulroney. After their initial discussions, President Bush let Mulroney know that he wanted an agreement with the Canadians to address the problems of acid rain. It was a major departure from the policy of the Reagan administration, which had steadfastly resisted taking any action on the issue until further studies had been completed. At the end of that meeting with the prime minister, the president left it to me to comment on the data I had provided him about Canada's less than stellar efforts to reduce its own industrial emissions.

Just one day before he met with the prime minister, the president presented his first budget to a joint session of Congress and said environmental legislation was right around the corner.

"If we are to protect our future, we need a new attitude about the environment," he told Congress. "We must protect the air we breathe. I will send you shortly legislation for a new, more effective clean air act. It will include a plan to reduce, by date certain, the emissions which cause acid rain—because the time for study alone has passed, and the time for action is now."

In mid-June the president formally announced clean air proposals addressing three specific issues: acid rain, urban air pollution, and toxic air emissions. "If this legislation is enacted, acid rain–related pollution will be reduced by nearly one half, all urban areas of the country will finally attain national air quality standards, and emissions of toxic air pollutants will be slashed," he said.

But it was clear that the battle was just beginning. Byrd and Dingell, along with the auto industry, the utilities, the coal industry, and their allies, had been through this many times before and they were ready.

The Clean Air Bill would turn out to be one of the most difficult pieces of legislation to negotiate with Congress. I asked Roger Porter to take the lead. He understood the nuances of the issues as well as anyone in government, or for that matter in the country. He came by my office often to review progress and discuss objections as they arose. His analysis was always accurate and he invariably had a list of recommendations on how we could resolve any differences we encountered. The Clean Air Act of 1990 was, to a great extent, Roger Porter's creation.

President Bush himself stayed fully engaged as the legislation moved through the congressional committees. About a month after his budget presentation, the president and the White House team went into heavy consultation mode with key supporters in Congress who could help move the environmental agenda along.

After one of the early meetings with the congressional leadership on the issue, the president took a moment afterward to speak with Senator George Mitchell, the Democrat who had replaced Senator Robert Byrd of West Virginia as Senate majority leader. Mitchell, from heavily forested and environmental-inclined Maine, was a strong supporter of acid rain legislation. The president said he wanted to establish a constructive working relationship with the senator on environmental issues, and Mitchell was quite responsive. It was left to me to keep them both in the loop and move forward on the subject from that point.

The state governors also played an important part in getting the bill done right. The National Governors Association had been trying for ages to reconcile the regional differences that stymied progress on the acid rain issue. In my last term as governor, I chaired the National Governors Association Task Force on Acid Rain, which managed, after some very difficult discussions, to put forward a compromise proposal that received the two-thirds majority vote required for formal support from the NGA. That proposal, like the president's, called for a reduction of ten million tons per year in the industrial emissions that cause acid rain. Although it did not include specifics on how to pay for this reduction, it did recommend a combination of "polluter pays" and support from general government funds.

That effort within NGA was followed by an agreement between the governors of New York and Ohio, a fact not lost on Senator Max Baucus, the new chairman of the Environmental Protection Subcommittee in the Senate. In comments to *The New York Times* in early March, Baucus said, "Things are clearly different this year. We have a new president who wants an acid rain bill. We have a new Majority Leader and a new mood to compromise on the bill. The states are less polarized this year than they were before. I just think that all the factors you look at tend to point overwhelmingly to passage of the bill."

It was clear that George Bush's leadership was creating the opportunity to break the stalemate on this long-contested issue.

Throughout the process, President Bush used the power and allure of the Oval Office to build support for his bill from parties that would be directly affected by it. We met a number of times at the White House with the leaders of utilities, manufacturing industries, and other industries. The president always put forward his arguments in as constructive and instructive a manner as possible, urging these leaders to be part of a solution instead of just opposing the legislation in a knee-jerk fashion. Although they didn't always jump on board, they appreciated the opportunity to discuss the issue directly with the president.

Two months after the president sent his legislation to Congress, some Democrats in Congress and their environmental constituencies began to ramp up the criticism. Even William Reilly, our

EPA administrator, was taken aback by how aggressive it was. Reilly thought the Democrats who controlled Congress would embrace everything he sent up to the Hill. He did not understand the politics of politics. "The truth is that nobody expected President Bush to come up with such a good bill," Reilly told *The New York Times*. At the White House, we ascribed some of the harsh language to tactical positioning as the legislation passed through the House and Senate committees.

Much of the actual resistance to the bill was Democrats battling among themselves. Henry Waxman, Democratic chairman of the House Energy and Commerce Committee's Subcommittee on Health and Environment, engaged in a not-too-private war of words with Democratic representative John Dingell from Michigan, chairman of the full Energy and Commerce Committee. Waxman wanted a more traditional command-and-control piece of legislation; Dingell, along with Republican representative Norman Lent from Long Island, sided with the president as a cosponsor to the legislation seeking market-based solutions.

The most difficult battles were over who would pay the costs associated with the legislation. Many members of Congress were looking to add amendments to the bill to shield specific groups in their districts, states, or regions from the impact of any new laws. The tug-of-war involved utilities, their customers, coal miners, automakers, and oil and gas companies. As all these lobbies descended on Congress, George Bush continued to use his powers of persuasion to generate support across even the most disparate of groups, and, through it all, Roger Porter continued to work with key members of Congress to keep the bill consistent with the president's initial proposal.

When questioned by the press on how Bush felt about all the amendments and exemptions the legislators were trying to add, I tried to emphasize that the president felt the bill as he presented it was well balanced and well thought out. "We're not going to be stubborn about adjustments of pieces that are in it," I told reporters, "but let's not make a drastic change."

With its emphasis on smog, acid rain, and airborne chemicals, a revised Clean Air Act was certain to have a serious impact on national energy policy, and especially on energy generated by burning fuels such as coal or natural gas. The battle among the different regions of the country that supplied those fuels was a legitimate and challenging part of the negotiations, the most intense being between producers of clean coal in the West and producers of high-sulfur coal in the East. Eventually, the White House was able to help find a compromise on the most significant differences.

By October 1989, the committees began voting on major provisions of the proposed legislation. That was when counterproductive internal squabbles surfaced. Some of the messages from the White House on proposed amendments were being contradicted by the EPA's lobbying. Although we eventually were able to bring the messaging back to a common track, press leaks from the EPA about the differences in positions within the administration were not helpful. On at least a couple of occasions I had to go to the president to get his help to keep us all working as one on his agenda.

The battle for a good bill continued through the end of 1989 and into 1990. For months, Roger Porter dutifully worked with our supporters and negotiated with our opponents on each and every detail of the bill. Finally, in the spring of 1990, the process took on a more positive tone as Porter and Boyden Gray worked out some of the more arcane details.

The president was pleased. It finally looked as if his legislation could and would be passed. By the fall, all sides seemed to be eager to find a compromise on the remaining positions. The last big hurdle was overcome when the Dingell-Waxman feud was resolved with both sides claiming victory in the negotiations.

In April, the Senate passed its version of the bill, and in May the House followed suit. But the struggle was not over yet. Senator Baucus was chosen in June to chair a joint conference seeking to reconcile the two chambers' respective versions of the bill. For the next four months, the tweaking continued and Roger Porter and Boyden Gray labored on. Finally, agreement was reached on October 22, 1990, seventeen months after the president sent his initial proposed legislation to Congress.

The bill that came out of this lengthy and cumbersome process was a great compromise. It was balanced and addressed all the major issues with provisions that responded to the concerns of all sides. Everyone agreed that it was a significant, important, and very effective piece of legislation. The House voted to accept the bill on October 26 and the Senate on October 27. On November 15 the president signed his Clean Air Act of 1990.

By signing into law a bill that updated and tightened federal air pollution laws for the first time since 1977, the president fulfilled a 1988 campaign pledge he had made on the shore of Lake Erie, that he would push for federal efforts to improve air and water quality. This bill was, the president proclaimed, "simply the most significant air pollution legislation in our nation's history."

The decades since then have borne those words out.

George Bush worked hard to address the environmental needs of the country, but he was determined to find an approach that balanced America's economic and energy needs. Not everyone in his administration shared that sense of balance.

Bush appointed William K. Reilly to serve as administrator of his Environmental Protection Agency, unaware at the time, perhaps, that Reilly was one of the smoothest self-promoters in

Washington. Nobody could have a telephone call or a private meeting with Bill Reilly without an account of that meeting showing up in the press within a day or two, biased, of course, to enhance Reilly's own personal environmental credentials and influence policy in the direction he favored.

On the Clean Air Act, Reilly was more of a hindrance than a help. He never really bought into the market-based trading system and, therefore, was never able or willing to be of any real assistance in creating and negotiating the balanced trade-offs required to get the legislation passed.

Quite often, after Reilly visited the Hill to talk to congressmen, I would receive distressed telephone calls from our friends there asking me to please send someone back to undo the confusion that Reilly had caused. Roger Porter is the one who deserves credit for writing the bill and negotiating through the problems. He was the one who worked tirelessly to hammer out the specifics and fine points in ways that mirrored the president's vision and enabled the Clean Air Bill to be passed.

Reilly also stirred up problems when we tried to deal with the wetlands issue. The president promised "no net loss" of wetlands during the campaign and intended to keep that promise. Instead of treating that as a mandate to protect existing wetlands, Reilly tried to use it as a mandate for overregulation and to prevent significant stretches of good property from ever being developed.

One of Reilly's great ploys was to use his relationship with the environmental press to highlight his "conflicts" within the administration and enhance his own reputation as a hero among environmental groups. I was always sure that Reilly's loyalty was less to the president and his agenda and more to the environmental groups to which he hoped to return to work after he left the administration.

Reilly's "off the reservation" approach contrasted with the much more effective and disciplined approach of Mike Deland, who served as the president's chairman of the Council on Environmental Quality. Deland was committed to the president's agenda and aimed his efforts at meeting those specific goals instead of freelancing beyond them.

Bill Reilly used leaks to the press as a tool to maintain his own personal standing in the environmental community and to leverage opinion on controversial policies. He raised leaking to an art form. Quite often, instead of doing it himself he would allow internal EPA memos to circulate among people who he knew had a habit of passing things on to the press.

Reilly had a few of his own favorite reporters, especially a couple at *The New York Times* and *The Washington Post*. I didn't recognize how diligently he worked the press until I got to CNN to appear on *Crossfire*. There, over Diet Cokes with the reporters and commentators passing through, I learned a lot about how the EPA leaked its memos.

If the EPA—or, that is to say, Bill Reilly—had a difference of opinion on any environmental issue, an unnamed source at the EPA would be spelling it out for reporters in no time flat, even though this self-serving tactic was a serious problem for the administration. Invariably, the premature presentation of positions undermines or embarrasses the president.

An especially unhelpful instance occurred when Reilly sent a memo to a large group of EPA employees complaining about the positions and performance of the administration team that went to Rio de Janeiro in June 1992 for the United Nations "Earth Summit." By then I was out of the White House, and the EPA had become more aggressive in poking the White House on policy differences. Reilly had to know that the widespread distribution of the memo within the EPA meant it certainly would end up in the press.

Even more egregious was that he did it in the middle of President Bush's battle for reelection against Bill Clinton and Al Gore. Reilly compounded this by contradicting one of the campaign's key messages. As reported in the *Times*, "William K. Reilly broke ranks with the White House and said Mr. Gore was not an environmental extremist."

It hadn't been easy for me to deal with Reilly's tactics, but I at least had them pretty much under control. It looked to me from outside the campaign that the administration was beginning to have trouble keeping the ranks in sync at the EPA. It was not an auspicious sign for the reelection campaign.

ENERGY

In 1989, the United States faced a mixed blessing. After the stratospheric oil prices of the previous decade, an oil glut precipitated by the Organization of Petroleum Exporting Countries (OPEC) brought the price of a barrel of crude down to under $30. While that was good for drivers, it also created some problems. Domestic oil production, barely profitable at that price point, plummeted, and the economic incentives for conserving energy evaporated overnight.

George Bush began his professional life and built a successful career in the world of energy. He understood how that industry worked and it was important to him to guide the nation toward a strong, sound, and forward-looking energy policy. He knew it would be a momentous challenge because of the many strong, competing agendas that intersect in any national energy policy.

His vision was for an energy strategy that recognized that America needed to use wisely all its own energy resources and to invest in new technologies and in conservation incentives. He saw that free-market incentives had to be a very important part of a long-term resurgence of America's energy might.

It was obvious in our conversations on the topic during the transition that he had a firm grasp of the nation's need to encourage and nurture each and every energy technology and resource available to it. Just a little more than six weeks into his term, at the swearing-in ceremony for Secretary of Energy James Watkins, the president summed up his thoughts:

> We need nuclear power, hydropower, oil, gas, and coal to meet the total energy requirements of the United States. And we need to improve energy efficiency as well as develop competitive renewable technologies. No one or two sources are sufficient alone, nor will they provide us with the flexibility that is necessary. For reasons of national security, we need to have domestic production in each area. And we will institute policies to promote that by restoring incentives and through deregulation. . . .
>
> I want to see a recovery in domestic oil and gas production. And I also want to see continued development of this clean-coal technology, a generation of safe nuclear energy, and also R&D, research and development, of alternative fuels and new technologies. And again, let me emphasize conservation methods as well. . . . For America's economy to be competitive, we need sound energy policies and competitive energy industries.

Bush immediately charged Secretary Watkins with the responsibility of developing a National Energy Strategy, or NES. Despite the timely start, the process of putting together all of the complex elements for a cohesive, meaningful and fair strategy took longer and became more controversial than the president ever imagined.

In the last week of July, President Bush formally announced that his secretary of energy would develop this national strategy, which would serve as a blueprint for future legislation and regulation. Secretary Watkins could see that there were two sides to the challenge before him, energy and environmental.

Watkins then went to work. First, he scheduled a series of public hearings to "find out what scientists, industry officials, political leaders, economists, environmentalists, and ordinary citizens wanted to do about energy and environmental policy." The Department of Energy ended up holding eighteen public hearings in cities across the country. The hearings revealed a wide range of differences in opinion from region to region.

In my conversations with the president on the topic, it was clear his greatest concern was the need for domestic production. He understood that conservation had to be a component of his strategy, but he wanted to make sure his commitment to energy production was distinctly and unmistakably noted. He repeated that message in subsequent meetings with Budget Director Darman and Michael Boskin, who headed the President's Council of Economic Advisors. The president charged the three of us with helping the secretary of energy over the political hurdles we anticipated.

In discussions with Watkins, I emphasized the president's concern that his policy proposals be crafted and packaged in a way that would influence Congress in our favor. We worked out a process in which the secretary would bring specific policy options, along with supporting data, for the president to consider and select. Boskin, Darman, and I were concerned about proposals that were too reliant on using higher taxes as a means of getting people to conserve energy, an approach that would be problematic in light of the president's "no new taxes" pledge.

Deputy Energy Secretary Linda Stuntz took charge of the process for Secretary Watkins. She collected the information, commentary, recommendations, opinions, and analysis, then created a list of what would eventually include nearly seventy potential NES options. She recommended that the entire package be reviewed by the President's Economic Policy Council (EPC).

The president tried at every opportunity to drive home the need for a national strategy. In December 1989, as he signed the Renewable Energy and Energy Efficiency Technology Competitiveness Act, he said of the legislation that it "will play an important part in our Nation's Energy Strategy. . . . The development of renewable energy resources and improvements in energy efficiency can provide many benefits to the United States, including a diversification of our fuel and technologies and increased use of less polluting energy resources." But he was fully aware that the bill he was signing then dealt with only a small part of what was needed to put the nation on a path to energy security.

Finally, in November 1990, the energy secretary's list of options was presented to the EPC. The policy paper that Linda Stuntz sent to the EPC was a very well-crafted document, one that clearly outlined the conceptual terms of reference on each of the issues. It was supported by exhaustive analytic detail, and proved to be a useful and objective decision-making instrument.

The policy framework addressed four major areas: energy security, electricity, the environment, and science and technology. Each of those areas included specific policy considerations to be debated and decided. Watkins and Stuntz made a detailed presentation on each of the four areas to the EPC. Watkins told the group that the ultimate goals were delivering energy at more reasonable prices, maintaining a safe and healthy environment, producing a stronger economy, and reducing dependence on unreliable oil suppliers in the Middle East and elsewhere.

A few days later at another meeting, members of the EPC debated, in some cases quite emotionally and with deep divisions, issues such as the costs, benefits, and political impacts of the strategy. This second meeting generated a fairly clear consensus around some of the difficult issues, including support for drilling in the Arctic National Wildlife Refuge (ANWR) and the Outer Continental Shelf.

A third EPC meeting followed about a week later. We discussed our nation's vulnerability to oil supply disruptions; enhanced environmental quality; availability and pricing of energy; deregulating portions of the gas industry; and issues related to enhancing and strengthening the electricity sector. Significant disagreements surfaced over issues related to mandatory energy conservation. I asked Secretary Watkins to rework the conservation provisions because many were based on taxes and mandates instead of the market-driven and incentive-driven measures preferred by the president. Nick Brady also sent a strongly worded memo to Watkins, indicating that unless the tax and mandate provisions were removed, Treasury would oppose the NES.

We scheduled two more meetings of the EPC, one for the end of December and one for early in January, this time with the president present. In an indication of how important the topic was to him, Bush attended those meetings even though they took place during the run-up to the Gulf War. The allied attack to liberate Kuwait took place on January 16, 1991, about a week after the second meeting.

Before the meetings, Darman, Boskin, and I briefed the president on the substance of the earlier meetings. He was satisfied that the production side of the strategy was broad and expansive.

We told him of the debate over the conservation measures and mentioned that Watkins had requested a one-on-one meeting with him before the next EPC meeting. The president agreed, and Watkins met with him over lunch on December 17.

The first EPC meeting with the president on the National Energy Strategy took place four days later, on December 21, in the Cabinet Room. More than thirty people crowded into the room, including cabinet members from all the departments except Defense. Secretary Cheney, immersed in Desert Storm preparations, was represented by his deputy secretary, Donald Atwood.

Secretary Watkins quickly went over items on which there was a clear consensus, then proceeded to cover the more controversial ones. The president listened intently and, after discussion, conveyed his decisions to Watkins. Bush supported the production-side components of the strategy, as well as the market-based incentives for conservation. He also made it clear that he didn't want to see any taxes or mandates in the strategy. Watkins asked him to reconsider. Bush said he would think about it, and the meeting adjourned. A couple of days later he came back to the secretary and confirmed his earlier decisions.

The final EPC meeting to affirm the National Energy Strategy took place on January 8. Again, the president agreed to meet Secretary Watkins for lunch on the preceding day. As before, the January 8 meeting had more than thirty attendees in the Cabinet Room. The final package was discussed and the president was very gracious in his remarks, thanking Secretary Watkins for having produced a good strategy. It was a program the president said he could and would support wholeheartedly.

With the NES formally packaged, the president solicited formal written comments from a number of key departments. With only one exception, the comments endorsed the market approaches woven throughout the NES. The Council on Environmental Quality, in its comments, indicated that it would have preferred more aggressive conservation strategies, but it supported the plan as a whole.

On February 20, 1991, at a gathering at the White House, the president released his National Energy Strategy. He acknowledged the prolonged process that had led to its preparation, but said he was happy with the results.

"We now have, thanks to all, a carefully balanced energy strategy, and it is designed to diversify America's sources of energy," he said. "It is designed to encourage efficiency and conservation, spur competition throughout the energy sector, give Americans greater choices among fuels, and enhance U.S. research and development in new technologies." Then, for added emphasis, he said, "It relies on the power of the marketplace."

Bush closed his remarks by saying that when considered with the Clean Air Act, his National Energy Strategy would "maintain an uncompromising commitment to energy security and environmental protection."

The next challenge was to convince Congress to enact those sections of the NES that required legislation to be implemented. The president sent Congress a comprehensive proposal to get the process started.

Through the remaining ten months of 1991, no energy bill ever made it to the floor of the House for a vote. In the Senate, a bill similar to the president's proposals came to the floor but was subjected to fierce lobbying by all the constituencies it touched and ended up being blocked by filibuster. By the summer of 1992, I had left the White House, but Roger Porter continued to work with both friends and foes alike to get a compromise solution out of the Senate.

Finally, the Senate agreed to a compromise that blocked drilling in the Arctic National Wildlife Reserve (ANWR) in return for the removal of increased auto efficiency standards that had been added to the bill by the Democratic leadership in the Senate. With those changes and a few other smaller differences resolved, the Senate passed the energy bill by a vote of 94–4. With those compromises in place, plus a few additional, smaller concessions, the House passed its version of the bill by a vote of 360–47.

The House and Senate bills then went to Conference Committee and, after an intense battle over provisions calling for fleets of alternative-fuel vehicles, a conference report was approved by both the House and the Senate. President George Bush signed the Energy Policy Act of 1992 on October 24.

The 1992 Energy Policy Act has often been dismissed by its critics as merely a "modest" policy, mainly because it failed to impose mandatory fuel efficiency standards, known as CAFE (corporate average fuel economy) standards, on automakers, and imposed no major taxes on fossil fuels. The critique, however, misses the real significance of this landmark legislation.

The act implemented virtually all of the major provisions of George Bush's National Energy Strategy. It addressed energy efficiency, energy conservation, and energy management. It included incentives for energy conservation with a variety of measures designed to reduce the nation's dependence on imported oil. It provided incentives for clean energy, and for renewable energy. Most significantly, it amended utility legislation to allow small utility companies to stay competitive with larger utilities, and provided for a broader range of resource choices for utility companies.

The act also restructured the regulatory system and replaced the noncompetitive model with one that promoted real competition by obligating existing utilities to make their transmission systems available to other sellers of electric power; this allowed consumers to shop around for the best prices and service.

George Bush relied on his understanding of the energy industry and years of real-world experience to craft legislation that provided meaningful changes in support of a strong and comprehensive national energy policy. Every one of those changes made for a more secure and more efficient American economy and, collectively, they have resulted in significantly reduced energy costs to consumers to this day.

The development and implementation of a National Energy Strategy and the passing of a Clean Air Act both yielded greater benefits for future generations of Americans than they did for the immediate political career of George Bush. The Bush Clean Air Act has been the most effective, most efficient, and most copied piece of environmental legislation ever. It is a great example of how conservative, market-friendly policies can be even more effective than liberals' big-government, command-and-control policies.

Bush may not have gotten the proper credit due him at the time, but the power of his approach is acknowledged now. The president pursued his priorities energetically, not for short-term political expedience, but because they were the right thing to do. He also had to consider our dependence on a competitive supply of energy in some of the foreign policy challenges he had to deal with. While energy policy was largely viewed as a domestic issue, the United States had become increasingly dependent on foreign oil. When Saddam Hussein threatened Kuwait, the implications of a global economy loomed as the foreign and domestic policy issues began to intersect.

7

Empowering Communities and Families

═══════════

Helping end the Cold War, fixing the budget crisis, getting historic environmental legislation, and unleashing America's domestic energy capacity were all great achievements, but George Bush was just getting started. The extended Bush family was large already, and getting larger every year. He and Barbara already had ten grandchildren when he took office, and he was determined that his legacy would benefit them and their peers long after he was gone.

For Bush, two sore spots stood out in America as the nation inched toward the end of the twentieth century—education and child care. The modern world demanded more effective classrooms for our children, but our schools were failing them. Throwing money at the situation and further meddling by bureaucrats in Washington were neither possible nor desirable in Bush's eyes. Real reform was necessary. It was a message he heard again and again from the governors.

Real reform was also needed to help women and families navigate the responsibilities of raising children in dual-income households. The number of women in the workforce had nearly tripled since the 1950s, and some of them needed help. But the help should be without strings and come from outside the K–12 system that was already failing them in other ways. Even while he was unwinding the Soviet Union and negotiating with Congress on the budget, Bush dedicated precious time to getting solid conservative solutions to the issues of education and child care through a reluctant, partisan Congress.

Addressing those needs might not have provided immediate political benefit and might even have expended valuable political capital. Great presidents take on important long-term issues without self-regard. Great presidents take on such challenges because that is the right thing to do.

EDUCATION

Young people, their futures, and their families were high on George Bush's domestic agenda. In fact, the Republican Party platform of 1988 was titled "An American Vision: For Our Children and Our Future." Achieving the results he sought on their behalf would require his determined attention, as well as—in at least one case—his around-the-clock commitment.

As early as 1987, George Bush began to address some of the slight differences he had with the Reagan agenda in ranking his priorities. In May, the vice president delivered at St. Louis University a commencement address in which he noted the problems many American families were having in sending their children to college.

"One of our highest priorities in the 1990s should be to help families finance a college education," he said.

Later that evening, in Kansas City, he elaborated on the theme, saying the federal government should spend more on education, but he added the critical caveat that improvements in education had to come not just from added funds, but from fundamental changes in the system.

"We've got to reform the whole education process," Bush said. "We are already spending more per kid than any country, and we are not number one in terms of achievement. I am looking for reform of the whole education system."

He acknowledged the value of education as an economic asset: "In the future, education will be America's most effective economic program, our most powerful trade program, our most productive jobs and anti-poverty program. It will be the way we outcompete anyone."

As Bush began to campaign in the state primaries, the press began to take note of his focus on education. In New Hampshire in January 1988, speaking to a group of high school students, he said, "I want to be the education president. I want to lead a renaissance of quality in our schools."

The same month, the education editor of *The New York Times* wrote, "Vice President Bush has made education his number one domestic policy. . . . This new emphasis on quality and accountability has given Republicans a chance to stick their noses under the education tent, and the GOP candidates find the all-important connection between education and the economy a natural." He noted that Bush "even wants to start up some new programs, including a college savings plan that would allow parents to put away tax-free dollars for their children's education." The *Times* even gave him credit for using education to differentiate his agenda from that of the president he served. "The vice president has made more of the education issue than anyone, using it as a relatively noncontroversial means of weaning himself from Ronald Reagan."

In speech after speech, Bush often repeated his commitment to be the "education president." His standard stump speech also included "Education has got to be the priority" and "Better schools mean better jobs." He was careful to be clear that the key to high-quality education—particularly in grades K–12—was to maintain control at the state and local level.

"I don't want the federal government taking over," he often insisted. "I think we can do a good job in helping the disadvantaged, or helping in Head Start, but I also think . . . the President ought to . . . use the bully pulpit to spell out excellence, to encourage—even though it's the responsibility of your school board here—support the good teacher, support those principals that are doing a good job."

George Bush knew the value of using the presidency to elevate expectations and standards for America's primary and secondary schools. During the campaign, I gave him a copy of a report from the National Governors Association titled *A Time for Results*. It was the product of a yearlong study by state governors under the leadership of then chairman Governor Lamar Alexander of Tennessee, who would eventually become George Bush's secretary of education. The report cited the deterioration of educational performance over the prior two decades and emphasized that it was a national concern requiring real attention and not just lip service.

The Republican platform Bush ran on contained a number of key components of his education agenda. It endorsed choice in education. It called for more spending on Head Start, and reaffirmed the primacy of the family and local schools in education. Each of these planks reflected his sense that better education would come not just from increased spending, but from improving the way the money was spent and empowering parents and communities to manage their own schools.

Recognizing that schools had to deliver more than just the three R's—reading, writing, and arithmetic—Bush stated, "I think we can stand up for values in our schools while maintaining the proper separation of church and state. We can agree on common values: decency, honor, kindness." During the campaign, Vice President Bush pledged that, if elected, he would meet with the nation's governors as early as possible to discuss education.

After he won in November, the president-elect continued his focus on education. The first event of his inaugural program was a speech to teachers. There, he repeated that education would be a top priority for his administration and reaffirmed his wish to be known as the "education president."

In December 1988, James Pinkerton, speaking for the president-elect, confirmed to the staff of the National Governors Association that Bush was planning to convene an Education Summit of governors, college officials, and business aides. During that period of transition, Bush indicated that Reagan's education secretary, Lauro Cavazos, would remain in office and include in his initiatives a process for recognizing and encouraging outstanding "merit schools" to serve as models for the rest of the country.

Less than a month after his inauguration, President Bush addressed a joint session of Congress and proposed a budget for fiscal year 1990. In that address he said: "The most important competitiveness program of all is one which improves education in America. . . . We must reward excellence and cut through bureaucracy. We must help those schools that need help most. We must give choice to parents, students, teachers and principals. And we must hold all concerned accountable. In education we cannot tolerate mediocrity." Bush asked legislators to join him as the "education president" by becoming the "education Congress."

The most significant step George Bush took as president to address America's educational needs was to follow through on his promise to convene an Education Summit with America's governors. The summit would establish a clear set of goals for our educational system. It was only the third summit between a president and the nation's governors in America's history. Franklin Roosevelt convened such a gathering to address the problems of the Great Depression, and before that Theodore Roosevelt had done so to talk about the environment and conservation. Its rarity alone made it a noteworthy event.

I had discussed the possibility of such a gathering with the president for some time, going back to when I was governor of New Hampshire. Bush recognized that governors could exert the most influence for improvements in education. While standing firm in his belief that K–12 schooling was primarily a local issue, he believed the federal government could provide key leadership by signaling that the inadequacies of the system constituted a major national crisis. President Bush wanted to try to build a national consensus on a broad commitment to achieve real improvement. He wanted to use the summit to begin to set nationally accepted goals.

As a former chairman of the National Governors Association, I continued to maintain good relationships with governors from both parties. With the president's approval, I asked Roger Porter to work with the NGA to organize the Education Summit. In the process, it became apparent that two of the governors, the cochairmen of the NGA Task Force on Education—Republican Carroll Campbell of South Carolina and Democrat Bill Clinton of Arkansas—would play an important role if the summit were to succeed. I knew Governor Campbell well; he served as chairman of the Bush campaign in South Carolina and proved helpful in organizing gubernatorial support for Bush. I also remained close to Governor Clinton, who had served as chairman of the National Governors Association the year before I took over that position.

Meanwhile, in April 1989, President Bush sent Congress his proposed legislation on Excellence in Education. He would, in each of his subsequent years, send Congress a similar package of legislation, and each time Congress would fail to act.

In his first attempt, the president laid out four principles central to his education policies and essential for reform: recognition of excellence, greater flexibility and choice, measured accountability, and careful targeting of resources. These four principles remained the hallmarks of the education packages the president sent to Congress each year.

On May 16, President Bush met with thirteen governors to discuss the details of the upcoming summit. Republican governor Terry Branstad was the chairman of the NGA at the time and was enthusiastic in his interest and commitment. With the governors at his side, Bush announced that the Education Summit would be held in September.

Besides the governors, President Bush also began to reach out to business leaders, seeking their participation in the effort to reform the system. In June, he challenged the Business Roundtable of many of America's largest companies to help the country's competitiveness by supporting improvement in education.

At the annual NGA meeting in Chicago in July that year, the president formally extended his invitation to the summit and set the dates as September 27 and 28 at a site yet to be determined. The NGA developed a proposed agenda, and in early September convened a meeting of nearly fifty representatives of education advocacy groups, business interests, and government officials. That preparation meeting, chaired by governors Campbell and Clinton, affirmed that the principal objective of the summit should be to set national education goals and create a strategy for meeting them.

In the week before the summit, now set to meet in Charlottesville, Virginia, Bill Clinton sent a letter to the Democratic governors across the country outlining his expectations for the gathering and the preparations that had been made to ensure its success. Clinton told his colleagues that, on the basis of his interactions with the White House, he sincerely believed the summit would focus on substance and not just on show.

"The White House has agreed to work with the governors to develop a set of national performance goals, for the first time in history, to guarantee that Americans will have an education system second to none," Clinton wrote. "John Sununu told Governor Campbell and me that he expects the governors to assume a leading post-Summit role in formulating the details of the goals in consultation with educators, business and labor, Congress, parents and other interested citizens no later than our midwinter meeting in February."

Roger Porter, the assistant to the president for economic and domestic policy, worked with the National Governors Association on both an agenda for the meeting and a plan for follow-up on the outcomes. Porter understood public policy as well as anyone and did a fantastic job of making sure that the summit agenda had a sharp and clear focus.

Addressing the governors at the Education Summit, President Bush told them: "There are real problems right now in our educational system, but there is no one Federal solution. The Federal Government, of course, has a very important role to play, which is why I'm here and why so many members of our Cabinet are here. And we're going to work with you to help find answers, but I firmly believe that the key will be found at the state and local levels."

There was some disagreement at the summit between the governors and the White House—most notably over levels of federal funding for schools—but, more significantly, there was solid agreement on virtually all other issues, so the group was able to release a joint statement endorsing the idea of national goals as well as the creation of a panel to help implement them.

The president and the governors set goals aimed at eliminating illiteracy, supporting early childhood programs, and holding teachers accountable for the performance of their students. They also agreed to develop, in support of those goals, specific action items that would be discussed when the NGA held its annual meeting the following February.

The results of the Education Summit were extremely gratifying. Even the press seemed to notice. *The New York Times* story on September 30, 1989, carried the headline "Teachers Praise Bush's Effort to Set a New Education Agenda." The article reported that "school superintendents, union leaders and teachers were virtually unanimous yesterday in praising the efforts of President Bush and the nation's governors in setting a national agenda for education."

The educational community also was strongly supportive of both the goals and the emphasis on early education, and there was virtually unanimous agreement about the need to balance a national call for action with the recognition that the key to success would be efforts at the state and local level.

At the conclusion of the summit, the governors and the president issued what they described as "a Jeffersonian compact to enlighten our children and the children of generations to come." They defined six national education goals that were later announced publicly by President Bush in his State of the Union address on January 31, 1990.

The six ambitious goals stated that by the year 2000:

1. All children in America will start school ready to learn.
2. The high school graduation rate will increase to at least 90 percent.
3. American students will leave grades four, eight, and twelve having demonstrated competency in challenging subject matter including English, mathematics, science, history, and geography; and every school in America will ensure that all students learn to use their minds well, so they may be prepared for responsible citizenship, further learning, and productive employment in our modern economy.
4. U.S. students will be first in the world in science and mathematics achievement.
5. Every adult American will be literate and possess the knowledge and skills necessary to compete in a global economy and exercise the rights and responsibilities of citizenship.
6. Every school in America will be free of drugs and violence and will offer a safe, disciplined environment conducive to learning.

Those six goals served as the basis for the reform efforts of successive administrations throughout the 1990s and into the twenty-first century. They also were the nucleus of the education proposals Bush sent to Congress every year throughout his term, but the Democratic-controlled Congress would never give him the legislation he asked for. Virtually the same goals ended up being codified during Bill Clinton's presidency in his Goals 2000 legislation.

Seven months after the summit, the president convened another gathering, this time at the White House, to help further his National Education Strategy. Congressional leaders from both parties, as well as members of the congressional education committees, attended. The president laid out the importance of high-quality education to individuals and to the nation, emphasizing that an educated population was one of the nation's greatest assets and resources.

Two months earlier, in February, Bush had met with the nation's governors, and now at this White House gathering he was formally asking Congress to act on the education strategy he had formulated with the governors' help.

The president spoke to the congressional leaders about the importance of innovation and modernization in education. He announced the formation of a private sector research and development fund within a new entity called the New American Schools Development Corporation that would disseminate successful new models for education in all the states.

At the end of 1990, the second full year of his term, President Bush was not satisfied with the pace of progress being made. He felt he needed a change in leadership at the Department of Education and replaced Lauro Cavazos with Lamar Alexander, the former governor of Tennessee.

Alexander had overseen the NGA's report *A Time for Results*, which sought to undo many of the bureaucratic constraints hampering education at the time. It stressed the need for accountability among schools and teachers, tying financial incentives to performance. That report fitted Bush's general perspectives on education to a T. It also appealed to the private sector, which was bemoaning the fact that too many high school graduates could not read well or do basic math. Some even had difficulty filling out a job application. Bush pressured Congress to understand that the system had to be shaken up in order to resolve those educational shortcomings.

The president saw that with Congress controlled by partisan Democrats, he would have to work directly with the governors to implement his programs. Congress blocked virtually all of his major education proposals. Bush came to understand that Washington could not, and should not, be involved in the control or management of our K–12 system of education. It was one area that had, to a great extent, withstood congressional erosion of the Tenth Amendment and he wanted to preserve that turf for the states. If Washington became the source of significant sums of money for K–12 education, Bush believed, then conditions could be attached to those funds to allow DC bureaucrats to begin controlling schools.

In order to sharpen the focus on what he was trying to accomplish, the president himself, by executive order, created the National Education Goals Panel. The panel included four members of the administration, six governors, two members from the House of Representatives, and two senators. Later, it also added four representatives from state legislatures. The panel was designed to work hand in hand with the National Governors Association, and the NGA selected Colorado governor Roy Romer as the first panel chairman.

With Secretary Alexander aggressively backing the president's education agenda, the president was able to push forward with a reform proposal he called America 2000. In May 1991, he sent Congress a bill titled America 2000: Excellence in Education Act. The bill included the latest proposals from the National Education Goals Panel, along with programs to develop national standards and tests to be implemented on a voluntary basis.

Additionally, America 2000 proposed the creation of model schools in each of the 435 congressional districts plus one hundred others. Those 535 New American Schools would develop innovative strategies and serve as models for other schools in their districts. The bill also included a controversial provision allowing parents to use federally issued vouchers to send their kids to better schools, including private schools, if they were unhappy with their own local, public schools.

A great deal of discussion and negotiation with key members of Congress took place before the bill was sent to Capitol Hill. Once it arrived, as expected, Congress was besieged by advocacy groups of all stripes. Liberal groups were wary of the testing and accountability provisions, and conservatives thought the proposed national standards and assessments would undermine state and local control.

Regrettably, America 2000 was swallowed up in the partisan black hole of congressional committees. The one piece of education legislation the president was actually able to get passed was the Excellence in Mathematics, Science and Engineering Education Act of 1990, which finally implemented a version of the National Science Scholars Program proposed by the president back in April 1989. It also contained a number of incentives to encourage students to pursue fields of study that the president and Congress agreed were critical to the nation.

Despite the hard work that went into crafting the legislation into something widely acceptable, the Democratic-controlled Congress and the liberal constituencies it represented were not enamored with many of the provisions of flexibility, choice, and accountability that the president included in America 2000.

Although Congress did not pass the major education legislation George Bush sent through, the president was able to have some significant impact by using the bully pulpit of his office and his constructive relationship with the nation's governors. By the time I left the White House as chief of staff in 1992, more than half of the states had begun to implement significant portions of the goals that came out of the earlier Education Summit.

The president's commitment to giving parents more choice, including the option to enroll their children in nonpublic schools with vouchers, also had a significant effect. Those nonpublic schools, dubbed charter schools, were a new alternative for K–12 education, and by the time Bush left office, nearly half the states in the nation had adopted some version of school choice and the charter schools structure. Today, many of those institutions are outperforming traditional public schools.

Bush's budgets also demonstrated his commitment to education. Despite being constrained by budget deficits, he managed to increase funding for the Department of Education by more than 40 percent. In his first three years, he bumped up our spending on math and science education by 70 percent, more than doubled the amount invested in Head Start programs, and quadrupled funding for early literacy programs.

Even into the fourth year of his presidency, Bush continued to press Congress hard to adopt his education reform initiatives. The House and Senate each worked on versions of the bill through the summer of 1992. Although the House and Senate were able to produce a conference report, President Bush was not able to get them to send it to him because by then the 1992 presidential election season had begun. Bush thought he might be better positioned to get a stronger bill in his second term, but unfortunately he never got the chance.

Although he never managed to get Congress to put quality, innovation, and performance at the forefront of American education, George Bush successfully used the budget process and the bully pulpit of the presidency to set America's schools on a course that over time would reflect his vision. His Education Summit of 1989 had a tremendous impact on the quality of education in America in both the short and the long term. It established for the first time a commitment to national goals, encouraged parental choice in education, and made consistent, measurable, reliable accountability an important component of assessing the performance of schools nationwide.

Although there would be no "education Congress," Bush had used every tool at his disposal to jump-start the process to review and improve education in America and fulfill his commitment to be the "education president."

CHILD CARE

It was gratifying working for a president willing to devote considerable time and attention to issues that might never make headlines, but nevertheless had a major impact on the day-to-day lives of Americans.

One of those issues was child care. The ever-growing number of women entering the workplace needed high-quality, affordable care for their young children if they were going to continue contributing outside the home to the nation's economic health. There was growing pressure to provide federal day care assistance, and Congress had tried in 1987 and 1988 to craft legislation addressing that, but in the end could not come up with either a program or the funding to accomplish the task.

During those two years, then vice president Bush heard from governors about the need for some type of federal child care program, but wanted assurance that whatever legislation came out of Congress would be structured in a way that would work for the states. The governors were especially supportive of a work component associated with welfare reform. In order for that work requirement to be effective, women on welfare with children would need assistance caring for their children.

A number of child care bills surfaced in the House in 1987: some with the support of Congressman Dan Rostenkowski, the chairman of the Committee on Ways and Means; and Congressman Thomas Downey of New York, the chairman of the subcommittee dealing with child care.

There was intense jockeying within Congress over the fundamental principles of the legislation, including whether there should be federally funded day care centers, direct voucher support to families, tax credits, or block grants that would let the states choose how to distribute the money. Much debate surrounded the question of whether the support—vouchers specifically—should be allowed for programs tied to religious facilities. An interesting subplot was opposition to vouchers from folks in the education community who were afraid that a voucher-based child care program would be a precursor to broad, voucher-based support for K–12 schooling.

George Bush continued his consultation with Republican governors on the child care issue shortly after he announced he was running for president in 1987. On one occasion in late 1987, I met with the vice president and Governor Thomas Kean of New Jersey to discuss a number of issues. Governor Kean brought up child care and the vice president agreed that his policy team would work with Kean's staff to generate a statement on the issue for the campaign.

In mid-1988, Bush outlined his Comprehensive Child Care Plan. In it, he called for assistance to all families with similar income levels whether or not the mother was working, putting top priority on low-income families. These families would have a wide range of child care options to choose from under his plan, including family-run and religious agencies. The proposal called for a $1.5 billion child tax credit and also provided $50 million in incentives for employers to develop child care facilities in the workplace. Support would be delivered in the form of vouchers given directly to families to alleviate concerns about excessive regulation from Washington.

Democratic governor Bill Clinton and Republican governor Tom Kean represented the National Governors Association at Senate hearings on child care in June 1988. Both governors argued strongly that federal standards could never account for the varied needs and capabilities of the states. Most of what they said strongly echoed the Bush campaign policy paper on the issue. During battles over the issue in the coming year and a half, enthusiastic support for the basic Bush approach also came from the United States Conference of Catholic Bishops, the National Association of Evangelicals, and other family values groups.

George Bush had heard concerned parents and family groups across the country fret that the federal government was expanding child care facilities without regard for the preference or role of parents in choosing the mode or provider of care. He always felt any program should strengthen the role of parents in providing for their kids, and was committed to build incentives and support for that in his proposals.

Once elected president, Bush signaled his support for child care choice in the budgets he presented to Congress. In March 1989, the president also sent legislation to Congress based on the principles he had enunciated the previous summer in his campaign and in the Republican platform. His plan would create a specific tax credit for low-income working families with children under the age of four.

"Child care is one of the key issues facing the nation," he said when he unveiled the package. "Our policy must have the family as its focus. We must put choices in the hands of parents and not in the hands of government."

In May the president asked his staff to develop a fact sheet outlining the basic principles of his proposed legislation and explaining why he opposed the proposals championed by most of the Democrats. Bush was concerned that the Democratic proposals put too much control in the hands of the federal government rather than in the hands of the parents, where it belonged. He wanted it made clear that he opposed federal standards that could have the unintended consequence of closing child care centers where services were provided by volunteers or religious workers, or standards that did not target low-income families or discriminated against those with one parent working at home to care for the family's children.

Bush knew it would not be easy to get these conservative approaches into legislation palatable to the liberal Congress, but he was prepared to fight for them. These were the principles he stuck to as he compared what he wanted to be passed with a variety of proposals that flowed into and out of congressional committees over the next year and a half.

The president's leadership in opposing any mandatory federal standards—he wanted the states to set those standards—sent a clear message to Congress and most of the constituencies lobbying in support of them. By May 1989, most of these groups abandoned their commitment to federal standards and were willing to accept state control.

In June, the Senate passed a compromise package on child care that included some of the president's provisions. The battle then moved to the House. President Bush made it clear that he opposed and would veto much of the legislation being considered in the House because it placed child care programs under the traditional educational bureaucracy. He firmly opposed placement of child care programs in public school systems, and said most of the bills being considered in the House "had too many federal mandates, did not give proper consideration to religiously affiliated services, and spent too much money creating excessive bureaucracy."

With the action back in the House, George Bush capitalized on his good relationship with Ways and Means chairman Rostenkowski to gain support for his principles in the child care debate. Earlier, in one of the meetings in 1989, the president asked Rostenkowski to help him on the child care bill. Rostenkowski's closest ally on his committee was Congressman Tom Downey of New York, so, at Rostenkowski's urging, I reached out to Downey and invited him to meet me at the White House, and together we laid out an agenda to move forward.

Although he was a member of the Democratic leadership, Downey was sympathetic to two of the most important principles of the Bush proposal: providing support directly to families via tax credits and allowing vouchers to be used at religious-based facilities. I continued to work with Downey throughout the summer and into the fall.

Every time there was an internal discussion on the status of the child care bill, the president emphasized that we should continue to work with Rostenkowski and Downey. Unfortunately, late in 1989, disagreements within the House—not only on specific features of the legislation, but also on the jurisdiction of different committees—kept the bill from coming to a vote.

As we moved into 1990, the president again asked us to refocus our efforts on child care. By then, though, the stalemate in the House was getting worse, so we asked Representative Bill Goodling from Pennsylvania, the ranking Republican member of the Education and Labor Committee, to visit us at the White House. We met in my office along with Tom Scully, who worked with Richard Darman at the Office of Management and Budget. We had a long, detailed conversation about how to get the process moving again. I agreed to spell out in writing, in a letter to Goodling, the specific provisions the president wanted in the legislation, along with some items on which he might be willing to compromise.

After discussing it with the president, I sent a letter that contained the following:

> The President strongly prefers a tax credit approach to child care policy [but] in the spirit of compromise he is willing to accept a carefully crafted grant program. If there is to be a grant component of the bill, the President's preference would be for a "clean" earmarked increase in the Title XX social services block grant program. By clean, I mean that the bill should not contain any federal standards, model or otherwise, nor should it require the states to establish standards.

With that letter in hand, Downey and Goodling were able to work out a compromise package. A year and a half after he sent his proposal to Congress, and after a dozen alternatives had been debated and discarded, Congress finally agreed on a program titled the Child Care and Development Block Grant. It met virtually all of the requirements the president had laid out. Procedurally, it became part of the Omnibus Budget Reconciliation Act, the budget agreement that had been so painfully arrived at through partisan negotiations.

The final version included more than $700 million to be distributed by the states, a tax credit for low-income families with children under the age of thirteen, and a significant expansion of Head Start that would provide child care for the full workday throughout the calendar year. It included religious organizations as potential providers and excluded public schools as providers. It also directed that standards were to be created and enforced not by the federal government but by the states.

Even then the drama was not over. A vote on the budget agreement was scheduled for October 16, and copies of the bill had to be provided to each member of the House early that morning before the vote. The evening before the vote, Tom Scully, Dick Darman, and I went to the office of Speaker Foley to make ourselves available to handle details and questions as the package was being assembled.

Darman and Scully, in their meticulous way, were poring over sections of the legislation as they were printed and brought in for assembly. We had reviewed with the president the major provisions of the package and were there to make sure nothing was compromised in translation. We wanted to make sure the "must have" provisions of a number of specific issues, including child care, didn't mysteriously get left out of the bill as written.

As we were going through the sections of the legislation in the Speaker's office, the package was being assembled painstakingly slowly. We remained there into the late hours of the evening— the *very late* hours. At around 2:30 a.m., the section of the bill with the child care provisions arrived. Tom Scully reviewed them and noticed that the provisions relating to vouchers and use of the vouchers at religious-based facilities were not what had been agreed upon.

I reminded Foley, who was also still there at that late hour, how strongly the president was committed to specific provisions in the legislation. The president would veto the bill if specific things weren't in there, I told him, and that included the features of the child care legislation.

The Speaker tried to persuade me that the mistake could be corrected in a later piece of legislation, that there wasn't time to make the changes to the package.

I repeated what I said earlier: the president will veto this bill the way it is now written.

Foley was incredulous. The president would never veto such a major piece of legislation because of the provisions of a child care amendment.

I said that I was positive he would, and that if Foley didn't believe me we could call the president, then and there at 2:30 a.m., to ask him.

Intent on calling what he thought was a bluff, the Speaker said he wanted to hear it directly from the president. So, despite the late hour, I picked up the phone and called the White House. One of the ushers answered and woke the president.

When Foley questioned the president, Bush confirmed that the provisions had to be in the bill or he would indeed veto it. The moment Foley hung up, he sent his staff scurrying to get that section reprinted and inserted back into the package.

George Bush had made a commitment and George Bush kept his commitment, even if it meant getting up in the middle of the night to do so.

8

The Compassionate Conservative

S ince the early days of the 1988 campaign, the Washington press corps and national media had been fixated on what they called "the vision thing." While many commentators acknowledged Bush's foreign policy prowess, few of them recognized the domestic philosophy that had been staring them in the face for months—honed over years, in fact. Bush articulated his domestic vision time and again on the campaign trail and in proposals from the White House, but journalists failed to appreciate how broad and encompassing the Bush domestic agenda was.

The Bush agenda had no shorthand phrase or snappy soundbite for them to get their heads around. No "Great Society" or "New Deal" catchphrase on which they could hang their headlines. Throughout his four years in the White House, President Bush was willing to take on even the most controversial issues—civil rights, crime and drugs, welfare and agriculture, immigration—despite the legislative odds he faced. He made sure any solutions he proposed were based on solid conservative principles and reflected what was best for all America, not just for the noisiest interest groups.

Although he did not always get his bills passed during his four years in the White House, his focus and persistence laid the foundations on which successors of both political stripes were able to successfully build. In many ways, the Bush agenda—his vision of a compassionate conservatism—outlasted the Bush presidency.

CIVIL RIGHTS AND THE AMERICANS WITH DISABILITIES ACT

After Lincoln's grand Emancipation Proclamation and the Thirteenth, Fourteenth, and Fifteenth Amendments to our Constitution, there was not much significant legislative implementation of equal rights for all Americans until after World War II. Then Presidents Truman, Eisenhower, Kennedy, and Johnson, in a series of executive orders and legislation, began to turn the promise of equality into reality.

In 1968 George Bush, as a Republican congressman from still largely segregated Texas, voted to support the Civil Rights Act of 1968, of which Title VIII, known as the Fair Housing Act, outlawed discrimination in the sale, rental, or provision of finance in housing based on race, nationality, or religion. He, along with 91 percent of his Republican colleagues in the House, supported the bill, compared with only 71 percent of the Democrats. In the Senate, 86 percent of the Republicans and 71 percent of the Democrats supported the legislation.

It's a little-known fact that similar patterns prevailed in virtually every piece of major civil rights legislation passed in the postwar period. But our liberal media have succeeded in stereotyping the Democratic Party as the principal champion of equal rights.

George and Barbara Bush's lives were guided by a strong moral and cultural compass. They grew up in New England and were deeply opposed to racial discrimination. Their four years in the White House were preceded by a long history of support for civil rights and opposition to discrimination on any basis.

For many years before George Bush became president, the Bushes were generous supporters of the United Negro College Fund. They both remained interested, supportive, and involved with that association throughout his presidency and remain so to this day. Barbara Bush served a term on the board of directors for the medical school of Morehouse College, a historically African American university in Atlanta, and she was instrumental in helping the president to convince Dr. Louis Sullivan, the founding dean of the Morehouse School of Medicine, to join the Bush cabinet as secretary of health and human services.

Barbara Bush has written that one of her most disturbing experiences occurred when she drove her children from Texas to their summer home in Kennebunkport, Maine, in the early 1960s. She sometimes was joined on those trips by two African American women, Julia May Cooper and Otha Fitzgerald. Barbara was horrified that her friends and companions were not permitted to accompany her and her children in some hotels and restaurants in the South. The reality of that bigotry angered her and she refused to stay or eat anywhere that excluded them.

As president, George Bush pledged to address two of his moral priorities: civil rights and a leveling of the playing field for disabled Americans. In one of my first morning meetings with the president, on January 23, just three days after the inauguration, we discussed items that he wanted to make sure would be included in the budget. On his list of "must haves," despite the

tough budget shortfalls he knew were ahead, was $60 million to
support historically black colleges and universities such as Morehouse College. Later, he established a new Presidential Advisory
Board on Historically Black Colleges and Universities to advise
him and the Secretary of Education on programs to improve and
strengthen those institutions.

Bush also had a history with the disabled community. As vice
president, he had been in charge of President Reagan's Task
Force on Regulatory Relief, and in that capacity became familiar
with the labyrinth of rules and regulations associated with disability legislation.

Vice President Bush and his legal counsel, Boyden Gray, were
tasked with reviewing the regulations as implemented under the
Education of All Handicapped Children Act. In order to better
fulfill those responsibilities, he sought advice on disability issues
from Evan Kemp, a lawyer and activist who experienced discrimination against the disabled firsthand in both the private
sector and government before becoming director of the Disability Rights Center.

Kemp, who was appointed by Ronald Reagan to serve on the
Equal Employment Opportunity Commission, helped Bush prepare for a speech the vice president gave to a disability rights
group, and over the years the two became quite close. Early in
1989, while serving as commissioner of the Equal Employment
Opportunity Commission, Kemp sent the president a supportive
letter, along with a copy of the Americans with Disabilities Act
(ADA) as it had originally been drafted.

Bush also learned about disabilities issues from Justin Dart,
a friend of his from Texas. Dart served on the Texas Governor's
Committee on the Handicapped. Confined to a wheelchair by
polio, he was a strong supporter of and champion for removing

barriers that made it difficult for disabled Americans to enter into productive employment or to enjoy full, meaningful lives.

In his speech at the Republican convention, Bush said, "I am going to do whatever it takes to make sure the disabled are included in the mainstream. For too long they've been left out, but they're not going to be left out anymore."

Gray knew how deeply the president felt on this issue, but he cautioned him that getting a bill that fulfilled his goal without overregulating and overconstraining businesses would be difficult. The president did not disagree; his experience with the regulatory process had taught him how true that was. He was ready to fight for good legislation he believed in, but he was also not afraid to buck the political tide to fight against legislation he thought unworthy.

When I met with the president a couple of days later with Gray and Attorney General Thornburgh, he told us of his earlier conversation with Gray and asked us to work together on suitable legislation. He wanted a plan for how the administration could and should interact with Congress on the ADA. Gray and Thornburgh explained to us that the battle over the legislation would be a war over the impact of a few dozen key words and how those words were interpreted in the courts. They warned us that the public would not appreciate our fighting against what might appear to be good legislation over a handful of words. Bush's answer to that was, "We have to get it right." Later in the month, Gray and I went to Thornburgh's office to put together some drafts of legislation for the president.

The three of us met with the president again in early spring to go over our recommendations. In that meeting, it became very clear that the difficult issues turned on legalistic and subtle interpretations of specific words and phrasing in the legislation—

those few dozen key words that Thornburgh first warned us about. That meant the president was completely reliant on his legal counsel and attorney general to advise him on what was acceptable in the language and what was not. As the bills worked their way through Congress, Boyden Gray and Richard Thornburgh were there all the way—meeting with key House and Senate members to get the wording exactly right.

George Bush remained focused on getting an effective Americans with Disabilities Act and a constructive civil rights bill passed by Congress. The last thing Bush wanted was to have to veto a civil rights bill or a bill supported by the disabled community. Perhaps because of that concern and his own strong support of the issues, the president often gave the status of those bills extra attention in our morning meetings.

To assist the efforts of Gray and Thornburgh, early in the process I began meeting with Senator Ted Kennedy, who had a strong interest in each of the issues and was the focal point for both bills in the Senate. I told the senator of the president's strong commitment to and support for the civil rights bill and the Americans with Disabilities Act. I also informed him that Boyden Gray had raised some legal and technical concerns about the initial draft. After that meeting, the senator and I exchanged several letters confirming what we had discussed and outlining an agenda to get the legislation through Congress. President Bush was quite pleased when I showed him the letters.

We were making constructive progress on the ADA, which pleased me as much as it did the president. As governor of New Hampshire, I had worked hard to modernize facilities and services for the developmentally disabled in the state. I worked closely with our state Council on Developmental Disabilities and our Granite State Independent Living Foundation to improve work and recreation opportunities for those with disabilities. In

New Hampshire I had even personally negotiated a state contract to replace our marginally qualified state psychiatric services professionals with private providers from the Dartmouth
Medical School who could offer a better quality of service, an
innovative approach in the 1980s.

In April, the president asked Gray and me to his office to discuss a memo Gray had prepared outlining the broad provisions of
the ADA and describing the legal and technical issues to be negotiated before the legislation was acceptable. The president again
indicated that he had to rely on his legal counsel and attorney
general to evaluate the complex nuances involved in both acts.

At times Bush was clearly frustrated because the negotiations
with Congress over critical legal nuances, word by word, created
long delays. Throughout the process, however, he maintained his
confidence in Gray and Thornburgh. I continued working with
Senator Kennedy to find a compromise.

Armed with detailed instructions from Gray, I met several
times with the senator, often just to haggle over a single word.
Justin Dart and Evan Kemp stuck with us as well, staying in close
touch with the White House. During our most difficult negotiations, William Roper, a senior advisor in the White House on disabilities issues, stepped in with memos about issues that needed
to be resolved.

Finally Gray, Thornburgh, and I were able to get agreement
with Senator Kennedy on all of the language. Once that was
accomplished in the early summer of 1990, Congress sent the
president an ADA bill to sign.

A Rose Garden gathering on July 26 brought together members of the disability community and longtime supporters of the
legislation. With Evan Kemp and Justin Dart sitting in their
wheelchairs on either side of him, George Bush signed the
Americans with Disabilities Act of 1990.

"This act is powerful in its simplicity," Bush said at the ceremony. "It will ensure that people with disabilities are given the basic guarantees for which they have worked so long and so hard: independence, freedom of choice, control of their lives, the opportunity to blend fully and equally into the rich mosaic of the American mainstream."

Success on the ADA did not automatically lead to success on the civil rights bill. The president was consistent in trying to appreciate the implications of the language of that bill as well. He met with the Commission on Civil Rights in May 1990 and invited key members of Congress to join him. The proposed legislation was designed to deal with a number of Supreme Court cases that had ended up limiting the ability of employees to sue for discrimination by employers. The challenge was how to craft legislation that restored those civil rights without creating an incentive for quotas in employment.

In that meeting he described how, over a period of weeks, he had sought advice on the bill from leaders representing "America's rich tapestry of cultural, religious, and ethnic diversity." He stressed that the shared concern to produce a bill should not lure the commission or the members of Congress into language that would either directly or indirectly require quotas. He urged Congress to work further to find a compromise he could accept.

The first version of the civil rights bill was pushed through Congress a little too quickly by some of its more liberal supporters. It contained language that the White House had, all along, said was unacceptable because it imposed unreasonable obligations on business and government institutions. The president was, regretfully, faced with a responsibility he did not relish: on the advice of Boyden Gray and Dick Thornburgh, he had to veto it.

Getting the most from the power of the veto is an art form, one that George Bush mastered quite handily. The mere threat of a veto is often as effective as the veto itself, depending on when and how it is wielded.

The process starts with messages to Congress, sometimes direct and sometimes sent through the press, suggesting that cabinet officers might be recommending to the president that he veto a particular piece of legislation unless it is adjusted to address his concerns.

That threat is ratcheted up when the entire cabinet, as well as the White House staff, signals that it too is recommending a veto. The entire administration is behind the threat, in other words.

At that point, it is ramped up even further by a signal that the president himself is considering the use of a veto. The last step is the clearest. Word gets out that "the president will veto the legislation" if this or if that is not added to or subtracted from the bill.

Most of the time the mere threat of a veto is sufficient to encourage members of Congress, who usually really do want legislation to be signed, to appease the president by modifying the bill.

On rare occasions Congress chooses to test a president's fortitude by passing a bill the way it wants instead of compromising. The president has to decide whether to veto it and send it back to Congress for reconsideration or whether it's smarter to live with the bill as submitted.

While I was chief of staff, there were about three dozen bills that George Bush decided he had to veto. And while I was there, every single one of his vetoes was sustained. Late in 1992, after I had left the White House, the one and only override of a Bush veto occurred on a bill related to the telecommunications industry.

As we were going through this process of deciding whether to veto the Civil Rights Bill of 1990, *The New York Times* ran an op-ed piece by Charles Fried, the distinguished professor at Harvard Law School who had been solicitor general of the United

States from 1985 to 1989. The president knew and respected Fried.

In his essay, titled "The Civil Rights Sham of 1990," Fried argued that the civil rights bill as passed by Congress was one that would allow plaintiffs to "prevail even over defendants who have done nothing wrong, who had not discriminated." Fried described the bill as "a miscellany of technical provisions . . . cooked up by a specialized plaintiffs' bar to make it easier for them to win their cases and recover fees from losing parties when they do."

With that added assurance of the bill's inherent flaws, the president vetoed it.

In order to minimize the political backlash from his action, the president accompanied his veto with a proposed new bill that he said he could and would sign. I immediately went back to the Hill with Gray to reengage with Senator Kennedy to produce a bill acceptable to both Congress and the president.

This process would take more than a few days or weeks. In fact, it took more than a year of long interactions with members of the House and Senate, and Senator Kennedy's office in particular. Finally, in the fall of 1991, we found common ground and reached an agreement. When Boyden Gray and I reported our success to the president, it was the happiest I saw him during that long, tough year.

I made a point of telling the president how impressed I was with Senator Kennedy. The senator always came to meetings prepared. He understood the nuances involved, yet stayed focused on reaching a compromise. The negotiations were serious. They were long, and often quite intense, but the senator and I came out of them much closer. In fact, we often fondly reminisced in the years afterward about the lengthy and difficult sessions leading to a rewarding conclusion.

The president considered the legislation significant enough to warrant a major signing ceremony. On November 21, he invited key players from Congress and major support groups to join him as he signed the Civil Rights Act of 1991.

"We had to work hard for this agreement," he admitted at the ceremony. "The bill passed both houses of Congress overwhelmingly with broad support from both sides of the aisle. A tip of the hat goes to Senator Kennedy and former congressman Hawkins who way back in February 1990 got the ball rolling."

He also thanked key members of Congress such as senators Bob Dole, Jack Danforth, and Orrin Hatch, as well as congressmen Bob Michel, Bill Goodling, and Henry Hyde, for working hard to pass legislation that "fulfills those principles that I outlined in the Rose Garden last year."

He then remarked on the angst he felt when he could not accept the bill last year.

"No one likes to oppose a bill containing the words 'civil rights,' especially me," he lamented. "And no one in Congress likes to vote against one, either. I owe a debt of gratitude to those who stood with us against counterproductive legislation last year and again earlier this year, as well as those that led the way towards the important agreement we've reached today. . . . I believe this is in the best interest of the United States."

Although it took more than half a year to work out the details for the Americans with Disabilities Act, and nearly three years from his inauguration to get a civil rights bill he could sign, George Bush delivered on his pledges. His commitment to moral principles, and his willingness to stand firm on those principles, gave the country two pieces of legislation that not only served minorities and disabled individuals well, but did so in a way that was fair to all Americans.

IMMIGRATION

In the 1980s, America faced an immigration problem remarkably similar to the one we face today. Millions of immigrants had illegally crossed the border into the United States, and there was a growing demand to give them some sort of legal status. Congress and the Reagan administration eventually agreed on an Immigration Reform and Control Act (IRCA) in 1986 that addressed some, but not all, of the issues.

The legislation was supposed to contain strong provisions to stop those border crossings and penalize employers for hiring illegal aliens, but did not provide enough resources to enforce the laws adequately. IRCA also offered amnesty for some illegal aliens who had been in America continually since January 1982. There were, additionally, some special case provisions, but fundamentally, the legislation was intended to legalize the presence of over three million people who were in the United States illegally.

By 1988, Florida, Texas, and California were facing problems stemming from the continued large inflows of immigrants, driven to some extent by the turmoil in Central America, especially Nicaragua, and Haiti. A week before his inauguration, while he was in Florida, Bush was asked about the situation and pledged to "take a hard look at our immigration policy." It was clear he was going to have to fix the failures of the 1986 legislation.

One of the principal sponsors of the 1986 bill was Senator Alan Simpson of Wyoming, a close friend of George H. W. Bush. Simpson acknowledged the failings of the bill, which was widely known as the Simpson-Mizzoli Immigration Act. Shortly after Bush took office, our domestic policy team gave Simpson a draft of legislation we felt had to be passed. Together, the president and Simpson agreed on what needed to be done and Simpson cosponsored, with Senator Kennedy of Massachusetts, a bill to implement the proposed solutions.

The president had a strong legislative affairs team working on the legislation. Roger Porter and Michael Boskin were both enthusiastic supporters of the new Simpson-Kennedy bill. They both felt that legal immigration was good policy and good economics. Porter collaborated with Simpson and Kennedy to try to pass a bill that met the president's conditions.

There were two provisions the president was adamant about: one that made it easier for families separated by borders to be reunited legally, and another that made it easier for highly skilled workers—especially scientists, engineers, and educators—to come to America. To deal with the failures of the earlier act, the president wanted real teeth and resources in the enforcement provisions of the new one and encouraged Congress to include them.

Porter deftly worked Congress, which finally passed a bill, Legislation to Amend the Immigration and Nationality Act, and sent it to the president for signature in November 1990. It increased the overall annual total of legal immigrants permitted entry into the United States to 700,000. In his remarks at the signing ceremony for the bill, Bush applauded the fact that it was "good for families, good for business, good for crime-fighting, and good for America."

CRIME AND DRUGS

Violent crime was a central issue during the campaign against Michael Dukakis, partly because Al Gore introduced the infamous Willie Horton issue during the Democratic primaries, but also because of the Massachusetts governor's tepid response to a question about the death penalty during one of the debates. Many pundits believed his robotic response to the question of whether he would support capital punishment if the perpetrator had raped and killed his wife had definitely hurt him in the election.

George Bush campaigned hard on the issue of crime and went into office ready to deliver on his commitment to do something about it. In June 1989, less than six months into his term, the president sent Congress a proposed bill: Legislation to Combat Violent Crime.

The president traveled around the country to lobby law enforcement groups directly. He proposed both legislative reforms and nonlegislative executive actions focused on four major objectives: strengthening current laws; augmenting enforcement; enhancing prosecution; and expanding prison capacity. He also wanted to modernize and strengthen the nation's laws and include a number of provisions dealing specifically with drug-related crime.

Attorney General Thornburgh took the lead in working with Congress to try to get a crime bill passed that would include all the Bush provisions. Although Congress thought the Bush proposals were too tough, Thornburgh was able to get the president a bill that included strong provisions on the prosecution of fraud, protection of children from abuse, and prosecution of child pornographers. That bill came to the president in 1990 and he signed it in November, making it clear at the time that he was doing so reluctantly, because he felt there was more to be done.

Bush would resend his proposals to Congress in 1991, and again in 1992. Although he was never able to get them back to his desk in the form of legislation, virtually all of them were separately passed in some form by the House and Senate. In the 1992 campaign, Bush said he would work in a second term to reconcile the various versions. Virtually all of his proposals—including the death penalty provisions—were included in a crime bill signed by President Clinton in 1994.

Drugs were a principal factor in much of the crime, so Bush placed great emphasis on that topic in all these negotiations. Bill Bennett, Ronald Reagan's secretary of education, served as the new, congressionally created director of the Office of National Drug Control Policy, better known as the drug czar. He and the president put together a National Drug Control Strategy, and Bennett, with the president's support, was able to get Congress to double the amount of money allocated to fighting drug-related crimes. Congress also nearly tripled the funding for state and local law enforcement to fight drug-related crime.

Bush often went out of his way to acknowledge fellow political leaders' taking politically courageous action in an effort to get things done. One such call was with President Virgilio Barco Vargas of Colombia. At great personal peril, Barco had taken on the drug cartels in his country and waged a tenacious and unyielding battle against drug production and trafficking. Bush felt he could help Barco in his battles by doing something public to acknowledge his efforts, and decided to attend a "drug summit" in Cartagena, Colombia, in February 1990 with Barco, President Alan García of Peru, and President Jaime Paz Zamora of Bolivia.

Our Secret Service was not thrilled to hear of the president's decision to attend the summit. The Secret Service officials had significant concerns about security in South America, and in Cartagena in particular. They had doubts about security everywhere in Colombia, in fact, but the president insisted he needed to attend to show support of and appreciation for the Andean presidents' efforts against the cocaine trade, so the Secret Service did the usual thorough job—and then some—to be sure he would be safe. We took some additional, unusual steps because of the security risks. With the help of the Department of Defense, I arranged for naval assets to be nearby in case the president had to be evacuated by air or helicopter to a safe haven or needed our finest medical facilities at hand.

I had a bit of fun during our preparation for the trip. In the week before we departed, a couple of press articles appeared quoting unnamed sources who claimed that the drug cartels might have obtained surface-to-air missiles and were planning to shoot down the president's plane as it flew into Colombia.

One afternoon, when a couple of members of the press were goading me on that issue, I told them we had the situation under control. I explained that we had learned the cartels actually had only one missile, so our plan was to paint the press plane to look like *Air Force One* and send it in first as a decoy. Needless to say, I ended up on the receiving end of a few press pads hurled at me for that one.

With his high-profile attendance at the drug summit, the president not only added credibility and support to Barco's efforts, but put pressure on both Peru and Bolivia also to be more aggressive in eradicating the coca cultivation that was the source of much of America's cocaine. At the summit the president secured a commitment from those countries to participate in a $2.5 billion, five-year program funded primarily by the United States to expand the battle against drug crops, drug processing, drug trafficking, and drug profiteering.

Recognizing that the drug issue was a problem as much of demand as of supply, Bush successfully increased funding for drug treatment programs by over $1 billion, doubling what had been allocated before. The additional funding enabled new programs to be introduced into schools, colleges, and universities. Bush also directed the Office of National Drug Control Policy to work with the Partnership for a Drug-Free America, a private group formed to help with antidrug education. James Burke, a former CEO of Johnson & Johnson, agreed to chair that partnership, and received the president's full support. To this day, that program successfully promotes an effective antidrug message through public service announcements in the media.

On the supply side, Bush increased funding to attack the importation of drugs into the country. He also worked diligently with Latin American governments to stem the tide at the source. He built on efforts here in the United States by increasing the level of cooperation with countries such as Colombia, Bolivia, and Peru, whose representatives Bush had joined at the drug summit in Cartagena. They agreed to expand their attack on drugs at every stage, from growing to processing to exporting.

HEALTH CARE REFORM, WELFARE REFORM, AND AGRICULTURE

George Bush wanted to solve the problem of the growth in health care costs, which was becoming a serious issue and was keeping a growing number of Americans from affordable health care. Bush had a vision for health care reform. His was a private sector, market-based approach consistent with his overall philosophy and designed to slow the growth in costs, relieve the states of the heavy burden of federal mandates, and make health care affordable for more American businesses and families.

His proposed legislation included provisions to reduce the excessive federally mandated benefits that had been pressed on the states by strong constituencies over the previous decade. His recommendations also included incentive-based reforms for malpractice, an allowance for small-business health insurance networks, increased tax deductibility of premiums for small businesses, tax credits and deductions for individual and family premiums, and a system to improve the availability of information to consumers.

The Democrats in Congress really didn't like any of his proposals and refused to allow his program to come to a vote. But when the Republicans won control of the House of Representatives in 1994, a lot of what Bush had proposed was incorporated into reform legislation sponsored by Senator Kennedy and Senator Nancy Kassebaum of Kansas.

Bush also wanted to get legislation to deal with an issue that had the backing of both Republican and Democratic governors: welfare reform. As he had traveled around the country, he had heard from both Republican and Democratic governors that the principal welfare program funded by the government, Aid to Families with Dependent Children (AFDC), was not working. Conservatives felt it was locking the poor into a life of welfare; liberals thought it failed to provide sufficient assistance. Both sides had come to recognize that AFDC was encouraging dependency.

The governors, in a bipartisan chorus, were also clamoring for flexibility in administering the program. The specific needs of their own states were not being addressed because of rigid rules imposed by Washington. Because of his conversations with governors, Bush understood clearly that all the welfare programs that had been enacted and modified over the past half century were just not working well.

Although Congress had passed, in the last year of the Reagan presidency, a Family Support Act to change a few of those rigid rules, everyone recognized that this was just a small step toward fixing a very large problem. In spite of the good intentions of the previous legislative efforts, the process was failing badly. Bush believed that good welfare reform should steer recipients into education, jobs, and training. He had come to feel that increasing support without a work or education requirement would condemn recipients to a life of dependency.

Bush built all these principles into a very comprehensive proposal for welfare reform, which he sent to Congress. Of course, he proposed the legislation to a Congress dominated by Democrats, many of whom had drafted the most ineffective components of some of these programs in the first place. His welfare proposals to Congress came back gutted. Bush's successor, Bill Clinton, caught a mixed blessing of a break when the 1994 midterm elections put the House back in the hands of Republicans for the first time in more than forty years. The new Republican majority was eager to enact the sort of changes that both Bush and Clinton saw as necessary, so America got a good welfare reform law. If George Bush had had the same Republican majority in Congress during his tenure, he would have been able to get a welfare reform package, which would certainly have paralleled what was eventually adopted during the next administration.

George Bush also worked with Congress to pass legislation to unwind some of the agricultural subsidy programs on which America's farm community had become chronically dependent. His approach was to replace subsidies, which were usually tied to planting quotas, with market-based initiatives that gave farmers more flexibility on what they could plant and helped to expand farm exports.

Increased flexibility allowed farmers to decide how to make the most profitable use of their land without being penalized for their crop selections. As a result, they were able to easily adapt to changes in market demand and consumer interest and respond to export opportunities as they arose.

The Bush initiatives stimulated farm income to record levels in both 1989 and 1990, and produced an agriculture export trade surplus of $15 billion in 1991. Bush's market-based strategy proved to be a turning point for the American agricultural economy.

POINTS OF LIGHT

One of President Bush's most enduring and far-reaching initiatives was actually a nongovernment initiative: his Points of Light Foundation. George Bush felt that one of the strongest and most effective tools to help people in need was America's deep commitment to volunteer service and charity work. In his 1989 inaugural address he said, "I've spoken of a thousand points of light, of all the community organizations that are spread like stars throughout the nation doing good. . . . From now on in America, any definition of a successful life must include service to others."

President Bush made voluntary community service one of his principal agenda items. In the first weeks of his administration, he established the White House Office of National Service, which was devoted exclusively to supporting community service across the country. We brought Greg Petersmeyer to the White House to set up the Points of Light Foundation as a private, nonprofit organization that would help coordinate and reward charitable service and volunteerism across the country.

The focus on volunteerism even won over a few Democrats. There was, however, a fundamental difference between their approach and his. The Democrats wanted to pay the volunteers, but Bush felt such a program would die when the funding ran out. However, seed money was needed to establish a permanent nationwide program, so the president and Congress compromised on a bill that provided about $250 million for service programs over three years, to be distributed by a presidentially appointed commission. Congress also agreed to provide an additional $22.5 million to establish the Points of Light Foundation.

Greg Petersmeyer developed the concept of a daily point of light. Since its initiation, the foundation has, every Monday through Friday, honored an individual or group for good work done in local communities. To date over five thousand Points of Light Awards have been given, and many additional programs have been implemented as the foundation continues to grow and serve the nation. The Points of Light Foundation lives on as an independent entity to encourage, coordinate, and facilitate America's volunteer programs.

As expected, many liberal critics carped: they criticized the president's effort as merely a short-term political ploy that had no value, but the impact and longevity of this effort have proved all those critics wrong. The foundation's work has helped to reinforce the value of volunteerism and public service, and now many public schools and universities across the country have adopted a requirement for some type of public service commitment from students before allowing them to graduate. Bush's inaugural vision of "a thousand points of light" continues to shine as brightly now as it did then, reflected in the many thousands of people who volunteer across the country every day.

9

Desert Storm

===

As we moved through the summer of 1990, the budget fight with the Democratic Congress was taking on a more confrontational tone when a different confrontation half a world away presented itself. In July 1990, the world watched as Saddam Hussein, Iraq's ironfisted ruler, taunted his Arab neighbors. Saddam was particularly piqued with OPEC, the oil-producing cartel of which Iraq was a member. Oil prices had plummeted, and Saddam accused his fellow OPEC members of exceeding their production quotas to make up for the lost revenue. He directed his most bitter ire at the United Arab Emirates and Kuwait. It was rapidly developing into a touchy and potentially explosive international situation, just as our negotiations on the budget began to heat up in Washington.

Saddam Hussein's beef with Kuwait went beyond the issue of oil production. They had been arguing over their common boundary, which happened to pass through the rich oil fields of the Rumaila area. Much of Rumaila's oil production, and its income, came from the neutral zone that Iraq and Kuwait shared. They

were also feuding over some islands in the Persian Gulf. In particular, Saddam wanted to maintain control of the large island
of Bubiyan, which would facilitate the Iraqis' access to the Gulf
shipping routes.

After publicly accusing Kuwait and the UAE of exceeding
OPEC production limits, Saddam Hussein warned them that
Iraq would take action to correct the situation. Soon he had escalated the militancy in his rhetoric, accusing Kuwait and the UAE
of "military aggression." Kuwait asked the Arab League to help
negotiate a solution to the dispute. As Saddam Hussein sharp-
ened his rhetoric, Kuwait put its small military forces on alert.

President Bush, in an effort to dissuade the Iraqis from doing
anything rash, arranged for a joint U.S.-UAE military exercise to
underscore America's support for the UAE and signal our concern for and interest in the region. Saudi Arabia also put its own
forces on alert, but insisted that the issue could still be settled
within the Arab community.

During the last ten days of July, George Bush took to the
phones in his signature one-on-one diplomatic efforts. He spoke
with President Mubarak of Egypt and King Fahd of Saudi Arabia.
He spoke with Jordan's King Hussein and with the Saudi ambassador in Washington, Prince Bandar bin Sultan. All of them were
of the opinion that, despite the sharp words from Baghdad, an
attack was not in the cards.

Bush continued his consultations with our allies, some of whom
were by then even flying to Baghdad for face-to-face meetings
with Saddam. Mubarak was especially active and remained confident that "accommodation can be worked out without delay."
He urged the United States to be temperate in its statements
and actions. The Saudis told Bush they were confident Mubarak
could defuse the situation.

On July 25, Saddam Hussein requested a quick meeting with

the United States' ambassador in Iraq, April Glaspie. With no time to get official instructions from the State Department because of the eight-hour time difference between Iraq and Washington, she went to the meeting primarily to hear what the Iraqi ruler wanted to tell the United States. In her report of the meeting, Glaspie said that Saddam had told President Mubarak of Egypt, "Nothing serious will happen" until after Saddam met with the Kuwaiti crown prince at the end of July.

Glaspie responded to Hussein with the standard State Department line: although the United States does not take positions on border disputes between friendly countries, it prefers that such differences be resolved by peaceful means. After the meeting, she summarized her talks for her superiors at the State Department. She told the department that she thought Saddam was beginning to worry a little about the concerns being expressed by many of the Arab countries, but she felt he remained rather belligerent.

Some critics have suggested that Glaspie's response did not make it clear that the United States would use force to expel an Iraqi invasion of Kuwait. Saddam Hussein needed no such reminders of American resolve, something the Iraqi prime minister, Tariq Aziz, later made made clear in a 1996 PBS *Frontline* interview. Aziz also noted that Saddam mistakenly believed that U.S. military action would be limited. He felt that since Vietnam, the United States government and its citizens had no stomach for any serious projection of American military power. He was confident that his army of 120,000 well-equipped troops, which was the third largest in the world at that time, could deal with any token U.S. response.

In 2008 Glaspie elaborated on the meeting and its aftermath in an interview with a Lebanese newspaper: "It is over. Nobody wants to take the blame. I am quite happy to take the blame.

Perhaps I was not able to make Saddam Hussein believe that we would do what we said we would do, but in all honesty, I don't think anybody in the world could have persuaded him." She was right.

Kuwait and the UAE, meanwhile, negotiated a new oil pricing arrangement that they hoped would placate Iraq. Mubarak again told President Bush of the assurances he had from Saddam that his military forces would remain far from the Kuwaiti border. But the president was hearing otherwise in his daily intelligence reports. The CIA had told the president that in the last week of July Saddam had massed nearly 120,000 troops on his southern border, far outnumbering Kuwait's own military.

The new oil pricing agreement failed to satisfy Saddam. He insisted that Kuwait and the UAE reopen talks on the boundaries of the neutral zone and that Kuwait write off debts incurred by Iraq during the Iran-Iraq war. On July 31, the two sides were meeting in Saudi Arabia under the auspices of both President Mubarak and King Fahd. They were at an impasse, but everyone expected the talks to resume soon in Baghdad.

Then, on August 1, 1990, Iraq invaded Kuwait. George Bush first heard about it from Brent Scowcroft around 9:00 p.m. Washington time. Although his friends in the region had been assuring him that an invasion was not imminent, Bush knew that moving 120,000 troops into an offensive position is not a signal of peaceful intent. Iraq swept into Kuwait, taking full advantage of its own larger, more powerful army. The Kuwaitis had no chance.

The president convened a meeting of the National Security Council for early the next morning. He had long been scheduled to go to Aspen, Colorado, the next day for an event at the Aspen Institute and to meet the British prime minister, Margaret Thatcher. Intent on keeping that commitment even in the face of crisis, Bush called the U.S. ambassador to the United Nations,

Thomas Pickering, and requested that he get, as soon as possible, a U.N. condemnation of Iraq. He also asked Pickering to press for an emergency meeting of the United Nations Security Council.

Energizing the United Nations to take the lead in condemning Iraq's actions could be important, Bush believed. He knew from his days there as U.S. ambassador what the United Nations could and could not do. Its effectiveness had been blunted during the Cold War years by antagonism among members of the Security Council—principally the United States and the Soviet Union—but Bush felt that the warmer relations with Gorbachev and the Soviets could make the United Nations a useful tool of diplomacy. He worried that the Soviet Union's status as a principal supplier of military equipment to Iraq might dash those hopes, but he was determined to try to urge Gorbachev to partner with the United States in dealing with this naked act of aggression.

That night Scowcroft convened a meeting of the Deputies Committee that started at 11:00 p.m. and lasted for three hours. Afterward, he recommended to the president that both Iraqi and Kuwaiti assets in the United States be frozen before Iraq was able to pull them out. The president had Boyden Gray prepare the appropriate executive orders and, at 4:30 the following morning, he signed them.

Intelligence reports of troop movements on the Iraqi side of the border with Saudi Arabia, the United States' principal ally in the region, also worried Bush. Our Arab allies were still telling us to maintain a measured position, however, and Bush felt it important to heed that advice and avoid unilateral action. To proceed without Arab support would destroy any credibility and influence the United States had in that part of the world.

It was still important for the United States, while waiting to consult with our Arab allies, to demonstrate support for the Kuwaitis and the Saudis. The president redirected part of our

regional naval fleet to the Persian Gulf and inquired about getting some of our aircraft into the region. Scowcroft said the State
Department was already trying to get the Saudis to host a squadron of F-15 fighters on their territory.

Later that morning the U.N. Security Council voted 14–0
on a U.S.-sponsored resolution condemning Iraq's invasion of
Kuwait. It demanded that Iraq immediately remove its troops
from Kuwait and insisted that the dispute be resolved with negotiations. Most important of all, the resolution was not vetoed in
the Security Council by the Soviet Union as had happened so
many times in the past. George Bush's friendly relationship with
Mikhail Gorbachev was paying off.

The president's core national security group gathered in the
Oval Office at 7:00 a.m. and half an hour later CIA Director
Bill Webster arrived to show us the latest intelligence reports. At
8:00 a.m. the president went to the Cabinet Room for a meeting
of the National Security Council.

Before the start of his NSC meeting, Bush addressed a reporters' pool escorted into the room for a few moments. He con-
demned the invasion and described the steps that had already
been taken in response. To the inevitable question of whether
he was considering military intervention, the president said he
was not yet contemplating such action. Even if he was going to
use force, he said, he would not announce it at an informal press
gathering.

The NSC meeting had been hastily put together. A major topic
of discussion was the global economic impact of the aggression,
particularly its effect on oil supplies. Iraq's biggest leverage was
its oil reserves, and we discussed the possibility of putting pressure on Saddam by blocking his ability to sell that oil. We wanted
to cut off his main source of financial support, but because Iraq
was such a major source of oil, accounting for as much as 5 per-

cent of the global supply at the time, blocking sales might seriously harm the world economy.

Toward the end of the meeting the president asked the chairman of the Joint Chiefs of Staff, Colin Powell, to lay out in general terms some of the potential military options. Powell had brought along the commander of Central Command, General Norman Schwarzkopf, who described in detail the air and naval assets we had in the region and how they could react.

Bush also wanted to know about the status of American citizens in both Kuwait and Iraq.

The meeting closed with a discussion of how to assemble partners for whatever action had to be taken. Much of it focused on gathering support at the United Nations and working hard to maintain the constructive response we had received thus far from the Soviet Union.

Immediately after the meeting, President Bush and Brent Scowcroft reviewed the information raised in it. Scowcroft was particularly disappointed that most at the meeting failed to appreciate the absolute "intolerability" of the invasion to U.S. interests. Then the president, Brent Scowcroft, and I jumped into a waiting car and rushed to Andrews Air Force Base to board a Gulfstream C-20 aircraft, which would be small enough to land at the Aspen airport. We focused on Kuwait all the way to Colorado. The president wanted his comments at Aspen to let the world know that America would not accept Saddam's occupation of Kuwait.

In Aspen, George Bush met with Margaret Thatcher and a small gathering of her team at the home of the U.S. ambassador to the United Kingdom, Henry Catto. Bush informed the British prime minister that Jim Baker was headed to Moscow to try to work out a joint statement condemning the actions of the Iraqis. He also briefed her on his conversations with King Hussein and Hosni Mubarak.

As usual, Thatcher was clear and direct. She was not complimentary in her comments about King Hussein of Jordan, who was refusing to join the coalition against Iraq, and she stressed the importance of getting the Saudis to sign on to whatever option the coalition chose to pursue. The president and Mrs. Thatcher then held a joint press conference at which they repeated their condemnation of the invasion and again warned the Iraqis to withdraw and allow the restoration of the Kuwaiti government.

Back at Catto's house, Bush got on the phone with King Fahd of Saudi Arabia. The king explained how he had tried to mediate between Saddam Hussein and the Kuwaitis. He was furious because Saddam had assured him there would be no attack. He said he had what he described as a "strict and strong" conversation with Saddam and had urged him to withdraw. The Kuwaiti royal family, he reassured Bush, was safe in Saudi Arabia. When the president asked Fahd to allow a squadron of F-15 fighters to be positioned at Prince Sultan Air Base in the desert near Al Kharj, the king was noncommittal. He said he wanted to discuss it with his advisors first.

The king's reluctance about the fighters did not please the president. Bush was worried that it might be an indication of the Saudis' unwillingness to be part of the effort to stand up against Saddam.

We flew back to Washington late that night. The president asked us to convene another NSC meeting for the next day. He and Scowcroft agreed that everyone there needed to fully appreciate the gravity of the situation, particularly the significance of Saddam Hussein's controlling the oil assets of both Iraq and Kuwait and the huge sums of money that came with them. With oil prices hovering around $20 per barrel in early 1990, the roughly five million barrels a day produced by Iraq and Kuwait together generated about $100 million a day for Saddam's government. Prices had spiked as a result of the invasion, so the sum was probably even higher by then.

At the NSC meeting, after a fresh assessment from the intelligence community, the president had Scowcroft make it clear that allowing Iraq to occupy Kuwait was not an option. That perspective was supported by Lawrence Eagleburger, sitting in for James Baker, and by Dick Cheney. Cheney, however, underscored the complexity of the challenge to our military forces if they were needed. The NSC also was informed that the Arab League was convening a meeting in Cairo to discuss the situation.

Discussion then returned to the military situation, with Cheney expressing a concern similar to the one that the president had noted the day before about the reluctance of Saudi Arabia to permit American forces to be stationed there. The last item we discussed was the worry that Saddam Hussein might use the American citizens remaining in Iraq as hostages; U.S. intelligence officials estimated that there were about fourteen or fifteen Americans already in custody in Baghdad. George Bush made it very clear that "American deaths and hostages will not be tolerated."

After the meeting, Bush invited the Saudi ambassador to the United States, Prince Bandar, to the White House to review the options. Bandar was not just the ambassador for Saudi Arabia in Washington; he was an extremely close advisor of King Fahd's. His father was the minister of defense for Saudi Arabia, and Prince Bandar made the trip back and forth between Washington and Riyadh frequently to brief the king face-to-face. I had known Bandar for a number of years before I came to Washington because of my involvement in the American Task Force for Lebanon and the National Association of Arab-Americans.

Bandar was scheduled to visit with Scowcroft at 11:00 a.m., and stopped by my office on the way. I shared with him our concerns about the king's hesitancy regarding fighter jets. Bandar said he thought the king was reluctant because he wasn't sure how committed the United States would be in the long run. I told him the president could make a clear and unambiguous commitment if that's what was required. Bandar and I then discussed the kind of precise language both sides would eventually have to exchange.

When he sat down with Scowcroft, Bandar heard more about the U.S. offer of military assets. Scowcroft later told the president that Bandar "seemed ill-at-ease and did not react with enthusiasm to the suggestion." When Scowcroft asked Bandar why, he repeated what he had told me just a few moments earlier. According to Scowcroft, "he explained that the Saudis were not at all sure they wanted to be defended by the United States. The United States, he said, 'did not exactly have a reputation in the region for reliability.'"

Bandar cited two examples. The first was from 1979, when the United States offered a squadron of F-16s to Saudi Arabia shortly after the shah was expelled from Iran during the Iranian revolution. It was only when the aircraft were being delivered to Saudi Arabia that the Americans announced publicly that they were unarmed. The second example he cited was that after American marines were killed in a terrorist attack in Beirut in 1983, the United States quietly withdrew its marines from Lebanon altogether.

According to Bandar, the king was concerned that America's verbal commitment would not really be backed up by actions. Scowcroft, speaking for President Bush, assured Bandar that we were committed to "stand with (the Saudis) to the end." To prove it, Scowcroft then arranged for Bandar to visit Cheney at the Pentagon and review CENTCOM's plan for responding to any Iraqi action against Saudi Arabia. CENTCOM is the U.S. Central Command, overseeing a zone of military operations comprising the Middle East, North Africa, and Central Asia. Following that visit, Bandar agreed on behalf of the king to receive a senior U.S. team in Saudi Arabia to continue the discussions and preparations.

By that time, Secretary of State James Baker had arrived in Moscow. He and Shevardnadze put out a statement jointly condemning the invasion of Kuwait. That statement must have shocked Saddam, because it made it clear that the Soviet Union, a principal supporter and supplier of Iraq's military, would stand with the rest of the world in opposition to his aggression. George Bush's careful nurturing of the relationship with Mikhail Gorbachev for the last year and a half produced this historic milestone—the two superpowers united in a common position on a major crisis for the first time since the end of World War II.

The phone calls continued. Bush spoke again with Prime Minister Thatcher in London and with Prime Minister Toshiki Kaifu of Japan. Throughout all this, Bush was also juggling meetings and telephone calls related to the ongoing and difficult negotiations with Congress on the federal budget. Later that afternoon the president left the White House for Camp David.

On Saturday, August 4, at Camp David, the president brought together his core group plus General Schwarzkopf; Paul Wolfowitz, the undersecretary of defense for policy; and Richard Haas, the senior director of Near East affairs for the National Security Council. We discussed, in breadth and detail, the general military options available. Cheney outlined the general capabilities of our airpower, naval assets, and ground forces. General Schwarzkopf briefed us on the strengths and limitations of Iraq's military capacity.

The president kept driving home what he felt was a principal point: we had to keep Saddam out of Saudi Arabia, and Saddam had to be expelled from Kuwait. By the end of the discussion, the president felt more comfortable with the military situation and agreed to the general concept of the military plans as presented.

None of these plans, however, would work unless Saudi Arabia allowed U.S. forces on the ground there. There was the rationale cited by Bandar earlier, but also the fact that, historically, Arab countries—and the Saudis in particular—were averse to hosting foreign forces of any stripe in the Middle East, Saddam or no Saddam.

The president called King Fahd again from Camp David on Saturday afternoon. Fahd remained noncommittal, and suggested that he needed to hear from that senior team the president promised to send from Washington to Riyadh before making a decision. The president kept pressing him gently, trying to get a definitive answer. He assured the king that any assets sent there would remain only with the Saudis' permission and would leave when asked to leave. Still, no luck.

Back in Washington, shortly after the president's conversation with King Fahd, Prince Bandar went to see Scowcroft and agreed on the composition of the team that would go to Riyadh. Secretary Cheney would lead the delegation, but a Cheney-led team should be going to Saudi Arabia, Bush believed, only to discuss how that deployment would take place, not whether it was going to take place. Bandar immediately called King Fahd and, after a lengthy discussion, told Scowcroft the king had finally agreed.

George Bush turned then to coordinating the next level of pressure: a series of sanctions and an embargo preventing trade with Iraq. After another intense round of telephone diplomacy, he secured support from America's major allies for the economic pressure on Iraq.

Among the calls was one to his friend Brian Mulroney in Canada. The prime minister had spoken with the Turkish president, Turgut Özal, who was prepared to shut down the pipelines traversing his country that were a critical path for Iraqi oil exports. Özal had also told Mulroney that Saddam Hussein was putting tremendous pressure on Turkey, telling the Turks that he had absolutely no intention of leaving Kuwait. Özal actually phoned Bush a couple of hours later with even more details about what he was hearing from Baghdad.

At about the same time, Ambassador Pickering was meeting with the five permanent members of the U.N. Security Council—China, France, the Soviet Union, and the United Kingdom, along with the United States—to get a sense of where they stood. Each could, with just one vote, block any anti-Iraq resolutions. Although the responses he got were generally supportive, it was by no means a certainty that if it came to a public vote they would all stand together. Pickering was able to get a resolution drafted and to arrange for a Security Council meeting on Monday, August 6.

Bush returned to the White House from Camp David, and as he walked across the South Lawn from the helicopter pad to the Oval Office he paused for a moment to speak to the press gathered there. He offered a short summary of the steps that had already been taken. In answering one of the questions, he ended by saying that "this will not stand, this aggression against Kuwait." The line "this aggression will not stand" became his rallying cry.

On Sunday, August 5, the NSC met once more in the Cabinet Room. Bill Webster told us the Iraqis were massing troops in Kuwait on the Saudi border. They were prepared and able to attack whenever they chose to do so, he said. Powell briefed the NSC on the progress of military deployments. The early focus had to be on airpower, since it would take time for ground forces to get to the region. Once again, at the end of the meeting, Bush expressed his concern for American citizens in the region.

On Sunday, August 5, George Bush heard from Dick Cheney, who was in Jeddah, Saudi Arabia. Cheney told him that King Fahd had approved the American plan, and would allow U.S. military forces into the kingdom. Bush immediately authorized moving the 82nd Airborne Division and two tactical fighter squadrons to Saudi Arabia as soon as possible. Cheney said King Fahd was eager to have other forces besides the U.S. forces involved, and had mentioned Morocco and Egypt specifically. The Saudis also agreed to increase their own oil production to blunt the impact of any embargo of Iraqi oil on the global supply.

Prime Minister Thatcher was in the Oval Office with President Bush when Cheney called from Saudi Arabia. They had been discussing the U.N. Security Council vote supporting sanctions on Iraq, and whether the resolution permitted a "blockade" of Iraq to enforce those sanctions—technically, an act of war not authorized by the resolution. Scowcroft came in and suggested that the way to resolve the issue was to use the word "quarantine," just as President Kennedy had done in 1962 during the Cuban missile crisis.

George Bush continued his telephone diplomacy. At 2:30 in the morning on August 7, he phoned François Mitterrand to tell him of the troop deployments. Bush attributed Mitterrand's strong support, in part, to the French leader's visit to Kennebunkport in the spring of 1989. His treatment of his fellow world leaders with courtesy and respect was paying off. The calls continued through the early morning hours. Hosni Mubarak. King Hassan of Morocco. Brian Mulroney in Canada. Mulroney was doing his own telephone diplomacy, and doing it well. He had learned from Mubarak that the Iraqis offered to buy Egypt's loyalty for $20 billion. Mubarak had rebuffed the offer, Mulroney told Bush, telling Saddam that Egypt "won't sell our principles." Mubarak believed the support Saddam Hussein was receiving from smaller countries like Jordan was clearly the result of payoffs.

At that point, George Bush felt he needed to communicate directly with the American public. We scheduled a television address for 9:00 the next morning, right after the 82nd Airborne Division would have arrived in Saudi Arabia. Bush himself has acknowledged that he was a bit nervous before this address and read through his prepared remarks a few extra times to feel a bit more at ease. Then he went on television to let the American people and the world know what the situation was:

> Four simple principles guide our policy. First, we seek the imme-
> diate, unconditional, and complete withdrawal of all Iraqi forces
> from Kuwait. Second, Kuwait's legitimate government must be
> restored to replace the puppet regime. And third, my adminis-
> tration, as has been the case with every president since Franklin
> Roosevelt, is committed to the security and stability of the Gulf.
> And fourth, I am determined to protect the lives of American
> citizens abroad.

He closed by putting the current crisis in the context of where the world stood now after the successful struggle for freedom in Europe. He emphasized, "If history teaches us anything, it is that we must resist aggression or it will destroy our freedoms."

That afternoon the president went, once again, to the phones. President Zayed of the UAE said he welcomed the presence of U.S. troops and recounted stories he was hearing about the atrocities being perpetrated by Iraqis in Kuwait City. Sultan Qaboos of Oman, another Persian Gulf neighbor, also was cooperative. Margaret Thatcher said Britain was sending naval and air forces to the Gulf. Robert Hawke, the prime minister of Australia, offered to send warships to the region, but said he would feel more comfortable with his commitment if Canada were also involved. The president immediately called Prime Minister Mulroney and soon both countries were on board.

Bush saw a pattern emerging in those calls. Most world leaders were committed to the cause, but said they preferred to be so as part of a broad international team.

"Everyone wanted some sort of cover to protect themselves against any backlash," Scowcroft wrote. "Ozal hoped his moves would be cloaked by NATO. Fahd did not wish to be the only Arab state opposing Iraq. Hawke didn't want to be the single Commonwealth country joining the coalition. We needed to demonstrate that this action was not a solo American effort against an Arab state."

The president left for Kennebunkport on August 10, and while there he received some good news from the Arab League summit in Cairo convened by Mubarak. The Egyptian leader had been able to enlist the support of twelve of the twenty-one members of the league to send a pan-Arab force to help defend Saudi Arabia. Surprisingly, Jordan had not backed Iraq in that forum. Egyptian and Moroccan troops already were on their way to Saudi Arabia and started arriving on August 11.

George Bush recognized the fragile nature of the coalition he was building. There was one thing that could quickly cause it to fall apart. It had to be seen as more than just a coalition of Americans and Europeans, as Scowcroft noted. It had to include Arab nations, and any Israeli involvement would antagonize the Arabs and torpedo the whole project. Saddam knew as much, Bush realized, and would do everything he could to drag Israel into the conflict. Bush took it on himself to personally discuss the need for forbearance with Israeli prime minister Yitzhak Shamir.

George Bush had a long and warm relationship with King Hussein of Jordan, so the king's support for Iraq disappointed the president, but Bush understood the pressure on the king by virtue of Jordan's geography and dependence on Iraqi oil.

King Hussein had asked to see Bush, so the president invited him to Kennebunkport on August 16. I myself had developed a good relationship with King Hussein over the years, and was hoping he was coming to somehow be more supportive than he had been. The meeting was a disappointment to all of us. The king tried to explain his support for the Iraqis but didn't make a very good case for it. He wanted the president to leave the Arab nations to work it out themselves. When Hussein left, I could sense how disappointed George Bush was at seeing his friend explain his appeasement of a tyrant.

King Hussein's visit was almost immediately followed by the arrival of Prince Bandar and the Saudi foreign minister, Prince Saud. Saud came bearing a message from the king that Saudi Arabia wanted the United States to force the Iraqis out of Kuwait as quickly as possible. George Bush tried to get him to appreciate the importance of properly timing any effort so that it would be successful.

Bush continued fretting about the U.S. citizens in Kuwait and Iraq. Many of the American citizens in Kuwait had been arrested by Iraqi troops and sent on to Baghdad. The Iraqis were saying that they would put the foreigners inside various strategic facilities, using them, in effect, as human shields to keep those facilities from being attacked. After the Security Council passed a resolution demanding that Saddam Hussein allow all foreigners to leave Iraq and Kuwait, Saddam offered to do so only if the United States withdrew its troops from Saudi Arabia. Saddam's dangerous actions and absurd demands, in violation of international law, made George Bush all the more resolute.

Bush began pondering how to prepare the coalition for the eventuality of war. The president and Jim Baker, the principal practitioners of personal and telephone diplomacy with the United States' allies, both sensed that its coalition partners were not yet ready for military action. Getting them to the point where they would be was the challenge.

Our coalition partners were not the only ones seeking more time before moving to overt action. Over at the Department of Defense, Dick Cheney already had concluded that force was probably in the cards. Cheney knew the highly professional American military leadership would want to make sure that if military action was required, it would be taken with ample forces and a commitment and capacity to go all out when those forces were unleashed.

Bush agreed. He was determined not to repeat what he thought were the failures of Vietnam and certain other conflicts in which the United States had been involved, when political leadership overruled sound military judgments. His own understanding of what needed to happen notwithstanding, he was determined not to micromanage his military leaders.

Besides building a coalition of moral and military support, George Bush and James Baker took on the additional task of urging countries to contribute financially to what was going to be a very expensive operation. After Bush spoke to Prime Minister Kaifu of Japan, that country delivered cash support that eventually totaled over $1 billion. Germany also came through with financial assistance as a result of the Bush-Baker outreach. Both countries had constitutional constraints preventing them from direct military involvement. They both faced tremendous political pressure from opponents of the anti-Iraq coalition at home, yet made the tough decisions to support the U.S. president. Bush even called on Mikhail Gorbachev to provide assistance to Eastern European nations that had peeled away from Soviet control by making up for any oil shortages they might face.

That cooperation convinced Bush that it was important to sit down face-to-face with Mikhail Gorbachev to thank him for what he had done thus far, and to prepare him for the more difficult decisions ahead. Gorbachev faced tremendous pressure from within his own government from factions, both military and industrial, with long-established relationships with Iraq. The two men agreed to meet in Helsinki, Finland, the week after Labor Day.

It was a rough, turbulent flight to Helsinki. None of us on the plane got much sleep. Jim Baker met the president when we landed with the good news that he had secured almost $7 billion in pledges from allies he had visited.

In his meetings with Gorbachev, the president let him know that the United States would probably have to use force if Saddam Hussein did not withdraw from Kuwait voluntarily. He acknowledged that the Soviet Union might not be able to send troops, but he asked Gorbachev to stand firm with the coalition on policy terms. He assured Gorbachev that no matter what happened, the United States had no plans to leave any of its troops in the Gulf area permanently and that the traditional U.S. policy of saying the Soviets had no role or business being in the Middle East at all no longer applied. Going forward, he wanted the United States and the Soviet Union to cooperate to resolve any issues that might arise in the region. Although the subjects at the meeting were tough and serious, the conversations were warm and friendly. It was at Helsinki that Bush and Gorbachev began addressing each other using their first names.

Gorbachev was uncharacteristically introspective at the meeting. "The question is, can we act and think in a new way?" Bush remembers the Soviet leader asking him at one point. "If not, the results are serious. Without the meeting in Malta, without the new relationship, Eastern Europe and German unification could have been much worse. It would have turned into a horrible mess. We now find ourselves with a problem no less difficult." He told the president his support was firm, though he did express concern that President Bush had been a bit late informing the Soviet Union when troops were first deployed.

The only downside of the meetings at Helsinki was that Gorbachev lobbied hard for a compromise with Saddam. He said one of his ministers, Yevgeny Primakov, knew Saddam well and might be able to convince him to withdraw from Kuwait. It was a tactic Gorbachev would use in many of his conversations with the president over the next few months. He always seemed to have another reason to wait before acting. Bush, eager as always to hear all sides, listened intently to Gorbachev throughout, but made it clear that the only compromise involved Saddam's withdrawing from Kuwait unconditionally.

By early fall, the president could look back with pride on what had been accomplished in the weeks since the Iraqi army had taken over Kuwait. He had, through a series of resolutions at the United Nations, clearly defined the need to undo the occupation. He had convinced our principal allies to participate in a naval "quarantine" to enforce economic sanctions against Iraq. He had persuaded our oil-producing allies to increase production to minimize the impact of the loss of Iraqi and Kuwaiti oil supplies. He was well on his way to building a broad military coalition, probably the broadest since World War II, to apply pressure on Iraq, or, if necessary, forcefully expel it from Kuwait. In short, Bush had succeeded in isolating Iraq and restraining it from using its military might any further than it already had done.

Inevitably, all presidents eventually discover how strong an impact the political pressure of public opinion can have on their capacity to develop and implement policy. They learn that doing what is right and doing what is popular don't always overlap. In Bush's case it was true not only in the complex and extremely partisan budget negotiations under way in Congress in late 1990, but also in the simultaneous preparations under way in the Middle East.

It soon became clear that partisan politics would attack both

the broad policy and the details of what the president felt had
to be done by the United States as the leader of this new coalition. Bush learned that, despite assertions of the Democratic
leadership in Congress to the contrary, partisanship was part
and parcel of the budget negotiations, and eventually that same
partisanship crept into the preparations for and execution of the
war in Kuwait, but public support was with him, even though his
critics were saying that he had not yet made the case for strong
action in the Gulf to the public or to Congress.

As we moved closer to the day when he would have to make a
final decision on whether to send men and women into battle, the
president met regularly with people outside the national security establishment to hear their thoughts and concerns. Some
of them, people he cared about deeply, came with impassioned
pleas not to use force.

Bush occasionally got frustrated when he met with members
of Congress—usually with the leadership, and virtually always
on a bipartisan basis—to explain the national security implications of the escalating crisis. He felt that pure partisanship was
influencing congressional leaders who should have known better,
such as Senator Sam Nunn of Georgia, who appeared fixated
on compromise even if it allowed Saddam Hussein to remain in
control of what he had taken in Kuwait.

On September 11, Bush addressed a joint session of Congress. As always, the chamber was packed and the speech was
televised nationally. Bush reported to Congress and the nation
where things stood with the coalition and our allies. He offered
a summary of his talks with Gorbachev in Helsinki. He hoped
Congress and the nation appreciated, he said, the long-term
implications of the fact that the two superpowers were handling
the situation cooperatively. It was, he said, a historic moment.

The address happened in the middle of the nasty partisan

battle over the budget. Brady, Darman, and I were able to report to the president that we were making progress. What the president was doing in the Persian Gulf was earning him strong public backing, and that support was putting pressure on the Democrats to work harder in search of a solution to the budget problem and the budget deficit.

Ten days after he addressed Congress, the president invited the joint leadership to the White House to discuss where Congress stood on the events unfolding abroad. Speaker Tom Foley and Senate Majority Leader Mitchell had supported the president in his coalition-building and the U.S. response to the crisis so far, but they warned the president that the issue of hostilities was a different question. They were very specific in making the point that, as Foley put it, "If we engage in hostilities, the War Powers issue would resume." This was their way of suggesting that the president could not use force to push Saddam out of Kuwait without getting a vote of approval from Congress. The president didn't agree, but listened to their presentation respectfully. On the Republican side, both Bob Michel, the House minority leader, and Bob Dole, the Senate minority leader, expressed strong support for all the president had done and might need to do. Even with that support, however, arming our allies in the coalition was a complex process. Providing military equipment to countries like Saudi Arabia involved a convoluted process of consultation, notification, concurrence, and approval from Congress. The president explained that the more we built up the Saudi military, the less we would need American forces. Even though he started the process in August, it wouldn't be until nearly the last day in October that an arms package would finally get through Congress.

At the end of September General Colin Powell asked for a meeting with the president. When he came to see us in the Oval

Office. I noticed that Powell seemed a bit more tired and tight-lipped than usual. There was none of the good-natured banter that usually started one of his meetings with President Bush. The chairman of the Joint Chiefs summarized the progress being made in the movement of materials and troops to Saudi Arabia, then got to the point that he wanted to make sure Bush heard.

"Mr. President, this is one of the biggest military offensives ever put together," he explained sternly. "And it is one of the most complicated. If you decide to liberate Kuwait by force, it is going to take half a million troops, a couple of thousand aircraft, thousands of tanks, a handful of carrier groups, a couple of hundred ships and billions of dollars of ordnance."

Like many military leaders, Powell was rightly reluctant to commit forces to combat. I had no problem with that, but he now was asking for essentially double what he and the Joint Chiefs had previously said they needed.

At first I thought Powell was testing the president's resolve. Then I realized he was just making it abundantly clear this was going to be a high-stakes, high-risk undertaking. In direct and specific terms, he was letting the president know that if he decided to go to war with Iraq, then it should be done—and must be done—with a large enough commitment of resources to ensure success.

The tactic, I suspected, was also an effort by Powell to cover his own back should things go wrong. I had noticed throughout his tenure that Powell kept an open line to reporters, such as his friend Bob Woodward at *The Washington Post*, to make sure his own achievements and perspectives had a clear outlet in the press. In his discussion that day with Bush, Powell was asking for virtually every available asset, perhaps with the expectation that Bush would not provide it.

The president took it all in. He sat quietly in his chair and listened intently. He could have balked at the request for additional resources. He could have sent Powell back to the Pentagon to find a way to do the job with less. He could have tried to minimize the cost and avoid the impact such a huge mobilization would have on public opinion.

George Bush didn't do any of those things. Without hesitation, President Bush committed. With eyes locked on the general he said, "All right, Colin. You've got it. And if you need anything else to get the job done right, you just let me know."

The Vietnam War had been managed by a president who seemed to always give the armed forces just a little less than what they requested. It had been a recipe for failure. I had seen it. George Bush had seen it too. And he would have none of it.

It took a second for it to sink in, but then I realized what Bush had just done. In his calm, low-key style, he had brilliantly navigated one of the most significant moments of presidential leadership since the end of World War II. It was the foreign policy equivalent of his admonition regarding the savings and loan debacle on the domestic side: "Fix it and fix it fast."

In that moment, with his deliberate and decisive words, George Bush changed the environment in which U.S. strategic responsibilities and resources would be committed. No more Post-Vietnam Syndrome. No more Paper Tiger. No more Reluctant Superpower. The die was cast, and the message to Colin Powell and the military was clear: get the job done, and get it done right. There would be no hesitation at or interference by the top of the chain of command from that moment on. You will have all the resources you need, he told Powell, but from now on there will be no excuse for failure.

Throughout October, the Soviets continued to try to broker a compromise with Saddam Hussein. Gorbachev sent his former foreign minister Yevgeny Primakov, a close friend of Saddam's, to

Baghdad to secure the release of more than five thousand Soviet personnel detained by Saddam Hussein because, Saddam said, they were "critical" to his military. Primakov also tried to get Saddam to withdraw from Kuwait, but didn't get far on that front.

Primakov then rushed to Washington to brief Bush on his discussions. He told us that part of the problem was that Saddam Hussein's advisors told him only what he wanted to hear. None dared inform him how internationally isolated Iraq was becoming.

In the following weeks, Primakov shuttled between Moscow and Baghdad a number of times. It was evident to Bush that political pragmatism on Gorbachev's part was behind many of these trips. Some in the Soviet leader's inner circle were still bitter over the "loss" of Eastern Europe and Germany. Gorbachev was under increasing pressure not to "lose" another strategic struggle with the West.

About that time, the budget agreement we thought had been negotiated with the Democrats fell apart following Newt Gingrich's betrayal.

On October 11, the president and his core group met in the situation room and heard from the Joint Chiefs and CENTCOM about how they proposed to take on the Iraqi army. The plan was to begin with an air campaign. However, Powell told us that airpower alone would not get the job done, that ground combat was almost a certainty. The Department of Defense's ground plan was basically a head-on charge through the middle of the Iraqi installations, with the aim of quickly capturing key roads in northern Kuwait.

During the presentation, I exchanged glances with both the president and Scowcroft, and saw that we all shared the same reaction. Scowcroft asked why there was no thought of using an envelopment action from the west to come in behind Iraqi forces and cut them off. The president was clearly unhappy with the plan as presented and asked Scowcroft to call Cheney and tell him to try again. Adding to Bush's unease was what he perceived to be a lack of enthusiasm or of commitment from the defense establishment.

"Long visit at lunch with Sununu, Scowcroft and Baker," he wrote in his diary on October 12. "I am trying to figure out how we handle the overall Iraq matter. Should we convene a group at the top—heads of all the countries that are supporting the Gulf—and make sure we are on the same wavelength when it comes to responding to provocation, or when it comes to using force without provocation? What do we do about declaring war, or getting congressional support? What do we do about the military?"

In our discussions, Jim Baker counseled us on the importance of working within the "international consensus." Continuous consultation with the allies was critical, he said, as was the backing of the United Nations. After that meeting, the president directed his national security and military teams to meet with their British counterparts. The president was getting a bit impatient, but he was also aware that acting prematurely could create serious problems and might even impede a constructive solution.

Then there was the political skirmishing—no small matter, either.

With midterm elections right around the corner, Bush, as leader of the Republican Party, was also bouncing around the nation on behalf of Republican candidates. Congress had already adjourned and would not reconvene until after the New Year. To keep themselves in the loop on the situation in the Gulf, the congressional leaders had named eighteen members to coordinate with the administration.

Speaker Foley and Senate Majority Leader Mitchell wanted to meet with the president before they all left town, which they were scheduled to do on October 30. That morning, at the meeting, Tom Foley handed the president a letter signed by eightyone Democratic members of Congress stating that they were opposed to any offensive American action in the Gulf. As many as fifty thousand American lives might be lost, they insisted. They wanted the president's assurance that he would not take military action without a declaration of war by Congress. In general, the Democrats were interested only in delaying things.

The only sliver of real support came from Democratic congressman Jack Murtha, a former marine from Pennsylvania who was the first Vietnam veteran to serve in the House. Murtha said he saw no alternative to the use of force. The meeting overall, however, was an unproductive, partisan exercise intended primarily to gin up statements for the leadership to parrot for the reporters and cameras waiting outside the White House. The only thing Bush promised them was that he would continue consulting Congress.

After the congressional meeting, Bush gathered his core group in the situation room and restated his firm "commitment to seeing Saddam leave Kuwait unconditionally." We debated how long to let the sanctions drag on, and whether there should be a specific deadline for the use of force should Saddam continue to ignore the will of the world. Powell reminded the group that our forces would not be completely in place before January 15, 1991. The timing was sensitive. The political side of the administration wanted to wait until after the elections to announce the deployments, but Cheney and Powell said they needed to know immediately whether and how to proceed. This huge acceleration of the mobilization of troops did not go unnoticed, obviously, and stories started popping up in the press.

The stories created problems for Baker, who was in Moscow to brief Shevardnadze and Gorbachev on our plans. The Soviets were irked that they had not been consulted prior to the buildup. Similar complaints came from some members of Congress back home on the campaign trail. This, despite the fact that at our last meeting, even Foley acknowledged that Bush had consulted with Congress more than any previous president. Scowcroft and I did as much as we could—calling the 435 members of the House and 100 members of the Senate as often as humanly possible to tamp down the complaints and keep Congress in the loop.

Beyond any partisan motivation for the Democrats' criticism, a historic constitutional battle was brewing between the executive and legislative branches over which had the power to authorize the use of force. To be sure, it is a complicated issue and has become even more so as the reaction time needed for that force to be effective shortens with the advent of new technologies.

In 1973, Congress passed a War Powers Resolution over a presidential veto, and every president since then has maintained that the resolution is unconstitutional. The resolution itself tries to provide specific guidance, but unfortunately contains an ambiguous framework that is, in the eyes of many, unworkable. There was no question that the War Powers issue would be a serious source of tension as the president got closer and closer to deciding on the use of force.

Another source of concern emerged from the same era as the War Powers Act—the so-called Vietnam syndrome. Ever since that long-drawn-out war in Asia, there was a sense that the American public was uncomfortable with, and could not sustain support for, another such conflict.

Since Vietnam, there had been no major crisis in which the United States had to mobilize and use its military power. There were accusations in some circles that the president contributed to this malaise by not adequately explaining to the American public why our troops were in the desert on the Arabian Peninsula. These accusations fueled factions that were determined to avoid force and rely solely on sanctions to get Saddam out of Kuwait.

About a week after the 1990 election, the president again met with congressional leaders and urged them to understand that, in his opinion, consultation was "a two-way street." He wanted to hear specific advice from them and said he would appreciate hearing it in private before reading it in the press. Such public dissent, he said, could, and would, embolden the Iraqis. Once again, at the meeting, Foley and Mitchell used the War Powers issue to badger the president, urging only conditional use of force—but the conditions were, in Bush's eyes, unworkable.

It was clear at that meeting, more than at any other, that the Democratic leadership had no real sense of how difficult it had been to pull together the international coalition, and how nearly impossible it would be to maintain that cooperation for any extended period of time. Time was of the essence, the president believed, and involving Congress in every decision only dragged things out. There were some at the meeting, such as senators Bob Dole and John Warner and congressmen Jack Murtha and Henry Hyde, who strongly supported the president. But it was clear that approval from Congress for the use of force was going to come with some significant partisan pushback, at least in the Senate.

While the president dealt with all of this in Washington, Gorbachev continued to push for compromise, and Bush continued to insist that diplomacy and sanctions were not working. He would return to the United Nations only once more for a new resolution authorizing action, he said. Since the United States held the chair of the Security Council during the month of November, the president wanted to sew up that one last resolution during that time.

Bush was due in Paris for a meeting of the Commission on Security and Cooperation in Europe (CSCE), and he hoped to meet Gorbachev again face-to-face there and seek his support for a last U.N. resolution.

We extended the trip a bit at both the start and the end. Before the CSCE, we scheduled stops in Czechoslovakia, another of the Eastern European nations wriggling out from under Soviet control, and Germany. After Paris, we scheduled time for the president to fly to Saudi Arabia to spend Thanksgiving with the troops on the ground and to meet with our Arab allies in the coalition.

Immediately after arriving in Prague on the morning of November 17, Bush met with the Czech president, Vaclav Havel. That afternoon, he addressed the Czech Federal Assembly in the presence of Alexander Dubček, who led the unsuccessful uprising against the Soviets in Czechoslovakia in 1968. Havel and the Czechs, Bush believed, understood better than most what Kuwait was going through. When asked at a press conference for his reaction to what was going on in the Gulf, Havel said, "It is necessary to resist evil. . . . It is necessary to resist aggression, because our own history has taught us ample lessons about the consequences of appeasement."

Late in the day, President Bush addressed a crowd estimated at about 750,000 people in Wenceslas Square in the middle of Prague. "Czechoslovakia," the president declared, "shall be free." As he spoke these words, a roar of approval from the crowd built up like a freight train rushing right at us. The noise seemed to rattle the buildings and shake the cobbled streets. When the president finished speaking, he and Mrs. Bush descended from the platform and into the mass of people, shaking hands and receiving grateful pats on their backs.

In Germany afterward, Helmut Kohl assured the president that he would stand with the coalition, but we all sensed his reluctance. In Paris, Mitterrand also remained steadfast but warned that the final U.N. resolution would be difficult to draft. Bush also met privately with Margaret Thatcher at the home of the American ambassador in Paris. Thatcher, facing a tough fight for the leadership of her Conservative Party at home, briefed the president on her own political battles before telling him that Britain soon would send additional forces to the Gulf. She and the president had a very long conversation about the hostages in Iraq and Kuwait, and the problems the United States and Britain shared because they still had embassies open in Kuwait.

For me the conference of the Commission on Security and Cooperation in Europe was an excellent example of how leadership protocol can sometimes create difficult problems. There were two full days of presentations by thirty-five world leaders, among them Havel of Czechoslovakia, Tadeusz Mazowiecki of Poland, and József Antall of Hungary. Each of the three men stressed the importance of resisting oppression and aggression. "All three had been in jail, all three knew firsthand about the crushing of sovereign nations," Bush would later remark.

Bush went above and beyond the demands of diplomatic protocol. He sat calmly and politely through all thirty-five of the speeches, some of them excruciating in their length and tedious in their depth. He passed some of the time creating limericks, some of them quite bawdy, about a few of the speakers on the podium. He passed them back to Scowcroft and me with a serious look on his face as if they were important instructions, and we all shared knowing glances. I made sure to destroy all the notes. The only lines I clearly remember, or maybe the only ones I am subconsciously willing to divulge, were one that started, "There was a big Chancellor from Bonn . . ." and another that ended "Only Dennis, her husband, could catch her."

On the evening of our first day in Paris, the president met

with Gorbachev at the U.S. Embassy. By this time, back in the
Soviet Union, Boris Yeltsin was beginning to aggressively criticize Mikhail Gorbachev. The president asked his friend how
things were going at home, and Gorbachev dismissed Yeltsin as a
nuisance but not a serious threat.

Bush then asked Gorbachev to support the proposed American resolution at the United Nations. Gorbachev agreed to back a
last, single resolution containing both an ultimatum and a deadline. Failure to meet the deadline, the resolution would state
clearly, would allow for "all necessary measures" to enforce the
ultimatum.

This was tremendously significant. Gorbachev added one
caveat, however. He wanted to delay an announcement of their
agreement. He said he wanted to speak to the Iraqis once more,
and needed time to do that. We and the Soviet team dined
together that evening and, considering the seriousness of the
situations with which we were all faced, it was a very convivial
event. Both sides shared stories and jokes poking fun at their
own political systems. Gorbachev even told some stories from
the old days of Stalin. George Bush and Gorbachev both said it
was the best meeting they ever had.

The next day Margaret Thatcher had to fly back to Britain to
participate in her party's leadership vote. She suffered a surprising defeat after having served as leader of the Conservative Party
for fifteen years. To her credit, she returned to France immediately after the vote for the closing CSCE dinner at Versailles. We
were all extremely surprised at how quickly and suddenly her
party had turned on her.

After Paris, the president headed for Saudi Arabia. He had
invited the four principal leaders of Congress to meet him

there: George Mitchell and Bob Dole from the Senate, and Tom Foley and Bob Michel from the House.

In his role as commander in chief, George Bush felt an obligation to demonstrate his appreciation to the young men and women—not only those from the United States, but the troops from all the allied nations now deployed to Saudi Arabia. Bush had been through combat himself. He remembered America's anguish over Vietnam. He understood the reality of personal sacrifice, of family sacrifice, and even the impact that sending men and women into harm's way can have on communities and on nations. He wanted them to understand that he knew that individually and collectively they were making a courageous contribution to an important effort.

The president also wanted to sit down face-to-face with King Fahd to discuss details of our plans that could not be reviewed in a telephone conversation. The president also wanted to sit, eye to eye, with the troops whom he would very likely have to order into battle in the near future.

We landed in the Red Sea port of Jeddah not far from Mecca and were greeted by the king himself and other senior members of the Saudi royal family. There, the president spoke with the emir of Kuwait, who was living in Saudi Arabia. The emir was pessimistic about the chances of Saddam's withdrawing from his country, and told the president of the terrible things being done to his people back home. The president urged him to be more public with his concerns.

That evening King Fahd hosted a state dinner for us in Jeddah. The president described the dinner this way: "It was an unbeliev-able meal. The only way to describe the amount of food was to say that if ever there was an occasion when tables groaned under a feast, this was it in every conceivable type of food."

Afterward the president, Baker, Scowcroft, and I spent a couple of hours with the king and his advisors reviewing, from the Saudi perspective, Saddam's deception in the days leading up to his invasion of Kuwait and the king's concerns about what the Iraqi dictator would do next. The president asked the king to speak with our Arab partners in the coalition about timidity in their public comments. The Syrians were saying their troops would not leave Saudi Arabia to engage the Iraqis; the Egyptians were saying they would not enter Iraq. Such comments, he warned the king, were unhelpful, weakening congressional and public resolve back in the United States. King Fahd and his advisors made it clear that they stood firm with the United States and would support whatever action was necessary to get Saddam out of Kuwait and to defend the kingdom.

The next day was Thanksgiving, and we flew across the Arabian Peninsula to Dhahran, in eastern Saudi Arabia on the Persian Gulf, to visit with our military. The president was greeted upon landing by General Norman Schwarzkopf, who took us all immediately to the military airlift command base. The president and Barbara Bush spent a lot of time walking through an enthusiastic crowd of men and women from the Air Force. With typical Bush warmth, they shook hands and posed for dozens of pictures.

Later in the day, we went into the desert to visit with a huge group from the US Army. Again the president worked his way through the crowd, taking his time to talk to and thank the young men and women there. He and Barbara then joined the crowd waiting in line for turkey, and sat down with them to celebrate Thanksgiving. Most of our troops were young kids wishing they were home for the holidays, and Bush wanted them to know that their commander in chief, who had once been a very young warrior himself, really cared about them and appreciated their service and sacrifice for America.

The next day we were in the air again, this time en route to Cairo to meet with Hosni Mubarak. Mubarak was very direct.

He told the president that he would do whatever was necessary to support the coalition. Then we all flew to Geneva for a meeting that few would have ever thought likely.

Mubarak, along with other Arab members of the coalition, had suggested we meet with Syrian president Hafez al-Assad. When we entered the meeting room, Bush and Assad exchanged pleasantries. As soon as we took our seats, the Syrian leader launched into a long tirade blaming Israel for all the problems in the Middle East and complaining about the Egyptian-Israeli peace process. President Bush raised the issues of terrorism and human rights. Most significantly, he tried to bring the focus back to Syria's participation in the coalition, and urged Assad to stop publicly suggesting that his troops would not advance out of their base in Saudi Arabia. The president strongly recommended to Assad that he have a conversation about that with Hosni Mubarak. The meeting confirmed to me how committed George Bush was to personal diplomacy, and how he would endure any discomfort to further a chance for peace.

While the president circled the globe in his burst of personal diplomacy, Jim Baker and Tom Pickering were gathering support for the resolution to be presented to the U.N. Security Council. Baker's lobbying continued all the way into the evening just before the actual vote, and the language was being tweaked until the very last moments. The president wanted the deadline to be January 1, 1991; the Soviets wanted to push it to January 31. Mitterrand said we should split the difference and settle on January 15. Bush knew our military would just about be ready by then, so he agreed.

In what was titled United Nations Security Council Resolution 678, on November 29, 1990, the Security Council voted 12–2 to authorize "any means necessary" to force Saddam to comply with its earlier edicts. Only Cuba and Yemen voted against it. China,

which usually vetoed such measures in the past, abstained. It was
the twelfth resolution passed by the Security Council since the
invasion of Kuwait, and the Iraqi leader had ignored all twelve.
Saddam now had a firm six-week deadline to comply or face very
real consequences. The president's hard work, along with that of
Baker and Pickering, had achieved this very significant victory,
one that would prove pivotal in the coming struggle with a disappointingly partisan U.S. Congress.

George Bush had set the stage for a genuine international
effort to deal with Iraq's act of aggression. He had built a coalition that included the two superpowers and also, amazingly, virtually all of the Arab nations. He had support from the United
Nations in the form of a dozen resolutions. At that point, George
Bush was leading not only his own nation but the world.

He might have the rest of the world on his side, but he still had
to bring along a reluctant and partisan Congress. In the weeks
between the final Security Council resolution and the New Year,
the struggle with Congress grew more intense. The War Powers
debate crept back into play. Democratic senator Sam Nunn convened televised hearings and paraded before the cameras a long
succession of witnesses opposed to the use of force. There was
no question in our mind that the hesitancy displayed in those
hearings was giving aid and comfort to Saddam Hussein. Senate
Majority Leader George Mitchell also continued the full-court
press. The president discussed with Tom Foley and Bob Michel
the possibility of holding a special session of Congress to discuss
the U.N. resolution and the use of force, but both of them recommended against it.

To demonstrate to the country and the world how much he
wanted to avoid the use of force, Bush called for one more set
of consultations and invited Iraqi foreign minister Tariq Aziz to
Washington. Jim Baker, he said, would visit Baghdad in return.

The reaction to this proposal, on the last day of November, from our coalition partners surprised the president. A lengthy series of phone conversations followed. King Fahd. The emir of Kuwait. Hosni Mubarak. Turgut Özal in Turkey. Margaret Thatcher's successor, Prime Minister John Major. They all seemed especially irked that they had not been consulted before Bush made the offer. The oversight was really the only serious misstep in Bush's long, complex run of diplomacy.

The proposal went over better at home. The tone of the conversations with Congress improved. The fact that Bush was willing to take that extra step added credibility to his assertion that he had done, and was doing, everything he could to resolve the problem without the direct use of force.

During a meeting with the congressional leaders in the Cabinet Room, the president asked specifically for a congressional resolution supporting Security Council Resolution 678. A united American government would add to the pressure on Saddam, Bush told them. Bob Dole and Bob Michel urged their colleagues to stand with the president, but Foley and Mitchell still wanted to "give sanctions more time." Positions were still being staked out along partisan lines.

The Iraqis spent December stalling as well. To curry favor in Moscow, Saddam allowed the detained Soviet citizens to leave Iraq. He also let more than 150 Americans leave Baghdad. The American ambassador in Kuwait, Nathaniel Howell, and his remaining four staff members left that country on December 13.

Bush remained concerned that Saddam would try to goad Israel into attacking Iraq in an effort to undermine Arab solidarity in the coalition. He invited Israeli prime minister Shamir to Washington on December 11 and expressed those concerns. He reaffirmed the United States' commitment to protecting Israel, and told the Israeli leader that we would aggressively retaliate against Iraq if Saddam tried to harm Israel. Shamir said he would cooperate, but made it clear that any such action by Saddam would put him under tremendous pressure at home. The men agreed to stay in close contact throughout the coming weeks to avoid any potentially dangerous misunderstandings.

Bipartisan support for Bush's efforts was starting to surface—finally. Democratic representative Stephen Solarz of New York organized a Committee for Peace and Security in the Gulf, a bipartisan group that included a number of significant Democrats from previous administrations and a few hawkish Democrats in Congress. Such bipartisan support gave the president a bit of solace.

"Finally we're getting some groups together to go out there and give the pitch," he wrote in his diary on December 14. "For too long, Sam Nunn, who they now joke about as 'Neville' and George Mitchell and others (have) dominated the scene. . . . But recent polls show the American people much more supportive than I thought they would've been."

His resolve was further strengthened in mid-December by an eighty-page Amnesty International report detailing some of the terrible things that had been happening in Kuwait. The president had copies of the report sent to the ambassadors of the coalition and to key members of Congress. He also encouraged Amnesty International to deliver it to the U.N. Security Council.

On December 20, President Bush wrote in his diary of sitting down with the presiding bishop of the Episcopal Church in the United States of America. "We had a very emotional meeting, at least for me, with Bishop Edmond Browning," Bush wrote that evening. "He had just gotten back from Jordan and Iraq. He was appealing for peace, and he was pointing out to me that everyone he encountered wanted peace. He felt that there was no way he could possibly condone violence." He showed the bishop the report by Amnesty International about atrocities taking place in Kuwait, but he could not get the bishop to agree that those violent acts needed to be stopped even if it took violence to stop them.

Although Bush could not get Bishop Browning on his side at that meeting, he did call him by telephone on the eve of the invasion, and they prayed together on the phone.

Just before Christmas, George Bush invited John Major, who had succeeded Margaret Thatcher as prime minister, to visit with him at Camp David. Unfortunately the weather required them to drive rather than fly there, but the long ride gave the president an opportunity to lay out for Major, in detail, our plans for the postdeadline period. Bush was impressed that Major never hesitated, and, Bush said, like his predecessor, "declared on the spot that the British would be with us all the way. I shall never forget that."

With December coming to a close, CENTCOM tried to push back the date at which it said it would be ready for hostilities. The president met with his national security team, including Powell and Cheney, and finally got the team members to reaffirm that they were prepared to move almost immediately after January 15.

On January 2 the president, Jim Baker, Brent Scowcroft, and I met to discuss the president's desire for one last face-to-face meeting to let Saddam hear directly what the coalition was prepared to unleash. This time, the president was careful to consult all his allies before announcing anything. The next day he offered to send James Baker to Geneva for a meeting with the Iraqis—if they would attend it.

Baker went to Geneva with a letter from Bush in hand, one making it very clear that the coalition was prepared to act after January 15. Two sessions with Aziz were scheduled for January 9. Aziz spent much of the first meeting ranting and raving about the historical conflicts between Iraq and Kuwait. Baker made it clear that he was there not to negotiate but to "communicate."

He handed Aziz Bush's letter, which was sealed, along with a photocopy so Aziz could read it on the spot. Baker told the president that Aziz merely skimmed the photocopy before shoving both it and the original to the center of the table.

The letter remained on the table between them throughout the second session. Baker continued his "communicating." The consequences of war would not be pleasant for Iraq, he warned Aziz, who just sat there stoically. Aziz never touched the letter again, and, in the end, refused to deliver it to Saddam.

On January 10 the House and Senate began deliberating resolutions supporting the use of force. Our initial count was that we were in fairly good shape on the vote in the House, but, to begin with, we had only about 35 to 37 votes in our favor in the Senate. Over the past month we had been working to try to get our required 51 senators. We tried to arrange to have the House vote first, hoping that a positive vote there would sway the Senate.

The votes were scheduled for January 12. The key vote would be the last one in the House, on a resolution jointly sponsored by Bob Michel and Steve Solarz supporting the use of force to carry out the United Nations' twelve resolutions, including U.N. Resolution 678.

Our lobbying for votes in the Senate continued. At one point, Bob Dole called to tell me that Senator Al Gore of Tennessee said he might vote to support the president if Dole would give up fifteen minutes of his own floor time so Gore's comments could be seen on television in prime time. Dole and I both laughed and lamented that a U.S. senator could be so shallow as to trade his vote on such a crucial issue for the chance to be seen on television. Dole did not give Gore the time, but Gore supported the resolution anyway. In the end, the Senate supported the president by a 52–47 majority.

One of the little-known heroes in the process of assembling the necessary votes in the Senate was the editor of a small newspaper in Nevada, William O'Callaghan. I had met him while I was governor in New Hampshire at the urging of William Loeb, the former owner and publisher of the Manchester *Union Leader*. As I was trying to get senators Harry Reid and Richard Brian of Nevada to support the resolution, I called O'Callaghan, a former Democratic governor of Nevada, and asked him to use his "powers of persuasion" on them. He was a real patriot. He understood how important it was to the country to get a positive vote in the Senate.

As far back as December, O'Callaghan began publishing editorials in his paper supporting the president's action. He also personally contacted the senators. In early January he called to tell me he had made a little bit of progress. He thought the senators would vote in tandem, though he still wasn't sure that the vote would be yes. Finally, on the day before the vote, he called with word that I could inform the president that both senators from Nevada would vote in his favor. They ended up being two of only ten Democratic senators to support the resolution, and we had O'Callaghan to thank for those two.

The partisan distribution of the vote made it clear that George Mitchell had tried very hard to have it defeated. In fact, all the Democratic leaders in both the House and the Senate voted against the resolutions. But the final outcome was nonetheless gratifying to George Bush and made him more comfortable as commander in chief about sending our troops into war.

The day after the vote in Congress, the president gathered his key defense and national security team at the White House residence and settled on an exact time for the attack to begin: January 17 at 3:00 a.m. Gulf time, which would be January 16 at 7:00 p.m. in Washington. We agreed that the president should address the nation right after the attacks commenced.

I knew all along how concerned the president was about his very serious responsibility of sending young men and women into war. He had thought through the decision and was comfortable making it, but that didn't diminish the burden on him. I could tell he had been dwelling on it more and more as the deadline drew nearer, and it was adding to the tension we all felt. In my conversations with him, I found that he already was thinking intently about the best way to bring hostilities to a close after the principal objective was achieved.

On the morning of January 15 we gathered in the Oval Office with the president to go over the final details of the attack. The meeting included the vice president, the secretary of defense, the chairman of the Joint Chiefs of Staff, Brent Scowcroft, and me. Bob Gates also joined us for part of the meeting. We decided that the president would go on television at 9:00 p.m., two hours after the launch of hostilities. We also parceled out responsibilities and processes for notifying the other members of the coalition of the launch time. When the meeting ended, it was obvious to me as I worked through the day with the president that he was counting the minutes until the midnight deadline.

January 16 was a difficult day for George Bush. We tried to stick to a routine calendar, which included a meeting on education policy, but I couldn't help noticing that although the president participated in the discussion, his focus was obviously elsewhere. The president invited Jim Baker to join him for lunch in the residence. After lunch, we spent most of the afternoon notifying our allies that the attacks would commence that evening.

The night of January 16 was one of the most surreal episodes during my time in the White House. Dan Quayle, Brent Scowcroft, and I went down to the Oval Office. Then, starting at about 6:30 p.m., we gathered around a television in the small office adjoining the Oval Office to watch CNN's live feed from Baghdad. At 7:00 p.m., the skies over Baghdad began to light up as the bombs started to land. It seemed as if we were glued to the set for an hour, but the official presidential log shows that we all left to get back to work after only twenty minutes. Two hours later the president spoke to the nation. Nearly 80 percent of the country watched.

The next day, as George Bush feared might happen, Iraq responded with an attack against Israel, launching the first of dozens of Scud missiles that would eventually land there. That evening, a number of us met with the president to discuss how to respond. It had been a hectic day, and we had some difficulty finding out what was actually happening on the ground there. We even had trouble reaching the Israeli leadership by phone.

When Jim Baker did finally get through to the Israeli prime minister, Shamir assured him and the president that Israel would refrain from launching any counterattacks for the moment. The Iraqi attacks on Israel would continue, and remained a concern throughout the war. The president eventually sent a team over to brief the Israelis on the details of the coalition military effort and arranged for a battery of Patriot missiles to be positioned in Israel, providing air defense against the Scuds.

The air war continued through the end of January. On January 29, the president delivered his State of the Union address to a joint session of Congress. The same day, the Iraqis actually attacked a Saudi border town and killed twelve American marines. A decision had to be made on when and how to launch the coalition ground attack, and it had to be made quickly. The air campaign had been very effective, and a quick follow-up on the ground would be needed to take advantage of the air effort.

Over those two weeks, in a series of core group meetings, the president focused his attention on the basic mission as defined in the U.N. resolutions: ending the occupation of Kuwait. It was unmistakable from those conversations that in George Bush's mind this meant no march to Baghdad. This was not an effort at regime change. Bush felt it extremely important that the coalition abide strictly by the letter of the law of U.N. Resolution 678.

The core group met again on February 3 at the White House to discuss a specific date for a ground campaign. Our military men kept pushing the date out. The president did not want to second-guess them, but he knew that too long a delay would undermine the coalition. The air strikes had been going on for more than two weeks, and had accomplished all the preestablished objectives. Any more delay would just allow the Iraqis to confuse the situation with diplomatic probes. At the meeting, Powell told the group that General Schwarzkopf wanted to wait at least another two weeks. The president, unhappy, sent Cheney and Powell to Saudi Arabia to speak with Schwarzkopf.

Finally, after continued consultations with our allies and with Schwarzkopf, we settled on February 23 as the start of the ground war. Saddam was still trying to stall. Through his friends in the Soviet hierarchy, he was pressuring Gorbachev to help arrange additional diplomatic talks. The president stood firm: leave Kuwait.

I still have in my own files a copy of a handwritten draft of a note the president prepared to send Gorbachev. He wrote it after numerous exhaustive efforts by the coalition to convince Saddam Hussein to leave Iraq. As Bush prepared to move the coalition into the ground attack, he wrote to the Soviet leader:

After accounts on the statement out of Iraq—when I first heard this I was hoping that S. H. had realized that he must now withdraw, unconditionally, from Kuwait—in keeping with the UN resolutions.

Regrettably the Iraq statement now appears to be a cruel hoax, clouding the peace hopes of people in Iraq and indeed around the world.

Not only was the Iraq statement full of unacceptable old conditions—S. H. has added several new conditions.

We have been in touch with several of our allies. All of them recognize that there is nothing new here with the possible exception of recognizing for the first time that they must leave Kuwait.

Let me state once again[:]

Iraq must withdraw without condition.

There will be no linkage to other problems in the area.

The legitimate rulers of Kuwait must be returned to Kuwait.

Until a credible withdrawal begins with Iraqi troops visibly leaving Kuwait the coalition forces, in compliance with UN Res 678 will continue its efforts to force compliance with all 12 UN resolutions.

George Bush was making it clear to Mikhail Gorbachev that the coalition would not tolerate Saddam Hussein's stalling any longer.

The complexities of notifying everyone about the launch of the ground war were daunting. The military wanted to delay any public disclosure of the operations for obvious reasons, but the president was mindful of his promises to keep everyone in the loop. To compress the time we needed to complete all our notifications, we distributed assignments. Since so many had to be called in a short period of time, the president made arrangements with some of the congressional leaders for them to accept calls from me and Vice President Quayle when the time came.

When the last deadline for the Iraqis' withdrawal had passed, the Air Force had flown nearly 100,000 missions. There were half a million coalition troops ready to go. At 8:00 p.m. Washington time on February 23, 4:00 a.m. the following day Saudi time, the troops began to roll. The notifications began almost immediately after that.

The first situation reports started arriving in Washington a few hours later on Sunday, February 24. They indicated that all was going as planned, and that there were a minimum of casualties on the coalition side. That afternoon we received reports that Saddam was withdrawing from Kuwait. Not surprisingly, the Iraqis began calling for a cease-fire.

On February 26 reports came in describing an Iraqi army in retreat. The US Marines were moving into Kuwait and approaching Kuwait City. On February 27, Cheney told the president that the southern half of Kuwait was occupied by marines and that much of the Iraqi armor had been destroyed. Cheney said it looked as if this might be the last day of serious fighting. Mitterrand called the president to review what was happening and suggested that it might be time for diplomacy again.

That afternoon the core group met in the Oval Office and reviewed the situation. It was clear by then that the ground operations had been smoother and more effective than anyone could have anticipated, achieving their objective with far fewer casualties than predicted. The president asked the group whether it was time to stop. The consensus was that the mission had been accomplished. Since Cheney and Powell had to brief key members of Congress on the progress of the action, the core group agreed to meet again later in the afternoon before making a final decision.

The reassembled meeting began at about 6:00 p.m. We received a telephone call from General Schwarzkopf. During the discussion, I pointed out that if we ended the ground war at midnight it would be exactly one hundred hours after we started. Without much more discussion, the president and the group agreed that it would be midnight.

Months of hard work had paid off. George Bush had forged an unprecedented coalition, a coalition that included virtually every Arab country as well as America's old Cold War opponent, the Soviet Union. The allies had all committed to the operation under the mandate of the United Nations. Bush knew it would not be the last time a coalition of nations might have to be assembled to deal with aggression in the post–Cold War era and that coalitions are built on trust. He did not want to jeopardize our capacity to build effective coalitions in the future by violating the "rules" under which this one had been formed; hence the decision not to chase Saddam all the way into Baghdad.

Bush himself has explained why he did not go to Baghdad. "Trying to eliminate Saddam, extending the ground war into an occupation of Iraq, would've violated our guideline about not changing objectives in midstream, engaging in 'mission creep,' and would have incurred incalculable human and political costs," he wrote in A World Transformed. "We would have been forced to occupy Baghdad and, in effect, rule Iraq. The coalition would instantly have collapsed, the Arabs deserting it in anger and other allies pulling out as well.

"Furthermore, we had been self-consciously trying to set a pattern for handling aggression in the post–Cold War world," he added. "Going in and occupying Iraq—unilaterally exceeding the UN's mandate—would've destroyed the precedent of inter-national response to aggression that we hoped to establish. Had we gone the invasion route, the US could conceivably still be an occupying power in a bitterly hostile land."

The press, historians, and academics are often self-serving, even when they have the benefit of hindsight. Their retrospective analysis of events is frequently based on whatever narrative is fashionable at a given moment. Critiques of George Bush's deci-sion not to march our coalition into Baghdad to oust Saddam Hussein from power in 1991 have varied from very negative at the end of the Gulf War to very positive then and also later, after 9/11, when America found itself mired in a half decade of con-flict and occupation following our second effort to deal with an Iraqi threat to international stability. *Barron's* summed it up per-fectly in the headline of its 2005 article: "The First Bush Got It Right in Iraq."

Operation Desert Storm was George Bush being quiet but tough at his best. Seven months earlier, Iraq had invaded and occupied a neighboring country. The president used his experi-ence and his relationships to evaluate the situation, sift through his options, make a decision, build multilateral support for what had to be done, and garner the support of the United Nations to do so. It was a smart, courageous, and deft application of super-power leadership, and was probably the most efficient, effective major response to aggression in history. It was what Americans always hope they are getting when they elect a president.

Bush had said that "aggression will not stand." It did not stand. Kuwait was liberated.

10

Panama, China, the Israeli-Palestinian Conflict

E ven as he had to maintain consistent focus on the critical issues and main priorities related to the big opportunities in Europe, the Soviet Union, and Iraq, George Bush always remained mindful of the fact that the United States was also the principal player in providing stability in the rest of the world. He understood the significance of our position and the benefit of using our influence to help cool hot spots as they occurred. Bush managed, while closing out the Cold War and liberating Kuwait, to deal with a number of other critical events around the globe to extend America's influence, support our friends, and promote democracy and economic reform.

PANAMA

Once the serious differences with Congress over Iran-Contra had been reconciled and the Brady Plan formulated, President

Bush began to focus on a developing trouble spot in Latin America: Panama.

Panama is important to America and the world primarily because of the canal. It was and remains the indispensable link between the Atlantic and Pacific oceans, a critical conduit for military and strategic assets, not to mention a huge chunk of the world's commercial goods.

Panama had been a longtime ally of the United States, but was at the time controlled by a Panamanian general, Manuel Noriega. Noriega, also our ally at one time, had devolved into a significant player in the world of international drug trafficking. Bush saw him for what he was—a repressive dictator whose corruption was undermining America's drug-control efforts and a blot on a region turning increasingly democratic.

As the United States pressured him to stop the flow of drugs through Panama, Noriega retaliated by allowing, even encouraging, his military to harass members of the American military and their families stationed there. The U.S. military's Southern Command, the locus of our entire military presence in the Western Hemisphere, was based in Panama at the time, partly to protect the canal but also because Panama served as an ideal logistics base. Because of these and other strategic considerations, Bush felt Noriega's illicit and provocative activities had to be brought under control.

The Reagan administration had tried to resolve these issues with Noriega diplomatically, but had little success. Noriega used a 1988 coup attempt as an excuse to replace many of the officer corps of the Panamanian Defense Forces with his own, more loyal cadre. The purge solidified the dictator's hold on the military and, consequently, the country.

Following the purge, President Reagan imposed sanctions on Noriega's government and tried to negotiate him out of power.

Noriega had an indictment for drug trafficking looming over him in Miami, and there was discussion about whether to offer to drop it in exchange for his stepping down. Baker recalled that in an NSC meeting in the spring of 1988, George Bush, then Reagan's vice president, argued strongly against dropping the indictment. Reagan rejected Bush's recommendation, and a deal was offered to Noriega. He ignored it and stayed on.

After Bush became president, in May 1989, there were new presidential elections scheduled in Panama. Noriega prepared well for them, manipulating the voter lists and making it difficult for opposition voters to cast their ballots. He also arranged for his supporters to stuff the ballot boxes with votes for his own candidate. Following the election, Noriega declared that his hand-selected successor, Carlos Duque, had defeated opposition candidate Guillermo Endara.

An international group chaired by former president Jimmy Carter was on hand to observe the elections and documented the obvious fraud. One of the more memorable images the group offered as evidence of the intimidation and violence accompanying the campaign was a photograph of an opposition vice presidential candidate being beaten by Noriega's security forces. The photograph showed Guillermo Ford, his shirt soaked in blood, being attacked by one of Noriega's thugs. It made the cover of *Time* magazine.

The day after the photograph was published, George Bush announced that he was withdrawing the family members of our military from Panama for their own protection. He also recalled our ambassador, reduced the embassy staff to a bare minimum, and reinforced our troops in Panama with another infantry brigade. In his comments to the press that day, he pledged that "the days of the dictators are over."

Bush then ordered a canal-wide military exercise to permit the movement of American military across Panama. It was a show of force allowed under the Panama Canal Treaty and, Bush hoped, a clear signal to Noriega that he ought to accept the Reagan-era offer and leave the country.

As was his style, Bush made every effort to bring our allies into the process. He took the case to the Organization of American States. The government of Venezuela, pro-American at the time, arranged an emergency meeting of the OAS at its headquarters in Washington. Even with that leadership, I was surprised at how difficult it was to get a good resolution through the OAS. Historical concerns about the United States' reach into Latin America persisted. Eventually, a watered-down resolution was passed and the OAS agreed to regularly review the situation in Panama. Even the condemnation from his Latin neighbors did not convince Noriega to leave.

Bush continued to put additional pressure on Noriega. Because Noriega had at one time supported U.S. efforts in Latin America and developed personal relationships with our military leadership, the Department of Defense went so far as to replace the head of Southern Command with a new leader who had no ties to the Panamanian general.

Part of the pressure on Bush came from the fact that the canal was, after eighty-five years, due to revert to Panamanian control in 1999 under the terms of a treaty signed in 1977 by Jimmy Carter. Bush was convinced that such an important asset could not fall under the control of an illegitimately elected dictator like Manuel Noriega. As a matter of principle, he could not, however, renege on a legitimately signed treaty.

Bush continued to put pressure on Noriega directly and indirectly, through traditional diplomatic channels and through friends in other Latin American governments. In the fall of 1989, forces within Panama again tried to overthrow Noriega, but failed.

Noriega tightened his stranglehold yet again, and increased his assaults on our servicemen and -women in the country.

Finally, in December 1989, Noriega went too far when his cronies killed an unarmed American marine. On Sunday, December 17, the president summoned his senior advisors to an emergency meeting in the residence of the White House after a well-attended Christmas party. Following a very short review of the situation, the president received virtually unanimous support to take strong action. It appeared to a few of us that his mind had actually been made up even before the meeting.

Our efforts to keep the preparations secret were unsuccessful. There was enough visible movement of equipment and personnel for outlets like CNN to notice and begin airing video of troops and matériel flying out of places like Pope Air Force Base and Fort Bragg in North Carolina.

We arranged for opposition candidate Guillermo Endara and his two vice presidents to be sworn in a few moments after midnight on December 20 at a U.S. military base in the Canal Zone. With the approval of Endara, as the new president of Panama, American troops were officially deployed to the country.

No one was surprised that our troops easily overwhelmed Noriega's Panamanian Defense Forces. We were slightly taken aback, however, by the dictator's determination to stay put. Even with thousands of U.S. troops surrounding him, he went into hiding and took refuge in the residence of the papal nuncio to Panama.

I was home in New Hampshire on Christmas Eve when I got a call from Scowcroft. The president wanted me to call the Vatican to express our dismay that Noriega was being given refuge on Vatican property. When I protested to Scowcroft that he, as National Security Advisor, should make that call, he said he and Bush had decided that I was the "in-house Catholic" on the team and that I should do it.

Early in the evening on Christmas Eve I called Rome and asked to speak to the pope. I hadn't taken note of the time difference between New Hampshire and Italy. I was slightly embarrassed when his assistant told me that His Holiness was preparing for the traditional midnight Mass. I left the message. Later, I found out that Jim Baker also had placed a Christmas Eve phone call from his mother's home in Houston. He, too, had forgotten about the time difference.

We were finally able to convince the Vatican that this was not a typical instance of political asylum, and soon Noriega was expelled as an unwelcome guest. He surrendered to U.S. forces and was flown to Howard Air Force Base in Panama, where legal proceedings against him for his drug crimes were initiated. He was convicted and jailed in the United States.

George Bush's actions in support of the democratic processes in our hemisphere had demonstrated to our friends and neighbors that the United States was committed to and would stand up for true democratic reform in the region. Eventually the Organization of American States endorsed a policy of collective action "anywhere democracy was threatened" in the region. With the additional help of Bush's Enterprise for the Americas Initiative and the economic revitalization of the Latin American economies through the Brady Bonds, Bush helped usher in a decade of growth and democracy in the hemisphere.

CHINA

George Bush surprised Gerald Ford by asking to be assigned as the U.S. liaison officer to China in 1974. He wanted to go there because he recognized that Richard Nixon's opening to China in 1972 would be just the first step in a long process of harmonizing and modernizing the relationship between two inevitably intertwined global economies. His assignment there was the first of many visits to the Middle Kingdom, and served him well later when he was vice president and then president.

After Jimmy Carter defeated President Ford in 1976, the Chinese government invited Bush to China again. He put together a group of ten to join him and Barbara on that trip. The group included his future secretary of state, James Baker. Bush would return yet again as vice president, when Ronald Reagan asked him to visit Deng Xiaoping and reassure the Chinese that, in spite of Reagan's hot campaign rhetoric, he would, as president, honor Nixon and Zhou Enlai's Shanghai communiqué of 1972 and its artful construction on Taiwan and "One China."

Throughout his service as President Reagan's vice president from 1981 through 1989, George Bush continued to be the administration's principal contact with China. He nurtured his strong personal interest and took advantage of every opportunity to gain a deeper understanding of an area that remained enigmatic to most westerners.

During our transition after his election, our conversations on the president-elect's broad foreign policy agenda invariably turned to China. He even explored the possibility of an early trip there. From the very start of his administration, it was clear that Bush was determined to pursue a stronger Sino-American relationship.

By the time he took office in 1989, that relationship was stronger than it had been at any period since Nixon's 1972 initiative. Many bilateral exchanges were under way, including economic, cultural, educational, and diplomatic missions. There were even conversations going on between the two countries' military bureaucracies.

In the opening days of the administration, George Bush was

personally involved in the selection of our new ambassador to Beijing, James N. Lilley. Lilley was fluent in Chinese, had been part of Bush's return trip to China in 1977, and had served as a CIA station chief in Beijing while Bush was liaison officer.

As much as President Bush wanted to accelerate engagement with China, the opportunities in Europe and the Soviet Union were at such a crucial point that it normally would have been inappropriate for him to turn away for an impromptu visit to China before visiting our European partners. Then, just before the inauguration, the Japanese emperor died. The loss of an emperor was a significant event in Japan, and an extensive funeral ceremony was scheduled for the last week in February.

Despite the regrettable circumstances, the event provided the opportunity for the president to appropriately alter his travel priorities and make a journey to Japan and China his first major trip outside North America. In the planning process, we decided to add a stop in South Korea. Bush was particularly pleased because he would get a chance to meet and briefly speak with Chinese leaders ahead of a trip to Beijing by Mikhail Gorbachev.

Since all of this was effectively "spur of the moment," the president decided to categorize the trip as a "working visit" instead of an official, full state visit. That designation did not diminish the importance of the trip, but allowed for less formality, less pomp, and more efficient use of the time available for serious discussions. Scowcroft, Baker, and their teams had to move quickly, but they were able to arrange meetings with Deng Xiaoping, Li Peng, and Zhao Ziyang. They were the three key government and political party leaders in China: Deng was the leader and elder statesman, Li Peng was the premier, and Zhao was the former premier and was, at that time, the general secretary of the Communist Party.

We landed in Japan on February 23, and while we were there

Bush took advantage of the auspicious gathering of heads of state to have about a dozen bilateral meetings, including some with the leaders from Turkey, Pakistan, India, Egypt, Italy, Spain, Jordan, and Israel. Two days later, we flew to Beijing, and Bush opened the visit by meeting with Chinese president Yang Shangkun. Their conversation was very cordial, and the president reported back to us later that Yang had told him, "China does not intend to have any military alliance or military relationship with the Soviet Union."

The big welcome continued. The first evening the Chinese hosted us all at a wonderful banquet of multiple courses in the cavernous Great Hall of the People. The dinner was cohosted by President Yang and Li Peng, and in addition to the usual pleasantries, the conversations included discussions about the Soviet Union and Gorbachev's perestroika. The Chinese were hopeful for Gorbachev, but thought they were handling political and economic change better than their Soviet counterparts.

Our meetings the next day were a bit more formal, first with Li Peng and later with the vice premier and the foreign minister. The Chinese emphasized that they wanted to normalize a relationship with the Soviet Union that had been strained for over a decade, but again they made it clear that they were not seeking any sort of alliance with the Soviet Union. That was good news to our defense strategists, because one of the great benefits of Nixon's original opening of relations with China had been the splintering of its informal alliance with the Soviet Union.

The Chinese deliberately pointed out some nuances of, and differences between, the way things were progressing in the Soviet Union and the way they had progressed in China. In particular, the Chinese noted that Gorbachev was emphasizing political reform and democratization. In China, the focus was on economic reform. The Gorbachev approach, they said, "might

provoke ethnic problems" in the Soviet Union. "In my view," Li
Peng told Bush, "the Soviet Union should mainly concentrate on
the economic problems in the country." Their opinions would
prove to be very perceptive in terms of some of the difficulties
Gorbachev encountered as he dismantled the Soviet empire.

President Bush and the Chinese were remarkably comfortable
being direct and blunt with each other. It was refreshing when
compared with the tap dance of diplomacy that usually was per-
formed at such events. The Chinese specifically emphasized, for
example, that America should not try to influence their internal
policies. The direct admonitions, however, were constructively
nuanced. The Chinese had no problem with observations and
comments within the United States about what was happening
internally in China, but those opinions had to stay at home. At
no point would they tolerate the United States' trying to impose
those views directly on the Chinese people. Bush graciously
took it all in—the old China hand in him clearly at work—but
countered that a successful relationship with the United States
depended on the free flow of ideas, goods, and people.

Li Peng was forward-looking in his approach. "We hope to see
the continuation of a good friend in the development of relations
between our two countries, so I particularly stress the above
points," he said in his closing statement. "As old friends, I feel we
can talk in this very frank way. With others, I might not approach
the question in this matter."

Shortly after that meeting, the president was told that we
could meet with Deng Xiaoping. The iconic leader looked even
older than his age of eighty-four. His face was worn and faded
but his eyes were bright. He was clearly not in the best of health,
and yet was both animated and energetic in his conversation
with the president. He was also the most voracious chain-smoker
I had ever seen, puffing expertly from one cigarette to the next.

Deng focused on the Chinese-Soviet relationship. He repeated what we had already heard—that there were no plans for an anti-American alliance with the Soviet Union.

Deng spent a great deal of time reflecting on George Bush's years in China. He was optimistic that Bush's personal history would set the stage for significant improvement in the relationship between the two countries. With Bush, Deng said he could envision building a relationship based on trust, not just on strategic opportunity.

A man whose generation had suffered through a century of Japanese aggression in Asia, Deng was still bitter about what he perceived as the Allies' betrayal of China at Yalta. Deng, undoubtedly aware of Bush's service in the Pacific during World War II, had no qualms about making his displeasure known, even at that late date. "Yalta not only severed Outer Mongolia from China, but also brought the northeastern part of China into the Soviet sphere," he complained through his translator.

Bush listened intently, then responded honestly. "You are not offending me, I don't like Yalta either," he told the Chinese leader. "In retrospect Yalta didn't turn out so well. It pledged free elections for Eastern Europe, and they still haven't occurred." The elections in Poland would not occur for another four months.

Deng also was not shy about expressing disdain for what he perceived to be the Soviet strategy of encircling China. That strategy was, in his words, extremely "unfavorable for China," and he was definitely displeased that the policy seemed to be continuing into the present.

George Bush was as direct as Deng. He stressed how important it was that China and the United States raise their level of engagement. He also wanted a relationship based on trust, and noted that further exchanges between the two countries were certain, now that China's economic focus was beginning to succeed. The two leaders had been able to speak frankly with each other, and Bush said he hoped this would lead to more discussions that would not be interpreted as interference. Through all of the exchanges, Bush was able to make tough points while keeping the exchange cordial and engaging.

Bush thought the meetings in China were more than worth the trip. "I had left Beijing optimistic that we had laid some important groundwork for productive and diplomatic relations, despite the threats of turbulence in China's domestic affairs," he later wrote.

His optimism was dashed in late May and early June when what started as peaceful demonstrations in Tiananmen Square led to a brutal crackdown on the dissidents and students gathered there. Several hundred people died, and there was no way the United States could fail to condemn the brutality. For Bush, the question was how to condemn what he knew was wrong, and react appropriately. He knew we had to remain engaged, even if the formal relationship had to be put on hold for the time being.

Following the repression in Tiananmen Square, Bush characteristically turned to the one former president he knew would be most helpful with the Chinese—Richard Nixon. Early on the morning of June 5, 1989, he spoke with his old friend on the phone.

"Don't disrupt the relationship," Nixon told Bush. "What's happened has been handled badly and is deplorable, but take a look at the long haul." Recalling our ambassador from Beijing was not a good idea, the two men agreed. A clear statement against the brutality might be in order, but a good relationship in the long run must be the primary goal.

A statement denouncing the Chinese government's actions came following a meeting between Bush and the congressional leadership later that day. With the full support of Congress,

Bush also laid out the actions that the United States would take in response, including suspending all military sales and visits to China. He was pleased that he had bipartisan support, for a change, on the tone of the United States' response. In the Oval Office afterward, Bush noted to me and Scowcroft that even Senator Jesse Helms, often a hawk about China, seemed supportive.

It was critical that any sudden complications in the relationship with China be handled deftly. Bush tried to call Deng Xiaoping. Scowcroft noted at the time that no American president before Bush had ever attempted to place a direct phone call to a Chinese leader. Unfortunately and surprisingly, the president was unable to get through. This frustrated the hands-on diplomat in Bush immensely. He had to settle for messages sent via the Chinese ambassador in Washington.

The overly emotional response by the American media also frustrated Bush and complicated things. "You have the networks, led principally by Dan Rather, pitching everything with the highest emotional content and driving to . . . almost break relationships with China, and that I don't want," he wrote in his diary on June 10.

Eager to find a way to communicate directly with the Chinese, Bush prepared a letter for Deng. It was, he put it, "Straight from my heart, so I composed it myself."

He wrote in "sadness, as one who appreciated the serious reforms that had taken place in China," the letter began. The letter referenced the meetings just a few months earlier, and spoke of his fondness and respect for China, its history, its culture, and its tradition. Then, as directly as he had in those earlier meetings, he turned to the issue at hand. He praised the early tolerance of the Chinese for the demonstrations but lamented "the turmoil and the bloodshed with which the demonstrations were ended."

He wrapped up by stating, "When there are difficulties between friends, as now, we must find a way to talk them out," and concluded with an offer to send an emissary to Beijing. "We must not let this important relationship suffer further," Bush wrote.

The next morning the president showed the letter to Brent Scowcroft, Jim Baker, and me. He insisted that no one else was to know about it. We all commented favorably on his effort, and Brent noted how important it was that the letter clearly showed that the sentiments expressed were "the president's own words."

After a series of missteps and missed opportunities, the letter made it to Deng's hands, and the Chinese agreed to receive an emissary. The president sent Brent Scowcroft and Deputy Secretary of State Lawrence Eagleburger. The trip was entirely secret, and Scowcroft and Eagleburger met Deng in the Great Hall of the People. Li Peng and the vice premier and foreign minister also attended.

Deng opened the conversation by reaffirming how much he valued his friendship with Bush because "his words are rather trustworthy." The premier spoke about Tiananmen, of course, downplaying the number of injuries and the deaths, then turned directly to the differences between the two countries that had surfaced as a result.

In response, Scowcroft remained faithful to the tone and the message that President Bush wanted to convey. He reminded the Chinese how far the two countries had come since the original Shanghai communiqué. Despite the inevitable ups and downs, the relationship had steadily improved. Bush wanted to continue that trend, Scowcroft said. How China chose to deal with its internal affairs was a matter for China to decide, he said, but its leaders must understand that those decisions had an impact on its relationships abroad and its options for dealing with America and the rest of the world.

Bush had directed Scowcroft to discuss the actions he had taken, but also to underscore the actions he had *not* taken. The president was being criticized in the press and by Congress and was under pressure to come down harder, he said, noting that the U.S. House of Representatives had voted, 418–0, to impose stiffer sanctions on China.

Both sides ended up agreeing to work their way through this very difficult period without sacrificing the progress that had been made in the relationship. When they sat down to lunch just before Scowcroft and Eagleburger were scheduled to leave, Li Peng waved off any efforts to continue the conversation. "Let us talk of something else," he said. His ease made it clear to Scowcroft that the Chinese were pleased the trip had taken place and pleased with the overall conversations.

In sending his heartfelt letter to Deng, George Bush had used his particular style of personal diplomacy to great effect. The visit by Eagleburger and Scowcroft affirmed the president's preference for face-to-face dialogue instead of diplomatic back channels. Through it, he was able to convey his forthright disapproval of the Chinese actions without being condescending. Bush was extremely pleased with the outcome—it had reopened and facilitated communication with the Chinese leaders he knew so well. A dark diplomatic cloud had dissipated and the president felt free enough to turn his attention, less than a week later, to Europe, NATO, and facilitating the end of the Cold War.

Though there was no significant or historic expansion of Chinese-U.S. relations during President Bush's tenure, his measured and wise response in dealing with the Chinese through this difficult crisis was significant and important in earning their trust and keeping the relationship intact. During the Gulf War, when China's vote and capacity to veto resolutions in the U.N. Security Council could have handcuffed his efforts to build a coalition against Saddam and work multilaterally through the United Nations, China stood aside and let Bush do what had to be done.

THE ISRAELI-PALESTINIAN CONFLICT

George Bush was a smart, experienced leader and diplomat with a full grasp of just how complicated and frustrating Israeli-Palestinian issues were. Both Bush and James Baker recognized the dispute for what it was—a "quagmire." Nixon warned the two men that Reagan's reputation as "the most pro-Israeli president in history" only made the challenge more difficult.

"It's time for some evenhandedness out there," Nixon said. "But basically, the Middle East is insoluble. Stay away from it!"

On the other hand, Bush believed that even small steps could make a difference in the festering problems in the Middle East. Once the American-led coalition ousted Saddam Hussein from Kuwait, Bush sensed an opportunity, perhaps a unique one, to get the Arabs and the Palestinians talking with the Israelis.

George Bush and Jim Baker both felt that the principle of "territory for peace" was a sound footing on which the dispute could begin to be resolved. Baker laid out the White House position in a speech to the American Israel Public Affairs Committee (AIPAC) as far back as May 1989. The speech was not entirely well received because it made clear that both the Israelis and the Palestinians had to make concessions if there was to be a comprehensive solution. Previously, as Nixon noted, the onus was almost entirely on the Arabs. Many supporters of Israel saw it as a pointed message directed at Israel.

The principal issue hampering any progress was the expansion of Jewish settlements in the Palestinian territories. Finding common ground on settlement activity in the West Bank and Gaza was, Bush believed, critical to any solution. He felt strongly that expansion of the Jewish settlements was wrong, not only because it wasn't fair but because it was hindering any possibility of resolving the problem.

There was a serious disconnect between Bush and Israeli prime minister Yitzhak Shamir, and not the least of its causes was the issue of Israeli settlements in the West Bank and East Jerusalem. On more than one occasion, Shamir had outright misled him on the topic. Bush rarely got honest answers out of the prime minister, and the commitments Shamir made were rarely fulfilled. Shamir told Bush he would halt expansion of the settlements, but never followed through. After every such promise, Bush would find out in short order that the Israelis had turned around and approved a new batch of settlements.

During the president's foreign policy briefings, he would occasionally be given maps of the region with Israeli settlements marked in red. Each time he saw a new map of the region, there was more and more red. The president considered Shamir untrustworthy, a feeling reinforced every time he looked at another map. Finally, after yet one more expansion of settlements, the president asked me to get him an exact representation of the "Green Line" boundary established in 1949 to demarcate territory the United Nations had divided between the Israelis and the Palestinians. To get the president a correct and accurate answer, I asked the CIA to send over some maps.

Any significant public initiative on the Israeli-Palestinian issue carried risk. Failure could stop the momentum and erode the credibility Bush had built through the first half of his term. But by 1991, Bush looked around the world and decided that perhaps the time was right.

The military might of Saddam Hussein, a consistently belligerent voice in the region, had been decimated during Desert Storm, giving Israel a new sense of security. The United States' rescue of Kuwait, in a coalition with Arab partners, enhanced our credibility in the Arab world. The new relationship with the Soviet Union meant the two superpowers could now cooperate on issues in that part of the world. Bush determined that the time was right and the potential benefits were worth the risk, so he directed Secretary of State Baker to begin the process.

The president decided the right vehicle would be a regional conference attended by both the Israelis and the Palestinians, as well as their Arab neighbors Saudi Arabia, Egypt, Jordan, and— though it may have seemed far-fetched at the time—Syria. Baker started with direct conversations with Prime Minister Shamir in Israel and representatives of the Palestinians. Baker's conversations were the first of many discussions.

The regional conference would be the next step. The president hoped that broad participation would help unwind the fabric of fear and distrust that had constrained such meetings in the past. We had no delusions about how difficult it would be to pull together such a conference, but it was a well-thought-out starting vehicle. The Arabs had long been pushing for a multilateral conference, and the Israelis had been saying publicly that they would participate in face-to-face negotiations as well. A regional conference seemed to satisfy both sides.

Baker's shuttle diplomacy was tireless—he sat through what seemed to be endless meetings with Shamir and the Palestinians. There also were face-to-face discussions with President Assad in Syria and King Fahd of Saudi Arabia, and Baker found an ally in Egyptian president Mubarak. When Assad said he would attend, it was a major breakthrough. With that commitment, Bush was able to convince the Israelis and the Palestinians to show up.

After that, it was relatively easy to get the Saudis, the Egyptians, and the Jordanians on board.

George Bush worked hard to get Gorbachev and the Soviet Union to cosponsor the conference, and they eventually agreed. Everything about it turned out to be difficult, however. Even selecting a title was a problem: after much hemming and hawing, the parties agreed to call it a "peace conference." Then there was debate about the location—also controversial. Finally, just eleven days before the scheduled opening, Madrid was proposed and deemed suitable by all participants. Baker and his team had to scramble, really scramble, to get the details in place.

The Madrid Conference (October 30–November 1, 1991) proved to be, as the president hoped, a turning point in Middle East relations. Unfortunately the path beyond that turning point was slow, tedious, and frequently interrupted. Madrid prompted some further dialogue between the Israelis and Palestinians leading to some progress on peripheral issues. Those meetings were followed by the Oslo Accords (1993, 1995), which led to a recognition of the State of Israel by the Palestinians and an acknowledgment by the Israelis that the PLO—and its successor, the Palestinian Authority—was the appropriate partner to deal with in resolving their differences.

Bill Clinton would probably have had a much harder, if not an impossible, time getting Yasser Arafat and the Palestinians to meet with Prime Minister Ehud Barak and the Israelis at Camp David in 2000 if not for the Madrid Conference. George Bush may not have succeeded in entirely solving the Israeli-Palestinian "quagmire," but he was the one who got them started talking about a solution.

11

The Supreme Court

Near the end of my first term as governor of New Hampshire, I made three judicial appointments: two to the superior court of New Hampshire and one to the New Hampshire supreme court. We decided to swear all the judges in together, in a ceremony in the Great Room just outside the governor's office in the State House. The large room was packed with family and friends of the three new judges, as well as other lawyers who might someday want to be judges themselves.

During my brief comments about how distinguished the selections were, I listed what I felt were the appropriate qualifications to be a judge in New Hampshire. Of course, I included all the usual attributes: talent, intelligence, integrity, character, and experience. Looking out across the room, I couldn't help noticing that all three judges were a little shorter than I am, so I added, "And of course, as you can see, you cannot be any taller than the governor."

Everyone laughed a bit, and then I swore them all in.

When I returned to my office a couple of staffers asked whether I had noticed what happened when I made the remark about not being any taller than the governor. My answer was, "When a governor makes a joke everyone laughs." But they pointed out what I had missed, "When you said you can't be any taller than the governor, all the lawyers in the room bent their knees a bit and scrunched down to look shorter."

One of the most important responsibilities of a president— also the least predictable one—is nominating judges, particularly justices of the United States Supreme Court. Once a particular justice is appointed to the Supreme Court, his or her votes can affect its decisions for many years, even decades. The process of selecting a judge is not as simple as it looks, and history has proved that presidents don't always get the kind of judge they thought they were appointing. Just like our lawyers in New Hampshire, lawyers and judges vying for a spot on the Supreme Court will often "scrunch down" as far as they need to in order to eventually attract a president's support.

In February 1989, a month after Bush took office, White House counsel Boyden Gray came to my office to talk about judicial appointments. Gray was a silver-haired attorney with an education from Harvard and the University of North Carolina Law School. He had clerked for the chief justice of the United States, and before becoming White House counsel he served as then vice president George Bush's legal counsel. Smart as a whip and loyal in every way, Gray had justifiably earned the trust of the president.

At our meeting, Gray showed me a list of potential Supreme Court nominees he had begun compiling. An appointment or two to the Court was all but certain at some point during Bush's tenure. Several justices were already in their eighties. Although the more liberal among them might have preferred being replaced with the appointees of a Democratic president, there already had been a Republican in the White House for eight years, and the whispers around Washington suggested that they couldn't wait any longer to retire. Gray wanted to be prepared when the time came.

There were nine names on the list left over from the Reagan days. Gray and his colleague Lee Lieberman added a number of their own recommendations to the list, then culled it down to fifteen potential candidates categorized as what Gray labeled "Qualified Candidates" and "Outstanding Candidates." The former included Senator Orrin Hatch of Utah; Carla Hills, who would later serve as Bush's U.S. trade representative; Appeals Court judge James L. Buckley; University of Texas Law School professor Charles Alan Wright, an expert on constitutional law; Ricardo Hinojosa of Texas's Southern U.S. District Court; and Clarence Thomas, a former chairman of the Equal Employment Opportunity Commission who had just been nominated to the United States Court of Appeals, D.C. Circuit.

In the memo, Gray described the criteria by which the president might want to judge the candidates. The nominee should, most important, have a first-rate intellect, sound judgment, and a "demonstrated understanding of the proper judicial role," as he put it. "Other important criteria include pro-life support, approach to separation of power, attitude toward the free enterprise system and private sector background." All the traits, in other words, of a solid conservative, just like the president.

Nine people fell into the category of "Outstanding Candidates," and Gray listed their particular strengths and weaknesses. Appeals Court judge Laurence Silberman had demonstrated a "strong commitment to separation of powers" and had an "attractive combination of private sector and government experience." Circuit judge Stephen F. Williams was "strong on both separation of powers and commitment to the free enterprise system."

Circuit judge David B. Sentelle had the fact that he was a southerner going for him and a "generally excellent" record on the
bench, but Gray noted that one decision of his "fails to give
proper deference to the president's foreign policy interests."
Appeals Court judge Pasco Bowman was also noted as a southerner, though living at the time in Missouri, with right to life support and commercial law expertise. "He would likely be strongly
opposed by organized labor," however, Gray noted.

Another southerner on the list with a strong private background was Patrick Higginbotham, a Fifth Circuit judge born
in Alabama "viewed with suspicion by National Right to Life
because of an opinion invalidating a statute prohibiting fetal
experimentation." Judge Edith Jones, also from the Fifth Circuit,
was described as a "Southern woman (Texas) with strong right to
life support and private sector experience." Appeals Court judge
Kenneth Starr, who would later be named independent prosecutor in the impeachment case that plagued Bill Clinton, was
also labeled "Southerner (born in Texas, lives in Virginia) who
has served in both the judicial and executive branches." Second
Circuit Appeals Court judge Ralph K. Winter Jr. was said to have
"a solid understanding of the separation of powers and the free
enterprise system." The list also included David Souter, whom
I had named to the state supreme court when I was governor.
The memo indicated Souter was said to have "strong right-to-
life support and experience in the New Hampshire executive
and judicial branches." Souter was on the list mainly because of
the aggressive lobbying of the Reagan administration by New
Hampshire's U.S. senator Warren Rudman.

My meeting with Boyden was followed by a lunch with the
president that included Attorney General Thornburgh, Gray,
and me. Bush stressed to us that he wanted to be well prepared
to act as soon as any Supreme Court vacancy occurred. Thorn-

burgh and Gray immediately set out vetting the list even further, reducing it down to a manageable number of nine prospective candidates—essentially, everyone on Gray's list of "Outstanding Candidates." They did a thorough job and we felt we were well prepared.

After a National Security Council meeting that afternoon I walked with the president to the Oval Office. It was about 6:00 p.m.—later than usual for our afternoon review meeting. Since the president had an hour and a half until he and Mrs. Bush were due at a dinner with his old friend Pete McCloskey, we weren't in too much of a hurry. We were also both a bit worn out by the day. Our conversation was less focused on specifics than our usual afternoon summaries.

The president referred back to our lunch earlier that day with Gray and Thornburgh, and again spoke about the chances of making at least one and perhaps two Supreme Court appointments. As we talked, Bush recalled, "I remember reading that Eisenhower said that his two biggest mistakes were his two appointments to the Supreme Court." After grumbling a bit on how unclear the process of picking judges was, he added, "Even if I ever felt that way about my appointments, I would never criticize any of those decisions in public."

He paused and grew thoughtful for a minute. He would get no argument from me about how onerous the responsibility for selecting judges was for either a governor or a president. I had found it particularly tough to do because I always seemed to have to choose without enough solid information on which to base a good decision. I added, "It gets hard because you're having to select someone from a group of people who have probably spent all their lives prepping themselves to be chosen." I recounted my story about the nominations I had made as governor and the "scrunched" lawyers in the audience.

"Mr. President, that is the problem with making appointments," I added. "Our friends spend all of their lives trying to look exactly like what they think is required to get the job. Only when they finally get where they want to be do they reveal their real selves."

Bush chuckled a bit, then got serious. "We just have to trust that Boyden and Dick will really be able to find us good people. All I can do is hope to appoint a really good person to the Court."

George Bush had a front row seat as vice president when the partisan Democratic senators and their extreme liberal constituencies had joined forces to reject Ronald Reagan's nomination of Robert Bork to the Supreme Court. Bork's opponents actually ran television ads narrated by Gregory Peck attacking him, and senators Kennedy and Biden led a Senate assault on Robert Bork's conservative positions. A new verb, bork, as in "to be borked," came into popular parlance in the aftermath of the hearings. Borking is defined as the process of obstructing someone, especially a candidate for public office, "through systematic defamation or vilification."

George Bush made it clear that he did not want his nominees to be borked. He wanted to be as prepared as possible as soon as possible with solid recommendations. By acting quickly, if and when the opportunity arose to make a nomination to the Supreme Court, we could minimize the time available for the opposition to organize and fund any partisan battles over the confirmation.

A few months later, when Justice Brennan stepped down from the court, Gray's preparation efforts gave us a big head start. Gray and Thornburgh met to whittle down the list even further, then Boyden and his deputy counsel Lee Lieberman quickly came to the president with four potential nominees: judges Souter, Jones, Silberman, and Thomas. I joined the meeting to discuss the candidates. The list of four was quickly pared down to just David Souter and Edith Jones.

The counsel's office went through its process of interviewing those two candidates and reviewing their detailed legal histories. Throughout that process, David Souter, who had been well prepped by Senator Rudman, shrewdly avoided taking any legal position on what was then the critical issue of abortion. At that time the topic had become prominent in the political tug-of-war that took place during the confirmation process for Supreme Court justices. Rudman had admonished Souter to give no hint of where he stood on that issue, and Souter artfully did just that.

David Souter knew George Bush was looking for a conservative judge, and that meant one who supported a reversal of *Roe v. Wade*. Souter carefully answered Gray and Lieberman's questions in vague terms, often couched in broad legal principles, to make them believe he fitted the conservative character they sought.

In my own one-on-one conversations with Souter, I tried to get a sense of where he stood on the major issues. Although Souter insisted he did not think it proper to discuss specifically any issue that might come before the Court, he did tell me that he believed "abortion was a violent act." Again, his tone, his body language, and the phrasing of his answers left me with the impression that he supported a change in *Roe v. Wade*. Of course, that would be great news for conservatives who believed there were already four votes on the Supreme Court to overturn *Roe*. If they were correct, then with Souter, that number would rise to the magic number five.

President Bush reviewed Boyden Gray's memorandum on the two finalists and asked Vice President Quayle, Attorney General Thornburgh, Boyden Gray, and me to review with him the merits of each before making a final selection. Quayle and I looked at both the philosophical and the political sides of the candidates, and made strong arguments for Edith Jones. I felt it important that George Bush name a second woman to the Supreme Court. Thornburgh and Gray supported Souter from a legal perspective.

Thornburgh's strong opposition to Edith Jones surprised me. Later, I learned that he felt Judge Jones "had a little too much of a hard edge to her for her to be an easy confirm." The president took about an hour to privately review what he had read and heard. Then he came back with Souter as his choice.

At the time, in spite of my personal preference for Jones, I was pleased to see someone from New Hampshire nominated for the Court. Armed with reassurances from solid conservatives like former governor Meldrim Thomson and some conservative judges from New Hampshire who had served on our courts with Souter, I worked hard to make sure the confirmation process went smoothly.

I sincerely believed Souter would be a good conservative justice on the United States Supreme Court. Boyden Gray and Lee Lieberman had pored over his decisions from both the New Hampshire superior court and the New Hampshire supreme court and deemed them conservative. The decisions were consistent, they said, with what they would expect from a judge who applied the law instead of trying to make it.

From my own experience as governor, I recalled an encouraging encounter with Souter. The state had been embroiled in difficult contract negotiations with the State Employees' Association of New Hampshire, and the union decided to strike, which was against New Hampshire state law. It announced the strike late one evening, while I was at a speaking engagement.

On the way back to the state capital, the state trooper driving me received a message on the radio asking me to stop at the next phone along the way and call my legal counsel in the governor's office. This was in the days before cellular phones. We stopped, and I made the call from a phone booth. My counsel, attorney Stephen Merrill—who later would become attorney general of New Hampshire and later still governor—told me of the decision by the employees' union to strike.

"Meet me in my office at the State House," I told him, and instructed him to find a superior court judge who would convene the court for hearings immediately. When I got to my office, Steve was already there and had arranged for a hearing at 1:00 a.m. The judge's clerk was in the process of notifying the lawyers of the state employees' union of the hearing.

At the hearing, the judge listened intently to both sides and then, after a short review in his office, rendered his decision. It was definitely illegal for the union to go on strike, he said, and every union member had to be notified to be at work the next morning. The officers of the union had to personally notify their more than ten thousand members to be at their jobs at 8:00 a.m., and had to maintain a log of those notifications. The judge was enforcing the law as written, and was willing to make a tough, possibly unpopular, decision to uphold that law. That judge was David Souter.

Souter's confirmation hearings before the Senate Judiciary Committee could not have gone more smoothly. The judge offered only broad answers to the committee members' philosophical questions and avoided any specifics on questions he said "might come before the Court." If the Democrats had any intention of doing to Souter what they had done to Bork, he wouldn't give them any basis for an attack. He was truly the "stealth candidate." Easily confirmed by the Senate by a 90–9 vote, he was sworn in by Chief Justice William Rehnquist at the White House in October.

The conservative community was devastated a couple of years later when, after he joined the Court, Justice David Souter provided the crucial fifth vote to save *Roe v. Wade* in *Planned Parenthood v. Casey* (1992). He cast that vote despite the fact that, as he indicated to me in our conversations at the White House and as was written in that decision, "Some of us as individuals find abortion offensive to our most basic principles of morality."

Souter also provided the fifth vote to uphold the constitutionality of race-based affirmative action and the fifth vote to bar the Ten Commandments from the lobby of a Kentucky courthouse. By the end of his career, he was consistently joining with liberals to thwart good laws and protect unconstitutional ones.

Over the years, I anguished along with my conservative friends as we watched David Souter become more and more liberal. To add insult to injury, Souter waited to retire until there was a Democratic president so he could be replaced with a justice as liberal as he was. As I watched Barack Obama replace David Souter with Sonia Sotomayor, I ruefully marveled at how artfully David had demonstrated, all those years ago, how easy it is to deceive by saying next to nothing.

On June 27, 1991, about a year after Souter was nominated, Justice Thurgood Marshall announced his retirement from the Court. Boyden Gray and his team again were ready with recommendations for the president.

The president was preparing to go to Kennebunkport for a long weekend when we heard about Marshall's resignation. I met with Boyden and asked him to join me at the Justice Department to meet with Thornburgh and come back with a short list of options for the president.

All along, I sensed that Boyden had been waiting for an opportunity to have the president nominate Clarence Thomas. Our conservative community had been waiting since Bork's defeat to get a justice on the Court with the strong, strict constructionist perspectives of Clarence Thomas. As soon as I heard that Marshall was stepping down, I was pretty sure that our nominee would be Clarence Thomas, and I thought him an excellent choice.

As expected, Gray and Thornburgh brought a very short list of two to the president: Judge Reynaldo Garza, who served on the United States Court of Appeals, Fifth Circuit; and Judge Thomas, who by then had been sitting on the United States Court of Appeals, D.C. Circuit, for more than a year. Before the president left for Maine, we reviewed our two candidates. This time, except for some early surprising objections by Attorney General Thornburgh, the president and our team quickly coalesced around Judge Thomas.

The next day I went up to Walker's Point to meet with the president. We were joined by Boyden Gray and Attorney General Thornburgh. After some discussion, the president confirmed that he was inclined to nominate Clarence Thomas but wanted to meet with him first. Arrangements were made to fly Thomas to Kennebunkport.

The judge arrived on a government plane, landing at Portland, Maine, and I was driven there to bring him back to meet with the president. We sat together in the backseat and chatted on the drive back to Kennebunkport. He appeared to be somewhat nervous. While we were driving, I was thinking about how difficult it was going to be to sneak past the reporters who always gathered around the single entrance to the president's compound when he was there. I saw an opportunity to try to help Judge Thomas unwind his nerves.

As we approached the gate, I told him, "You know the press will all be gathered near the entrance trying to see who's driving in and out, so when we get close I'm going to give you my glasses. If you put my glasses on, then, when they catch a glimpse of who's in the car they'll think you're me."

Clarence looked at me for about five seconds, and then the absurdity of my suggestion hit him and he burst out into that wonderful, deep laugh of his and settled down. Somehow we did manage to get onto the Point without the press getting a good glimpse at who was in the car.

Once we passed through the checkpoint, we drove up the water side of the drive to the main house, and slipped through the side door and out onto the deck. Judge Thomas himself described to Doro Bush what happened there: "President Bush introduced me to everybody on the deck and when I arrived Mrs. Bush was standing there wearing a big hat and she said, 'Judge, congratulations.' Then catching herself, she said, 'I guess I let the cat out of the bag.'"

"Bush said, 'I'd like to ask you a few questions,'" Thomas recalled the president saying to him after they had settled in. "'First, can you and your family go through the confirmation?'"

After Thomas answered yes, the president continued: "If you go on the Supreme Court, can you call them as you see them?"

Thomas again answered in the affirmative.

"Look, if you become a member of the Supreme Court, I will never publicly criticize any opinion of yours," Bush then told Thomas. "At two o'clock I'm going to nominate you to the Supreme Court of the United States. Let's go have lunch."

Thomas said he was slightly shocked. "That was the totality of our discussion about the Supreme Court."

The nomination of Clarence Thomas did not go as smoothly as Souter's. It was, from the beginning, a protracted, bitter, partisan battle. Less than a week after the announcement, an officer of the National Organization for Women (NOW) vowed that the group was "going to Bork him." NOW was joined by the National Education Association and other extreme liberal groups that pressured the Democratic majority in the Senate to reject another conservative Republican nomination.

It is the responsibility of the Senate Judiciary Committee, at that time chaired by Senator Joe Biden of Delaware, to review all judicial nominations and make a recommendation to the entire Senate. Although as recently as a year earlier the Senate had confirmed Thomas's appointment to the Federal Appellate Court, Biden decided to delay the hearings until late September, probably to give the liberal interest groups time to organize and fund their assault.

When the committee hearings began on September 10, 1991, the Democrats lit into Thomas for his conservative perspectives. They tried to pin him down on the positions he might take on cases related to *Roe v. Wade*, but didn't get very far. The first hearings did not really produce any damaging testimony, but the committee defeated a motion to recommend his confirmation, and on September 27 sent the nomination to the floor without a recommendation. A full Senate vote was scheduled for October 8.

On October 5, Senator Jack Danforth of Missouri, who had been championing Judge Thomas and mentoring him through the process, received a call from Senator Orrin Hatch, the ranking Republican on the Judiciary Committee. Hatch told Danforth that one of Thomas's former employees at the Equal Employment Opportunity Commission had come forward alleging that Thomas sexually harassed her. Danforth, who knew Thomas extremely well, did not believe it.

When word of the allegations was leaked, probably by Biden's staff, the extreme liberal groups rallied their troops and pressured the Democrats to reopen the hearings. We asked Boyden Gray to review the statements and accusations that had been given to the investigators. He told us that the FBI had interviewed Anita Hill before the allegations became public, and during those interviews she was relatively temperate. After being promised anonymity, she told the FBI that she did not feel it necessary to testify before Congress. More important, Boyden Gray told the president and me that the FBI had determined that "what she was complaining about had occurred—based on her own timeline—two or three months before she had ever met Thomas."

Unfortunately, the floodgates were opened. Democrats on the committee grilled Thomas as if he were guilty as charged. They reopened hearings to allow additional testimony on the harassment allegations. The Democrats trotted out friends of Anita Hill to testify on her behalf; the Republicans brought in witnesses who knew Clarence Thomas and testified in support of the judge. Of the witnesses who knew both Thomas and Hill personally, all testified in support of Thomas.

Clarence Thomas's supporters noted in the hearings that Anita Hill followed him to another job well after the time during which she claimed to have been harassed. Among the many women who testified supporting Clarence Thomas was Diane Holt, his personal secretary for half a dozen years. Holt made it clear that she never once saw any hint of the kind of behavior Hill claimed. Senator Alan Simpson said he found it puzzling that Hill would have continued her interactions with Thomas well after the time she accused him of harassing her—interactions that included meetings, dinners, and telephone conversations, all of which continued even after they no longer worked together.

The Democrats on the Judiciary Committee accepted none of these doubts and continued their badgering of Thomas. At one point, under intense grilling and wild accusations from the committee, Judge Thomas referred to what was happening to him as a "high-tech lynching."

Throughout the ugly process, George Bush watched, listened, and remained completely supportive of his candidate. In the White House, Boyden Gray and I met with the president and our congressional liaison team on a daily basis to review what was happening. "Judge Thomas is a good man," Bush said repeatedly. "We're sticking with him."

One week after the originally scheduled vote, the Senate finally met and voted to confirm Thomas by a margin of 52–48. Senator Hatch told us that he knew of a handful of Democratic senators who believed Thomas, but felt they had to vote against him.

Later, Thomas himself gratefully acknowledged the president's strong support. On the day of his swearing-in ceremony, he recalled the president asking him once again, "Can you call them as you see them?"

Thomas, of course, confirmed that he could. His mother was at the ceremony and felt faint, she said, having suffered terribly through the arduous confirmation process. Thomas said the White House physician took his mother aside to check her blood pressure, and he noted that Barbara Bush left the ceremony to spend time with her.

"Go on with the rest of your family and I'll look after your mom," she told Thomas.

The respect and kindness Clarence Thomas received from the Bushes throughout his confirmation moved the judge deeply, he later said. "The oath that I took to do this job and that promise to [George Bush] are the two things that keep me going in the difficult cases. I will not break my word to that man. I get real emotional about it. Because when you are at your lowest, you can really get the measure of the people who are there—and President and Mrs. Bush were there."

George Bush recently brought up the topic of Thomas's confirmation. He told Doro, for her book, that Clarence Thomas "got brutalized in the hearings."

"In the view of the liberal opponents of Clarence Thomas, there is no such thing as a distinguished conservative black person," Bush said. "If you're conservative, they'll turn on you, and Clarence Thomas was turned on by the community. . . . I found it very offensive and the more they piled on him, the more determined I was to stay with him and to support him.

"I remember him coming down to the White House with John Danforth saying, 'Do you think it's time I got out of the race? I think it may be hurting you, Mr. President.' I put my arm around him and I said, 'You can't do that. You've got to stay in this fight. And you're going to be confirmed, I'm sure of it. You'll be a great justice.' And he has been."

At the time of the nomination there was a great deal of discussion as to whether or not Thomas was nominated solely because of his race—because Thurgood Marshall, whom he replaced, also was a black jurist. Although I understand the reason for the questions, I know that regardless of who the retiree had been, our process was already stacked to nominate Clarence Thomas as the next Supreme Court justice, as he had come close to being chosen for the previous opening. Even though the press never believed George Bush when he said race was not his principal consideration, he was being absolutely truthful and correct.

The accusations leveled against Clarence Thomas in his confirmation process are an amazing illustration of how the liberal establishment and the liberal press can, over time, reshape public perception. In 1991, right after his confirmation, public opinion polls showed that the vast majority of Americans believed Clarence Thomas rather than Anita Hill. But the liberal press and its friends have continued repeating the refrain of harassment to the point where they have been able to actually change that balance of public opinion.

In the nearly quarter of a century that Clarence Thomas has served on the Supreme Court he has been the kind of justice we all hoped he would be—exactly what David Souter wasn't. Thomas has been true to what his past suggested, and consistent with the positions he took in his interviews and confirmation hearings.

That is all George Bush ever asked him to do.

12

An Embattled 1992

For George H. W. Bush, the first three years of his tenure had been among the most productive of any modern presidency. He had masterfully managed the end of the Cold War and the collapse of the Soviet Union. He had fixed a collapsing savings and loan system and propelled the movements toward democracy and free markets in Latin America. Both of his nominees to the United States Supreme Court were confirmed. He had organized an international coalition, led by the United States, to expel Saddam Hussein from Kuwait, and rid the Western Hemisphere of a drug-dealing dictator in Panama. He signed START, a major nuclear weapons reduction treaty, with the Soviet Union, and succeeded in getting major domestic legislation passed by an overwhelmingly Democratic-controlled Congress. Those legislative successes included the Clean Air Act of 1990, a five-year deficit-reducing budget agreement, the 1990 Civil Rights Bill, the Americans with Disabilities Act, energy deregulation legislation, a major crime bill, and child care legislation. He also had energized a partnership with the nation's governors to establish significant achievement standards for our K–12 education system.

The legislative battles over those bills had certainly been partisan, and we all knew it would get even worse during the 1992 presidential election year. The Democratic leaders of both the House and the Senate were determined not to let the president have any serious legislative victories that year.

When the president sent an economic growth package to the Hill, one that included tax cuts to stimulate the struggling economy, the Democrats returned to him a package of spending and tax increases that he had to veto. Although the veto was sustained in the House, the pattern was set and he would have to deal with an intransigent election-year Congress from that moment forward. The only major legislative initiative he was able to get out of Congress was his Energy Policy Act, which the Democrats finally signed off on just two weeks before the election. It was an important achievement for the country and the economy, but it came too late to boost the president's standing with the voters.

The only other notable victory of the year was his charter for the Multilateral Investment Fund, a major component of his Enterprise for the Americas Initiative. The agreement was a capstone of the president's effort to revitalize the economies of the Western Hemisphere. Fortunately, he was able to sign that agreement under the authority of legislation that had been passed a year earlier. Otherwise, it too probably would have fallen prey to the Democrats.

Not only was there a legislative stalemate, but the president's campaign operation was bogged down. He was being encouraged to dwell on a weak economy just as it was starting to turn around. His new team had him say that his 1990 budget agreement had been a mistake instead of emphasizing the fact that the spending caps he won in those negotiations were keeping the spendthrift Democratic Congress in check.

His foreign policy triumphs were being ignored. He had resolved several large, lingering problems left by the prior administration. He put the budget process onto a more responsible track that would generate surpluses within just a couple of years and put the dollar back on a sound footing, not to mention reinvigorate the economy. Bush got credit for none of this. The press ignored it all.

The campaign team seemed to have forgotten as well, and was instead battling with the White House team over control of the president's time and effort. The problems persisted until James Baker came back to take control of both operations, and they would take a tremendous physical and psychological toll on the president before being righted.

The political squabbling played out despite the tough election facing him. Not only did Bush have to face an aggressive Republican challenger in the primaries, Patrick Buchanan, but he also had to deal with an abrasive, obnoxious third-party candidate in the general election, Texas billionaire H. Ross Perot.

Perot, upset that Vice President George Bush had not been more supportive of his international intrusions in Vietnam over the issue of prisoners of war, ran as a self-funded candidate with more money than sense. His economic platform consisted of significant increases in both personal income and gasoline taxes, yet he still attacked the president for accepting taxes in the 1990 budget agreement.

Arkansas governor Bill Clinton ran an aggressive campaign, claiming that Bush had failed to deal effectively with the country's economic slowdown. "It's the economy, stupid," was his team's rallying cry. With the Iowa caucus and the New Hampshire primary starting the election cycle in February, the campaign challenges meant the president had to be in an aggressive campaign mode himself from the very first days of 1992. He wasn't.

PREPARING FOR THE CAMPAIGN

To prepare for reelection, I started meeting in late 1990 with key Republican political operatives outside the White House. I wanted to coordinate their efforts and weave together a good political team for the president. Any good presidential reelection campaign needs to have its policy, scheduling, and issues emphasis led from inside the White House, but there has to be close coordination with a first-class campaign team working on the outside.

By mid-1991 we were having those gatherings about once a month. In one of the first meetings, with about a half dozen players present, I asked the question, "Whom do you think the Democrats will nominate to run against Bush?"

Virtually everyone there answered, "Mario Cuomo."

I didn't think Cuomo had the stomach for the challenge. To me, it looked as if Cuomo wanted a coronation—the task of actually working to challenge a sitting president was more than he was willing to take on.

The group then turned the tables on me, asking who I believed would get the nomination.

My answer was Bill Clinton.

Surprisingly, a couple of the team members didn't know very much about Clinton. I had to remind them that he was the governor of Arkansas who had given the overlong keynote address at the last Democratic convention. I knew Clinton—we had worked together as governors—and I told them, "Bill Clinton has the fire in his belly. He is tough politically. He wants to be president.

He *really* wants to be president. And he's willing to go through a grueling fight now in order to position himself, if he loses, for the next cycle."

We went through this "Who do you think . . . ?" routine at each of our meetings over the next few months. I never could budge any of them from their firm belief that the Democratic nominee would be Cuomo, but I became even more convinced it would be Clinton.

By the second half of 1991, the discomfort of some of the political operatives who hoped to run the president's reelection effort was palpable. They were not happy that we in the White House controlled the president's schedule and agenda. They wanted more control over his day-to-day activities, so I brought them in more often to try to build their comfort with the balancing act required of a president. One typical meeting in my office included Andy Card, Roger Porter, Ron Kaufman, Dick Darman, Bill Kristol, and Tim McBride from the White House, and Bob Teeter, Charley Black, Craig Fuller, and Mary Matalin from the outside political team. We spent nearly two hours trying to work out a framework and a coordination process. In hindsight, I should have recognized the signals of discomfort as a sign that some of them preferred to see me out of the picture entirely.

To make sure we had accurate, up-to-date information for our campaign messaging, I asked Roger Porter to continuously add to our roster of George Bush's significant domestic achievements. We even included some talking points and dialogue that might be used by the campaign. Roger kept memos identifying each of the achievements to be used in an aggressive campaign communications effort.

We asked Dorrance Smith to join our White House team to handle media affairs. His first assignment was to tackle the complicated logistics of a president fulfilling the duties of his office while simultaneously campaigning for a second term. Dorrance was a very smart former ABC producer who understood how to use television effectively. He suggested that we build a small TV studio in the Executive Office Building so the president could be interviewed live, regularly and easily, from anywhere in the country.

The studio was a great tool that allowed George Bush to bypass the elite Washington press corps and give regional and local television stations direct access to the president. Dorrance reasoned that these stations would be thirsting for material; they would love an opportunity for their own anchors and interviewers to speak one-on-one with the president. Dorrance was right. I approved the plan, and in short order he set up a fantastic facility in a corner of an upper floor of the Executive Office Building.

We also beefed up the speechwriting team with talent that could focus primarily on the campaign. I convinced Tony Snow, who at that time was writing editorials at *The Washington Times*, to join us, first as a speechwriter, then to manage the entire speechwriting staff. Tony brought a sharp, conservative perspective to the president's speeches. That style would serve the president well as we tried to increase appreciation not only for his foreign policy, but for all his domestic policy successes.

Each of these steps was designed to facilitate running a campaign from the White House, which had to be done by any president seeking reelection. As comfortable as the president was with the staff additions, and as comfortable as he seemed to be about shifting into campaign battle mode, I could see that terrible press coverage involving me personally was beginning to weigh on him.

As chief of staff, I had the job of deflecting all the partisan attacks. In 1990, after I had handled that responsibility for about a year and a half, *Time* magazine had run a cover story branding me "Bush's Bad Cop." My efforts, the magazine said, allowed Bush to continue to present himself as the "good cop" in the process. At the time, I took it as a compliment, but the supercharged partisan atmosphere of Washington politics presented too many openings for the press to ratchet up the negative coverage.

The coverage about my travel while I was chief of staff would prove to be the impetus for my eventual stepping down. I probably could have—should have—handled it better, but at the time I really believed that because I had done nothing wrong it would all work itself out. Unfortunately, I failed to follow the advice I had given George Bush's brother, Prescott, shortly after taking the chief of staff job: in Washington, you don't necessarily get into difficulty for doing something wrong. You get into trouble for doing something right in a manner that your enemies can portray as wrong.

Shortly after we moved into the White House, Brent Scowcroft informed me that the Reagan administration had established a requirement that the national security advisor and the chief of staff not fly commercial. Reagan wanted them to be accessible at all times, with secure communication, so he directed them to fly in government aircraft. I told Brent, "Let me find out from President Bush what he wants to do going forward."

At our morning meeting, Brent and I presented the issue to the president and asked for guidance. Bush told us to find out exactly what the policy had been in the Reagan administration, and said we should "continue doing exactly what they did."

There was, indeed, a Reagan Presidential Directive, still in effect, *prohibiting* the chief of staff and the national security advisor from flying commercial. Attached to that directive was a memo from George Shultz explaining to then chief of staff Howard Baker that "prohibited meant prohibited." The chief of staff was required to use Department of Defense aircraft when he went anywhere. "No exceptions."

The reason for this policy was understandable. In a world where critical events come to a head almost instantly, the president needs to reach his key staff immediately. Since President Bush wanted to stick with the Reagan directive, we asked our staff and DOD to set up a procedure to manage those flights going forward.

Before we had our procedures in place, I flew home to New Hampshire to take care of a few issues related to my taking temporary residence in Washington. I flew home commercially and, as luck would have it, while I was waiting for a connection, the president tried to reach me, but in those days before cell phones were ubiquitous, he was unable to track me down for a few hours.

The next day, Colonel Charles Krulak—who eventually became commandant of the Marine Corps, but was at the time the military liaison in the White House—and Bonnie Newman, who was the assistant to the president in charge of handling all the administrative details in the White House, asked to meet with me.

Colonel Krulak was an ideal military liaison for George Bush. He was smart and a dedicated career marine. He also became a great member of our White House team. In fact, he and his wife dressed up as Mr. and Mrs. Easter Bunny for the annual White House Easter Egg Hunt in 1989. Krulak was probably the toughest Easter bunny to ever walk the White House grounds.

Colonel Krulak was very marine-like in informing me that the presidential directive regarding travel, which he stressed was still in effect, was there for a reason, and that the reason it was there was demonstrated by the president's difficulty reaching me over the weekend. He reminded me I did *not* have the choice to fly commercially. I was *prohibited* from flying commercially.

We quickly moved to firm up the procedures for requisitioning flights and to determine a reimbursement protocol. The Department of Defense, *not* the White House, evaluated the costs of the flights, and the charges varied depending on the purpose of the trip: government business, a political trip, or a personal matter. Under that presidential directive, I was required to use a government plane for any and every trip regardless of purpose—and the only thing distinguishing the trips was how much they would cost and who would be responsible for reimbursing the Department of Defense.

When *The Washington Post* began to write stories about my travel, it mentioned only in passing that I was required by presidential directive to use government transportation. In retrospect, I probably should have gotten a lawyer to represent my perspective and to put out a formal analysis of the "how, what and why" associated with the travel, but I naively believed that because we had been doing it under presidential directive and correctly following the guidelines issued by the Department of Defense, everything would eventually work itself out. *Big mistake.*

A couple of years after I left the White House, Colonel Krulak wrote to me and expressed his disappointment that the articles about my travel had been so badly distorted. He was concerned that his best intentions in our first meeting led to my difficulties. A while later, Bonnie Newman told me something that surprised me: during the entire process of reviewing the procedures, not a single person had come to talk to her about the process. No reporters. No White House staffers. No one. She had never been asked how the presidential directive was administered or how it was set up, even though she was in charge of those operations.

The Washington Post ramped up its reporting on my travel as we prepared for the 1992 campaign. I began to worry that my problems would become an even bigger problem for the president and his campaign. I raised the issue with him during a couple of our morning meetings, but each time we discussed it, the president said, "This too shall pass. Just keep doing your job well."

Around Labor Day 1991, I had conversations with Dan Quayle and Andy Card to get a sense of whether they thought my continued presence as chief of staff would be problematic for the campaign. In November, I had a similar conversation with the president's oldest son, George W. Bush, during one of his visits to the White House. He seemed much more concerned than either the vice president or Andy had been. At that time, I attributed it to the personal concern of a son for his father. I assured the future president that I would continue my discussions within the White House as well as with a couple of key folks outside the White House, and promised him I would do whatever was in the best interest of his father.

The pressure in the press continued to build, and I saw it had become a problem for the president. I called Senator Dole and Bob Michel, who were both very supportive, but I was beginning to feel that it was finally time to go.

Through the autumn, I received a couple of encouraging calls from former president Nixon and Canadian prime minister Mulroney. The prime minister's advice was to stay and support the president. Nixon reminded me, "Catching the flak is part of the job description for a chief of staff."

I went to New Hampshire for Thanksgiving weekend and spent most of that quiet time pondering the situation. I finally decided that I did not want to burden either the president or the campaign. On the Monday after Thanksgiving I decided it was in the best interest of the president's chances for reelection if I stepped down.

The next morning I went to see the president as soon as I arrived at the White House. I told him I was going to step down as chief of staff. He, too, had seen the pressure build and agreed that perhaps it was a good time to go. We both felt it would be useful if I stayed on to help put together the State of the Union message and the budget for the following fiscal year. We decided that I would resign as chief of staff effective December 15, but stay on through March as counselor to the president.

That afternoon, I gave him my handwritten letter of resignation. It was somewhat longer and more detailed than most resignation letters, but I wanted to thank him for the incredible opportunity of serving in the White House and to let him know how much I appreciated being part of his first three amazing years. I hoped all the lightning being flung at the White House by the liberal press and the Democrats would follow me out the door and that things would get significantly easier for President Bush.

George Bush, ever kind and thoughtful, wrote some letters of his own, as is his way. He wrote to my wife and kids—a long, warm letter—thanking them for having been a part of the whole process and saying some wonderfully generous things in support of my service to him. He sent a similar letter to my parents because he knew they would have seen only the unpleasant press version of the events leading to my departure. I'm pleased and proud to say that my family and I felt as close to George and Barbara Bush on the day I resigned as we were on the day I accepted the responsibility of chief of staff, and that the relationship has gotten even closer over time.

When I first came to Washington in 1989, I expected my tenure would last less than a year. I ended up serving a bit more than three years—much longer than all but one or two other chiefs of staff. Though disappointed about not being able to complete the full first term of the president, I was not angry, bitter, or upset. I was sorry to have to leave the first-rate team that I had a hand in assembling and that I thoroughly enjoyed working with.

My biggest concern was over who would replace me and whether that person would be able to provide the support, assistance, and, frankly, the strong defense of the president's record required to move the campaign into a winning mode. My recommendation to President Bush was that my deputy, Andy Card, replace me. Andy had been through the political wars of the campaign and had a complete understanding of the operational side of the job of chief of staff. The president ended up selecting his transportation secretary, Samuel K. Skinner, to be his new chief of staff. I liked Sam, but was a little concerned because he lacked "political combat experience."

As I prepared to shift gears and focus on the State of the Union message and the budget package, I moved to an office in the Executive Office Building adjacent to the White House and met regularly with Tony Snow and Dick Darman to ensure that the speech and budget came out right. I made sure to limit all my efforts during the last couple of months to those two tasks to make sure nobody felt I was butting in while the new chief of staff got his bearings and put his own team in place.

Regrettably, what I saw in the White House and on the campaign from the sidelines was painful to watch.

In its December 16, 1991, issue, *U.S. News & World Report*, in a column labeled "Irony Department," reported the following:

In his first trip after being named last week as the new White House Chief of Staff, Transportation Secretary Samuel Skinner demonstrated his determination to avoid the mistakes of his predecessor. Instead of commandeering a government plane for a trip to Chicago, where he was scheduled to make a speech to a citizens group, Skinner flew coach class aboard a commercial airliner. The irony, however, is that he ran into one of the chief problems John Sununu often cited to justify his flying ways: the need for secure communications. On Skinner's return trip to Washington, he was unable to make a promised important telephone call, first because he was hurried to catch his flight; then the cellular phone aboard the airliner malfunctioned.

Sam Skinner came in and, astoundingly, decided that one of the first things he needed to do was bring in an efficiency consultant to tell him how the White House should be run. I was shocked. First, because there were only about nine months left before the election—not nearly enough time to put in any new structures and procedures that this "efficiency expert" might recommend. Second, because no private sector consultant is ever going to understand how to operate in the complex political bureaucracy of a White House fully exposed in the fishbowl of Washington, DC. The consultant's efforts proved to be monumentally nonproductive, and cost many precious weeks at just the wrong time.

A CAMPAIGN IN DISARRAY

During my final weeks in the White House—not as chief of staff, but as counselor to the president—the buildup of internal strains became more and more conspicuous. My heart bled for the president, who patiently hoped things could be worked out. I could see the president's frustration, not only with the campaign but also with the deteriorating management of the White House. I began to sense that although he had the conviction and enthusiasm for a second term, the pressures of internal disorganization and a campaign with no fire were sapping his energy.

It was upsetting to hear from old administration friends how the growing turmoil was making life difficult and stressful for the

president. One of the calls I received was about the messy process
of naming a new administrator at NASA to replace Admiral Richard Truly. The bickering had gotten so confusing that the mess
was dumped directly into the president's lap for him to sort out. It
pained me to hear that the president said in a private conversation,
"Sununu would have never let it come to this." I felt that I had let
George Bush down by not being able to be there.

As the new chief of staff, Sam Skinner made two very serious mistakes right from the beginning. The first was to try to
marginalize the president's budget director, Richard Darman.
Darman got the job in the first place because Jim Baker championed him for it and Baker, the president's closest confidant,
still supported him. Skinner should instead have used Darman's
strengths, which included an understanding of the arcane budget
process and how to effectively work the bureaucracy. Darman
also knew how to deal with Congress and had a wide network of
friends in the press.

Skinner tried to cut Darman out by bringing in a new set of
advisors to blunt his influence. In late January, *The New York
Times* quoted "an administration official who attended a meeting
with the two men last week" as saying, "The tension between
Darman and Skinner was so obvious you can see it." Instead of
attempting to direct Darman's participation, Skinner was alien-
ating him, and Darman was a very effective political infighter.

Most of the early internal problems were highlighted in the
headlines: "Bush Aides Divided on How to Correct Slip in Popu-
larity" (January 21, 1992); "Bush Camp on New Strategy Debate"
(January 25); "New Chairman Installed to Invigorate GOP"
(February 2); "Problems at White House Persist Two Months
into a New Chief's Tenure" (February 11).

Skinner's second mistake had to do with political messaging.
Less than two weeks into the job, he convinced the president to

start talking about the "sluggish economy." Unfortunately, this was just as the economy began growing again. In reality, 1992 would turn out to be a year of strong economic growth, but the White House's own careless language masked the upbeat trend. The inability to communicate the good economic news and the president's real record of achievement was the most serious problem in the 1992 campaign. The failure was only emphasized by Pat Buchanan's primary challenge and Ross Perot's persistent, but unanswered, attacks. They would prove to be factors in the president's loss in November.

My amazement and concern grew as I continued to get almost daily calls and visits from staffers inside the White House expressing their concern over the slide into an unmanaged and unresponsive routine that had become downright chaotic. Pretty soon, it was abundantly clear to everyone that my friend Sam Skinner was in way over his head and, unfortunately, the problems inside the White House were compounded by similar ones within the campaign being managed from outside the White House.

The campaign leadership troika consisted of chairman Bob Mosbacher, who had been secretary of commerce; campaign manager Fred Malek, who had run the 1988 Republican Convention and was vice chairman of Northwest Airlines; and chief political strategist Bob Teeter, who had been the pollster for the 1988 campaign. After the 1988 election, *The Washington Post* had reported that Teeter wanted to be chief of staff. All were good people, but none had the political focus and aggressiveness we had in the 1988 campaign. The hard-edged old trio— Lee Atwater, Roger Ailes, and I—were no longer part of the campaign effort. Lee had passed away, Roger was on his way to changing the face of cable news, and I had stepped aside hoping the lightning would follow me.

In 1988, the campaign had fearlessly launched direct attacks when necessary and faced the important issues head-on with strong messages on taxes, the environment, foreign policy experience, crime, and our differences with a "liberal Michael Dukakis." This time there appeared to be no focus or fire in the messaging.

The members of the political team who pushed to manage the campaign with significant independence from the White House soon discovered they had made an enormous mistake. It is all but impossible to effectively manage a campaign for a sitting president without serious, capable leadership within the White House to provide discipline on schedules and policy. The candidate's obligations as president, including dealing with the issues of the day and travel schedules, mean that all final decisions, even for the campaign, need to be made by the president's staff.

Unfortunately for George Bush, the same ambitions that drove individuals to muscle their way into leadership roles in the campaign also resulted in bickering among themselves and with the president's staff. It imposed so much stress on the White House that the new Skinner team could never get into an efficient functioning mode.

As the Bush camp's internal disorganization and stress mounted, Bill Clinton charged through the key states. He recognized how important New Hampshire was in the Democratic primary process, and invested a lot of time and political capital establishing a solid campaign operation there. Governor Clinton and I had become friends as fellow governors, and while I could never support him for president, I enjoyed watching him outmaneuver his Democratic rivals. Always a smooth operator, he even called me in October, when it looked as if Cuomo might be his toughest challenger in the primaries, to ask about some Democratic political leaders in New Hampshire.

By December 1991, the Clinton effort looked pretty strong. He was joined in the fray by Massachusetts senator Paul Tsongas, former governor Jerry Brown of California, Senator Bob Kerrey of Nebraska, Governor Doug Wilder of Virginia, and Senator Tom Harkin of Iowa. By the end of the year, Mario Cuomo decided, as I expected, that the battle for the Democratic nomination would be more demanding than he had anticipated, and on December 20 he announced he would not run for president in 1992.

Patrick J. Buchanan, the former Nixon speechwriter, decided to climb on the bandwagon of anger that grew from George Bush's having accepted taxes in the 1990 budget. He challenged the sitting president in the 1992 New Hampshire primary, and I watched in horror as he managed to lock up the endorsement of the Manchester *Union Leader*, the state's most conservative newspaper.

In his campaign rhetoric, Buchanan exploited George Mitchell's success in forcing Bush to accept new taxes in the 1990 budget agreement. He picked up 38 percent of the vote, enough to create a split in the party that became a serious problem for the Bush campaign. After New Hampshire, Buchanan hung on through all of the early primaries, continually attacking the president, harping on old misperceptions of Bush, and arguing that these were proof he was not a true conservative.

It was not a good omen for the campaign.

Eventually, even Buchanan's old boss Richard Nixon asked Pat to come and visit him. There, Nixon told him, "It's probably time for you to get out of the race. From now on, you can't win and you can only hurt Bush." Buchanan refused to take Nixon's advice.

By May, H. Ross Perot also had effectively entered the presidential race as an independent, third-party candidate. He hired a fairly complete campaign staff, but his campaign manager, Ed Rollins, resigned in frustration in mid-July. The very next day, on *Larry King Live*, Perot said he had changed his mind and would no longer seek the presidency. Nevertheless, he continued to spend money, building up campaign assets. Two weeks later he released a fifty-page economic plan. I puzzled over the fact that most of his supporters joined him because he criticized Bush for breaking the "no new taxes" pledge, yet they continued that support despite the fact that Perot's plan advocated far more taxes than Bush had been forced to accept.

By Memorial Day, the drifting and confusion within the White House were out of hand. The president pressed Jim Baker to resign his post as secretary of state and come serve as chief of staff. The press also reported that Robert Mosbacher, the nominal head of the Bush reelection campaign, along with many of the president's key campaign fund-raisers, had recommended that he remove Sam Skinner from his post as chief of staff and get Jim Baker on board as soon as possible.

Eventually, Bush was able to sway his old friend. Baker had held off leaving the State Department until August 13, though he surely had known for at least two or three months that he was going to have to make the change. Baker brought his very able undersecretary of state for economic and agricultural affairs, Robert Zoellick, with him to serve as his deputy chief of staff, and the deputy secretary of state, Lawrence Eagleburger, then took the helm at the State Department.

Baker's new responsibilities extended well beyond managing the White House. He also was there to control and provide strategic direction to the reelection campaign. Baker wisely reestablished contact with some of the political strategists from the 1988 campaign, among them Roger Ailes, and was able to restore order in the White House. Eight weeks, though, were not enough time for him to reverse all the failings of a broken and dispirited campaign.

On the Democratic side, Bill Clinton continued to pile up primary victories, and by the beginning of summer it was clear he was going to be the Democratic nominee. Shrewdly, he campaigned as a more conservative Democrat than any Democratic presidential candidate in fifty years. His strategy to present himself as a credible moderate was carefully thought out. Years earlier he had created and assumed leadership of a group he called the Democratic Leadership Council, which advocated much more moderate policies than the far left agenda of the traditional Democratic Party. Clinton began to formulate his own public agenda, and one of the issues he targeted was an issue that George Bush had championed on the advice of the governors, including Clinton: he laid out a fairly conservative agenda for a complete reform of America's welfare program.

Clinton and Perot both continued their aggressive attacks on Bush. They claimed the economy was still in recession in spite of data showing that it was growing at a healthy 4 percent clip. The Bush campaign responded ineffectively to the attacks, and Clinton was boosted by press outlets that ignored the recovery and repeated the negative claims put out by him and Perot.

Finally, Bush was assured of the nomination. He won big majorities and virtually all the delegates. Now, however, the campaign had to figure out how to undo the damage of the primaries. The team sought out Buchanan's endorsement, and Pat agreed to give it in exchange for a prime-time speech at the Republican convention in Houston.

That endorsement and the speech it cost turned out to be a mixed blessing for Bush. Buchanan gave what is now referred to as the "culture war" speech on prime-time TV. The hot rhetoric of the speech rallied the extreme conservative wing of the party, but it frightened voters in the middle of the political spectrum and became an easy target for the nation's liberal press corps.

Buchanan, even in endorsing the president, played into Bill Clinton's hands.

As the two parties moved through their conventions and firmed up their platforms and agendas, Clinton opened up a five-point lead over Bush in the polls, give or take a bit depending on whether or not Perot was included in the polling. On October 1, Perot decided to reenter the race, just in time for three presidential debates scheduled for October 11, October 15, and October 19. Throughout October all the way through to the November 7 election day, Perot continued to pound Bush and scarcely even mentioned Clinton's name.

I had offered to help the campaign in any way possible, and eventually received a phone call asking me to play the role of Ross Perot in the preparation for the debates. Of course I agreed. I even wore a set of "big ears" to one of the sessions, hoping to add a little spark and levity to the process.

When I visited the White House to participate in the debate preparations, I urged senior members of the campaign staff to run more ads extolling the tremendous domestic achievements of the president, but my appeals fell on deaf ears. They never quite got around to it. In fact, they barely got around to reminding the public of the president's foreign policy achievements, either. I even tried to convince the president himself to brag about his achievements, though I knew his modesty would probably make him reluctant to do so.

The second of the three debates was set in the town hall format Bill Clinton loved, and Clinton was working the audience with his charm and smile. It had been a difficult evening for Bush, as both Perot and Clinton pounded away at him on economic issues. With only about ten minutes left in the debate, just as he was to receive a question from a member of the audience, George Bush glanced at his watch.

When I saw him do that, I gasped and cringed.

My reaction was not because of any concern over the impact that gesture might have on the debate or the campaign—there was no way I could have anticipated the ridicule it would get from his opponents and the press over the next two weeks. I knew the president well, and that gesture was a clear expression of impatience and frustration. I could almost hear what was going through his head: "Only ten more minutes of this crap." My hunch was correct. Those were the exact words Bush himself would use to describe the moment to Jim Lehrer of the Public Broadcasting Service in a postelection interview.

The campaign made a serious mistake by not responding aggressively to Ross Perot from the beginning. He was known to be thin-skinned, and was in the campaign just to spite George Bush. I always felt that going after him would have been extremely effective. Had Atwater still been in the game, I feel certain he would have nailed Perot between the eyes with a two-by-four every time he opened his mouth—particularly since Perot, who continually criticized government, had made his fortune by providing very expensive services to the federal, state, and local governments. But the 1992 Bush campaign gave Perot a free pass, and focused most of its efforts on Clinton.

The overarching liberal bias of the national press didn't help the president, either, and dogged him throughout the campaign. One glaring example of some reporters' tendency to highlight the negative despite the facts was demonstrated during a campaign stop at the National Grocers Association meeting at Orlando, Florida, in February 1992. An NCR Corporation systems analyst was showing George Bush a state-of-the-art grocery product scanner—the device that reads bar codes on product labels—which had some new technological wrinkles. The scanner he showed Bush was able to read a bar code that had been ripped

.to five mangled pieces. Ever polite, Bush said, rather drily,
.sn't that something." Nothing more.

The Associated Press, as part of the press pool at the event,
ran the story straight and factually. The spin soon followed from
The New York Times, however. The *Times'* reporter, Andrew
Rosenthal—the son of its executive editor—was not even in
Orlando; he wrote his story from the press pool report and
claimed Bush was "amazed" by the fact that a machine could
scan bar codes and automatically enter the price into the cash
register. The gist of the story was that Bush was so out of touch
with everyday America that he hadn't set foot in a grocery store
in more than a decade. Nowhere in the report did it mention
that the new technology could weave together mangled labels—a
genuinely new and advanced technology that any normal person
would marvel about.

The *Times* played the story on its front page. It was clearly
erroneous, but even after other outlets like *Newsweek*, CBS, and
Time magazine pointed out the error, *The New York Times* stood
by its story. The report quickly took on a life of its own, however,
and became part of Clinton's campaign rhetoric, reinforcing the
Arkansas governor's mantra about Bush not being one of the
"common folks."

One more factor contributed to Bush's loss, one that no one
saw coming. On October 30, four days before the election, Special Prosecutor Lawrence Walsh indicted Caspar Weinberger,
who had been secretary of defense in the Reagan administration,
for his role in the Iran-Contra affair. Walsh's protestations to the
contrary notwithstanding, the timing was obviously designed to
hurt Bush. At the very least, even if the indictment itself did not
affect public opinion of the president, it sucked all the energy out
of the closing efforts of his campaign.

People inside the campaign, who had access to the daily polling, have pointed out that Bush was virtually tied with Clinton in the closing days. They maintain that the Clinton people must have seen the same numbers, and that somehow Walsh "sensed" their concern. Fred Steeper was the Bush campaign pollster. His tracking numbers had the race dead even on the Thursday and Friday before the election. That meant Bush was trending up and Clinton was trending down. At about the same time CNN had a poll that had Bush down by only one point.

Walsh released his announcement of the indictment of Caspar Weinberger at 11:00 a.m. on Friday. The polling numbers turned around over the weekend. I've never seen any evidence to confirm the concerns about malevolence or conspiracy raised at the time, but I do find Walsh's claim that the timing of his announcement had nothing to do with the election somewhat hard to swallow.

The Churchill Effect manifests itself in many interesting and unpredictable ways. In 1992 it was Pat Buchanan, Ross Perot, Bill Clinton, Lawrence Walsh, and the lackluster campaign and tepid messaging of George Bush's reelection effort that produced a Churchill-worthy result.

On November 7, Clinton won with 43 percent of the popular vote, Bush came in second with 38 percent, and Perot got 19 percent. Most of Perot's voters were antitax Republicans, at least two thirds of which, I am confident, would usually have voted for the Republican candidate. Perot's advertising money and direct, vicious attacks on President Bush also had a huge influence on public opinion overall. Perot skewed not only the vote but also the debate leading up to it. His campaign enabled Clinton to win the election. He got his revenge, and America was the big loser.

Postscript:
Completing the Mission

A t the end of 1990, before a single jet had flown into Iraq and as the assembled coalition of nations waited to give Saddam Hussein one more chance, *Time* magazine selected President Bush as "Man of the Year," commending his handling of the Gulf crisis. It was the halfway point of Bush's presidency, and the editors at *Time* magazine had the story half right. While they praised the president for his "bold vision" in assembling and leading a world coalition, they counterbalanced their praise with the headline "At Home: No Vision—A Case of Do Nothing." It was a myopia prevalent across all the media at the time, and it fostered a misperception that persists even today.

To be fair, the blindness of Bush's critics to his array of domestic achievements is due in part to his remarkable success on the international stage. He began by righting the disjointed policy in Central America and reestablishing a constructive relationship with Congress that nurtured the emergence of democracy in Nicaragua. His willingness to use force to capture and replace itary dictator Manuel Noriega and restore the democratic ess in Panama was unwavering. He masterfully handled e unraveling of the Soviet Union and the move to freedom, independence, and democracy in the once occupied countries of Eastern Europe. The process went so smoothly, in fact, that Bush was able to help reunify Germany and bring it under the NATO umbrella without serious objections from the Soviets— much earlier than anyone dreamed possible.

History also has judged George Bush's quick and decisive steps to drive Iraq from Kuwait to have been handled adeptly. The president assembled a coalition—the first such coalition since World War II—that included not only the Soviet Union but the vast majority of Arab nations, most of Western Europe, the British Commonwealth nations, and notable outliers like Japan, Argentina, and Bangladesh. The coalition's resolve and firm action assured our allies in the Middle East that the United States was ready to protect them, even when the aggressor was an Arab neighbor. Later, George Bush brought the Israelis and Palestinians together in Madrid to talk face-to-face in a historic opening that led to the Oslo Accords and defined a framework for negotiations to resolve the lingering conflict.

George Bush's overall impact on the world of his time is unparalleled in postwar America. Regrettably, his expert handling of his broad foreign policy agenda changed the world so dramatically and rapidly that friends and rivals alike seemed able to focus only on those successes. They failed to see or appreciate his equally tremendous record of achievement on the domestic front.

Consider an analogy—an analogy from the baseball world George Bush loved. The president would never have offered it himself because he was far too modest, but it's an instructive one. How many of us remember that George Herman "Babe" Ruth was a truly great pitcher, one of the greatest of all time? He still has the eighth-best win-loss percentage in baseball history, and had the best earned run average in the league in 1916. For fifty years he also held the record for the most consecutive scoreless innings pitched in the World Series. Does anyone recall that Ruth led the league in strikeouts in two of his five full seasons as a pitcher? Babe Ruth began as a great pitcher and later grew into such a magnificent slugger that he is rarely remembered for his pitching prowess.

Similarly, George H. W. Bush's foreign policy wins were so impressive that they overshadowed his dramatic domestic policy achievements and the dexterity he displayed in reaching those milestones. He pitched prolifically and effectively on the domestic front even while hitting one home run after another in a rapidly changing and challenging international arena.

In January 1991, following the *Time* magazine cover story, I met with Roger Porter and Dick Darman to discuss Bush's image. We all lamented the fact that Bush's international success was overshadowing his energetic and determined work on domestic issues and discussed how to address this anomaly. It was discouraging, among other reasons, because what was being achieved domestically required just as much, if not more, effort on the president's part. Porter tried to put all those achievements in context in a detailed memo that we gave to the press, but their position had already been cast in stone.

During the second half of his presidency, Bush added another layer of solid results onto his already impressive accomplishments. Nevertheless, a contrast of great success abroad with little achievement at home remained the public narrative for the Bush presidency, and it spilled over into his campaign for reelection. It even lingered for several years after he left the White House. No matter how often or how clearly his distinguished record of

...as discussed, the press, the public, and even many ...tical academics simply refused to acknowledge the evidence ... before them.

...one of these achievements, domestic or foreign, came easily. ...he preceding chapters have contrasted the strategic, personal approach of the president's foreign policy efforts with the heavy lifting and hard, partisan negotiating he endured in order to get his domestic agenda enacted. The president's challenges in foreign policy were immense, but in facing them he usually had to deal with only one rival—usually the nuclear-armed, communist Soviet Union. His struggles on the home front were an entirely different story. Bill by bill, issue by issue, sometimes even word by word, the president butted heads with a very partisan and sometimes cunning Democratic leadership armed with large majorities in both the House and the Senate and backed by an array of politically connected liberal interest groups.

It could have been a recipe for failure, but despite this embedded opposition the president achieved extraordinary things. In the more than two decades since Bush left office, the significance of these accomplishments finally has been recognized. Ripple effects such as the budget surpluses of the 1990s and the decade of economic prosperity that started during his last year as president have been acknowledged and appreciated. The achievements are even farther-reaching than any of us had originally anticipated. By any measure, they constitute the equivalent of a world-class pitching record. Just because his foreign policy triumphs are the equivalent of an all-time batting record, there is no justification for denying Bush the credit for the pitching prowess that was his domestic legislative agenda.

There are two interesting historical facts that apply to the American presidency since Dwight David Eisenhower was first elected in 1952. The first is that in only one election over those

sixty-plus years has either party been able to hold on t
White House for more than two consecutive terms—that is
more than eight years. That exception was the victory of Geo
H. W. Bush in 1988 following Ronald Reagan's two terms
president.

The second fact is that, as often as not, for well over a half
century, all of our presidents have had to deal, for at least part
of their tenure, with a Congress in which at least one body was
controlled by the opposition. Except during Jimmy Carter's four
years in the White House, every president since Eisenhower has
had at least one two-year period during which one body of Congress was organized by the other party.

These two realities reflect a tendency on the part of the
modern American electorate to avoid giving too much power for
too long either to the Republicans or to the Democrats.

For George Bush, his two terms as vice president had reinforced his understanding that our Constitution created our
American system as one of shared powers, not separated powers.
Neither the president nor Congress can do much without per-
suading others in that tent of shared power to respond and cooperate. Our presidents discover quickly that they cannot break the
tendency of divided control of government to end up in gridlock
unless they spend some of their own political capital. Gridlock
in Washington, DC, cannot be broken unless the president is
willing to do the hard work and take the political risks of actively
taking the lead to resolve political differences.

During his entire term George Bush faced one of the most
heavily disproportionate dominations of House and Senate by the
opposition. In the House, the Democrats were a one-hundred-
vote majority in his last two years, and nearly as large a majority
in his first two years. They also controlled the Senate by ten votes
in his first two years and twelve votes in his second two years.

...res of George Bush's capacity to lead
...islative results even in the face of control
...rocess by the Democrats. It is truly regret-
...t get the chance to work with the Republican
...the House and the Senate that came to Wash-
...e 1994 elections.

...ld a second George Herbert Walker Bush term have
...e? What could he have accomplished in the second
...th the benefit of the Republican control of the House
...enate that occurred after the 1994 election? The answer to
...se questions must begin with a review of his basic agenda and
of the principles that guided George Bush the man.

On the domestic side he certainly would have continued to
focus on issues in which he won only partial victories over the
Democratic Congress. Among those were welfare reform, health
care reform, education, crime, and immigration. Although his
successor was able to build on the Bush initiatives to get additional legislation in those areas, George Bush, with a Republican
House and Senate after 1994, would certainly have been able
to get more free-enterprise, market-driven, cohesive programs
into law.

The more significant impact of a 1992 Bush win would have
been his ability to use his global leadership to recast and frame
the international coalition he built for the Gulf War to stably and
effectively shape the world in a one-superpower environment.
Bush also would have continued to build on his breakthrough
Madrid meeting to guide a continuation of the progress on the
Israeli-Palestinian conflict.

A second-term George Bush would have been more timely
and aggressive in providing guidance and assistance to the
emerging governments in Eastern Europe. The budget stability
he achieved and the surpluses later generated by his own budget

deal would have given him the capacity to provide early and tar-geted financial incentives to the new democracies, something he regretted not being able to provide in 1991–92.

His political capital and credibility in the Middle East after Desert Storm would have helped refocus more mutually benefi-cial commerce and development in the region. That alone could have dramatically altered the intensity of the anti-American cabals that eventually did grow into Al Qaeda and its offshoots.

Bush also would have used his standing with the Chinese leaders to forge a more beneficial relationship there, and his early focus on revitalizing the Latin American economies and democracies would have been expanded to undercut the Cuban mischief that later set back progress in the Western Hemisphere.

Of course, even if he had been reelected, reality, most likely, would have been very different from those scenarios. We never really do know what changing one event might do to the future. All we know for sure is the impact one Quiet Man did have at a very crucial, pivotal moment in history.

On October 10, 1995, in Colorado Springs, Colorado, I attended a most extraordinary gathering of personalities from the final days of the Cold War. In a one-day pair of sessions mod-erated by Jim Lehrer of PBS, George Bush, Mikhail Gorbachev, Margaret Thatcher, François Mitterrand, and Brian Mulroney discussed how they changed the face of the earth in a few short months.

The gathered leaders exchanged personal reflections on how their relationships brought about this historic change. In all the discussions of that day, it was undeniable that these world-class leaders respected each other—cared for each other, even. They spoke of the political risks they themselves took and acknowl-edged those of their colleagues. They all agreed that Mikhail Gorbachev went above and beyond. There was something else they all agreed about, too. In their presentations, Gorbachev, Thatcher, Mitterrand, and Mulroney all insisted that none of it would have happened without the deft, sensitive diplomacy of the American president, George Herbert Walker Bush.

Mitterrand's praise for Bush was noteworthy, not only for its effusiveness but for the fact that he was there at all. As befitted the master French statesman, he presented a brilliant and eloquent historical analysis of the evolution of the Cold War conflicts and the eventual peace attained in Europe. He spoke as part scholar and part participant. It was all the more impressive that Mitterrand made the effort to attend the gathering because he was clearly quite ill at the time. In fact, he died two months later. His supreme effort and sacrifice to be a part of the event were testimony to his respect and affection for George Bush.

They all were proud of what they had accomplished. Their egos allowed them to beam about what they had achieved. Each of their presentations made it abundantly clear, though, that what happened between 1989 and 1991 was by no means foreordained. The seamless transition to peace required a deliberate, determined, and experienced master to urge it along. George Bush was the best man for the job. The Colorado Springs event was unique, and the most amazing history class I ever attended.

These were leaders who were not afraid to make tough decisions. These were leaders who understood the risks in making those tough decisions. These were leaders who understood that they were in office to make those tough decisions. George Bush stood tallest among them.

We are all lucky that they were all there. The world is extremely fortunate that the right man, with the right experience, with the right disposition, with the right sense of history, and with the right self-discipline, was president of the United States at that particular moment in time.

At that event I was once again reminded of the Churchill Effect. Every one of the leaders there had lost office virtually immediately after the end of the Cold War. All of them had achieved the impossible and then had been replaced by their constituencies with new faces to deal with their new, more immediate, and ordinary problems of the day.

Two years later, in 1997, there was another gathering—this time at Hofstra University on Long Island—to examine the presidency of George H. W. Bush. More than two hundred scholars, journalists, foreign dignitaries, and alumni of the Bush administration were there, and Bush himself gave the convocation address. In that address, he reflected a bit about his tenure. He commented on his difficulties in dealing with Congress, but then cited his notable legislative victories, including the Americans with Disabilities Act, clean air, the 1990 budget, civil rights, energy policy, deregulation, the farm bill, crime, savings and loans, and education. He summed it all up by saying, "Thanks to our team we were able to make progress on many fronts, and when we left office after four years, we did so with our heads held high. Our nation was at peace, our economy was strong, our environment was cleaner, and our future was brighter."

The day after the 1992 election, George Bush sent a note to his old friend President Nixon. In it he said, "The dust has begun to settle. It hurts still, but we Bushes will do fine. I just want to thank you for the Tom Dewey letter and, of course, for your kind words. I want to finish the course with no rancor, no blaming of others. Then Barbara and I will go back to Houston. . . . As I contemplate private life, the way in which one Richard Nixon has conducted himself in his post President life will serve as a fine example of how to do it."

George Bush has conducted his own postpresidential life as his mother would have expected—with no bragging, always generous and kind, with an unabashed love of America and its values, and brimming with decency, grace, and class.

I am thankful to the president for allowing me to do the bragging on his behalf, and hope this book will spark a realization of, and appreciation for, the remarkable legacy of this strong, quiet man.

ACKNOWLEDGMENTS

This is my first book. I quickly discovered that, at least in this case, a big writing project cannot get done without a lot of help—direct and indirect—from a number of people. I wish to acknowledge and thank them.

President George H. W. Bush and Barbara—for letting me ride with them for a while on their extraordinary journey.

My family—Nancy and the kids and the grandchildren—they, with great patience and understanding, put up with me for my year as a recluse as I dictated into my computer and scratched away to get this done.

My daughter Cathy—she kept track of my lost notes, typed in my edits, tracked and sorted the photographs, formatted the manuscript, and made great suggestions through it all.

The George Bush Presidential Library and Museum, especially Robert Holzweiss, the deputy director, and his great team, who led me to the nooks and crannies of the calendars, diaries, and memos that cleared the cobwebs from my memory; and Mary Finch, the library's audiovisual archivist, who, with her staff, found and scanned the great photos in the book.

The Miller Center Presidential Oral History Program at the University of Virginia—the oral history records collected by the program from more than two dozen cabinet members and staffers from the George H. W. Bush White House were a great reference. Reviewing my own two rather extensive interviews brought the details of those years in the White House back to me in a most meaningful way.

The great White House team I served with—their hard work and loyal support of President Bush helped make his presidency one of the most productive in history.

My principal assistant for nearly thirty years, Jackie Kennedy, who kept the administrative side of my responsibilities working smoothly throughout my years as governor and chief of staff, and for so efficiently helping me gather the early outlines of this book.

David Valdez, our White House photographer and dear friend, who took most of the photos a quarter of a century ago, and was kind enough to send me a few of the better shots.

My friends at Saint Anselm College—Professor Gary Bouchard, who helped edit my earliest drafts; Neal Levesque, the director of the Institute of Politics; and six bright students there who fact-checked those early drafts: Lyndsay Robinson, John Pearson, Kristine Adams, Brian O'Connor, Tara Sennick, and Abigail Smith.

My editors at HarperCollins—Adam Bellow, whose quiet but firm suggestions made it more readable; and Eric Meyers, whose thoughtful comments helped guide this to a better finished product.

I also want to acknowledge the writers of the dozens of books on George H. W. Bush—some good and some not. I read as many as I could get my hands on, and they too refreshed my memories, directed me to resources, or inspired me to correct the misperceptions that are out there in print.

With a little more appreciation for the authors of the world,
John H. Sununu
Hampton Falls, New Hampshire

REFERENCES

My definitive resource for this book was the George Bush Presidential Library and Museum in College Station, Texas (bush41.org). Its archives contained the documents and resources needed to confirm the accuracy of the myriad details of the president's daily schedule, events, calls, and discussions. I would also like to acknowledge the ease of use and utility of the online archives of *The New York Times* and *The Washington Post*. Both resources were invaluable in confirming dates, meetings, and players, as well as reminding me of the joy of my days in the White House and the pace and pressure of cramming it all into a few short years.

In preparing to write this book I went back to read or reread a number of books and reviews of the Reagan and Bush presidencies, including the following:

Adelman, Ken. *Reagan at Reykjavik: Forty-Eight Hours That Ended the Cold War.*

Baker, James A., III. *The Politics of Diplomacy.*

Bush, Barbara. *A Memoir.*

Bush, George H. W. *All the Best, George Bush: My Life in Letters and Other Writings.*

———. *The China Diary of George H. W. Bush*, edited and introduced by Jeffrey A. Engel.

———. *Heartbeat: George Bush in His Own Words*, compiled and edited by Jim McGrath.

Bush, George H. W., and Brent Scowcroft. *A World Transformed: The Collapse of the Soviet Empire, the Unification of Germany, Tiananmen Square, the Gulf War.*

Darman, Richard. *Who's in Control? Polar Politics and the Sensible Center.*

Feldman, Leslie D., and Rosanna Perotti, eds. *Honor and Loyalty: Inside the Politics of the George H. W. Bush White House.*

Greene, John Robert. *The Presidency of George Bush.*

Himelfarb, Richard, and Rosanna Perotti, eds. *Principle over Politics? The Domestic Policy of the George H. W. Bush Presidency.*

Koch, Doro Bush. *My Father, My President: A Personal Account of the Life of George H. W. Bush.*

Kuhn, Jim. *Ronald Reagan in Private: A Memoir of My Year in the White House.*

Levantrosser, William, and Rosanna Perotti, eds. *A Noble Calling: Character and the George H. W. Bush Presidency.*

Naftali, Timothy. *George H. W. Bush.*

Parmet, Herbert. *George Bush: The Life of a Lone Star Yankee.*

Quayle, Dan. *Standing Firm: A Vice Presidential Memoir.*

Reagan, Ronald. *The Reagan Diaries*, edited by Douglas Brinkley.

Regan, Donald T. *For the Record: From Wall Street to Washington.*

Rudman, Warren. *Combat: Twelve Years in the U.S. Senate.*

U.S. Government Printing Office. *Public Papers of the Presidents of the United States: George Bush, 1990, Book II, July 1 to December 31, 1990.*

They were very helpful as I tried to convey the accomplishments of the forty-first president of the United States.

INDEX

About the Author

John H. Sununu was a three-term governor of the state of New Hampshire. He served as chief of staff and as counselor to President George H. W. Bush from 1989 to 1992. While governor, he helped organize, and served as cochairman of the 1988 Bush presidential campaign. Prior to serving as governor, Sununu was associate professor and associate dean of the College of Engineering at Tufts University. When he left the White House in 1992 he served for six years as the conservative host on CNN's *Crossfire* and won a Cable Ace Award in that role. Since 1992 he also served as president of JHS Associates Ltd. During the 2012 presidential campaign he was the principal surrogate for Governor Mitt Romney and made nearly two hundred radio and television appearances on his behalf. Governor Sununu continues to make frequent appearances on the issue discussion shows and is a much-sought-after guest on television, including programs hosted by Bill O'Reilly, Sean Hannity, Megyn Kelly, Greta Van Susteren, Neil Cavuto, Joe Scarborough, Chris Matthews, Chuck Todd, and Wolf Blitzer, and on virtually all of the major radio talk shows.